Sustainable Energy
and the States

Sustainable Energy and the States

Essays on Politics, Markets and Leadership

EDITED BY DIANNE RAHM

McFarland & Company, Inc., Publishers
Jefferson, North Carolina, and London

LIBRARY OF CONGRESS CATALOGUING-IN-PUBLICATION DATA

Sustainable energy and the states : essays on politics, markets and
   leadership / edited by Dianne Rahm.
      p.   cm.
   Includes bibliographical references and index.

   ISBN-13: 978-0-7864-2768-0
   ISBN-10: 0-7864-2768-X
   (softcover : 50# alkaline paper) ∞

   1. Renewable energy sources— United States— States.   2. Energy
policy— United States— States.   I. Rahm, Dianne.
TJ807.9.U6S87   2006
333.79'40973 — dc22   2006018557

British Library cataloguing data are available

On the cover: Wind resource map (Renewable Resource Data Center, U.S. Department of Energy); windmill photograph (Photodisc)

Manufactured in the United States of America

McFarland & Company, Inc., Publishers
  Box 611, Jefferson, North Carolina 28640
   www.mcfarlandpub.com

Contents

Introduction

In an era of global climate change and international fossil fuel insecurity concerns, finding ways to increase our utilization of sustainable energy is of vital importance. If the United States is able to develop domestic sources of reliable sustainable energy that pump only small amounts of green house gases, or none, into the atmosphere, we will have addressed two serious national issues—global climate change and energy security. Transitioning to greater usage of sustainable energy is not easy, though. New technologies have to be deployed, many of which are not yet market competitive. To move these technologies into wider adoption, a broad array of government incentive programs have been created.

Efforts to increase sustainable energy utilization in the United States make up a story that cannot be separated from politics, markets, or leadership. Politics is involved as policy makers devise and implement programs to support sustainable energy. Markets are drawn in because most of the country's energy is provided by the private sector and sustainable energy must survive in the competitive marketplace. Leadership is critical because policy entrepreneurs have been the catalysts that continue to drive the transition to sustainable energy. This book provides detailed snapshots of sustainable energy development efforts in the states. Each of the cases presented highlights the importance of the political climate, the impact of markets, and how the exercise of leadership (or the lack thereof) made a difference in the emergence of sustainable energy as a viable alternative to fossil fuels.

The book begins with an overview of national and state policies and programs currently in place. On the federal level these consist of the National Energy Act of 1978 and the Energy Policy Acts of 1992 and 2005. The chapter then explores the variety of financial programs and policy mechanisms the states have used to support the development of sustainable energy. Drawing on a survey of sustainable energy program officers from the fifty states, the chapter explores attitudes towards sustainable energy as well as the role that politics and market forces play as barriers

1

to or facilitators of the widespread use of sustainable energy in the states. The chapter concludes with a discussion of the perceived effectiveness of government efforts at both the state and national levels.

The rest of the book consists of case studies. A number of states are discussed including California, Colorado, Iowa, Massachusetts, Michigan, Minnesota, New York, New Jersey, and Texas. Offshore wind development is provided as a separate case. In each of these cases, the role of politics, markets, and leadership can be seen as critical for understanding development efforts.

W. Henry Lambright, Sarah Pralle and Jessica Boscarino present the case of New York. They argue that New York is playing a policy leadership role in developing and deploying sustainable energy technologies. They discuss three of New York's sustainable energy programs: the transition to hybrid electric buses, the development of wind energy technology, and regional greenhouse gas mitigation. The chapter shows that politics, markets, and leadership each played a role in the success of renewable energy programs in New York. The political support of environmental groups and the market support of private developers are significant factors in the New York story. The chapter further suggests that the political will and policy entrepreneurship of New York's Governor Pataki was critical in achieving success.

Dianne Rahm presents the case of Texas. The chapter argues that Texas, long a player in energy production, forged a cutting edge policy strategy to maintain energy leadership after the governor and legislature realized that Texas had become an energy importer in the early 1990s. After briefly discussing the renewable energy capacity of Texas, this chapter explores the Renewables Portfolio Standard (RPS) policy initially established by Texas and discusses its provisions, how it was implemented, and the problems it faced. The chapter explains how the Texas RPS was first in the nation at the time in terms of its requirements and was very successful in achieving desired results long before legally required. But while the Texas RPS was a model to other states especially because of its innovative market-based provisions, politics and markets soon took their toll on the policy's effectiveness. Transmission issues resulted in political squabbling and market hesitation to move forward with increased renewable energy capacity. The chapter discusses a subsequent amendment to the initial law which may address many of the problems associated with the initial legislation. The chapter concludes with the comment that given the enormous capacity in Texas to produce renewable energy, Texas RPS goals are being set too low to fully encourage the growth of renewables at an adequate pace.

Catherine Horiuchi describes California's movement toward sustainable energy through the adoption in 2002 of a California RPS. The chapter argues that leadership failures and markets played a critical role in the California story. One unintended outcome of the California RPS was that energy efficiency and load management programs were ignored. In the end this, along with the rules governing supplemental energy payments, increased the average cost of energy, reduced sustainability, and challenged the stability of the electric grid. The chapter argues that the RPS, counterintuitively, may actually increase California's consumption of energy from all sources, thus heightening rather than reducing reliance on fossil fuels.

Justin R. Barnes and Barry D. Solomon consider the renewable energy policies of Minnesota, Iowa, and Michigan, with an emphasis on the goals and effects of specific policies. They argue that while these states have large potentials for renewable energy development, their commitments and approaches to addressing barriers are quite different. Three different strategies for supporting renewable energy through state programs are identified. Minnesota has a broad mixture of policies that cover most aspects of renewable energy development from research, development, and demonstration to distributed generation and large-scale commercialization. Iowa, likewise, has this broad range of sustainable energy programs but uses less strident means in implementation. In Michigan, however, support for renewable energy is almost nonexistent. Concern in Michigan is almost completely about economic development rather than renewable energy. The chapter concludes that overall what is most apparent from this region is that political leadership is essential if sustainable energy efforts are to gain support.

Clinton J. Andrews provides the case of New Jersey. With a history of its energy economy mostly in private hands, New Jersey has tended to allow the private sector to lead while the government rarely intervenes. The chapter argues that this tradition of conservative and careful government partnership with the private sector has resulted in New Jersey developing a professional, cost effective, and aggressive sustainable energy program. Driven largely by regulatory agencies run by progressives and environmentalists, the New Jersey case is a story of leadership exercised by professionalized state regulators, this chapter maintains.

Paul Komor writes about Colorado, a state that has in the past decade taken some significant steps toward sustainable energy. The chapter asks the question: How and why did a fiscally conservative state with politically and economically influential fossil fuel interests decide to invest in wind? The chapter shows how small steps toward sustainability, taken in a non-threatening way, paved the way toward larger ones. The chapter concludes that the Colorado experience suggests that sustainability and environmental protection are not effective arguments when it comes to the harsh reality of political negotiations, as they do not easily translate into polit-ically motivating factors such as economic development and increased employment. The chapter concludes that wind power, however, can com-pete economically with fossil fuels and can gain political backing when it is presented as a tool for rural employment and economic development.

Nicholas A. Hiza presents the situation in Massachusetts. He argues that the most important supports of sustainability in Massachusetts are the measures to increase the use of renewable energy that came out of the deregulation of the electrical markets in the 1990s. These included well designed policies to encourage demand, such as its RPS, and programs investing in supply. Despite these well formulated policies, the develop-ment of a sustainable energy industry in Massachusetts has been slow. Because of the slow development, Massachusetts is exploring two initia-tives to expand the supply of renewable energy available under the RPS. One would allow limited development of wind resources on state land while the other would allow currently ineligible biomass facilities to be considered new and renewable. The chapter argues that if Massachusetts' policy moves in this direction, it would send the unfortunate signal to the development community that state requirements are too fluid to be trusted. The chapter concludes that without the assurance of fixed and firm state mandates, market forces will be reluctant to invest the necessary time and capital to pursue projects in the state.

Christine Santora's chapter on offshore wind explores an emerging form of renewable energy generation in the U.S. The chapter argues that shifting traditional wind farms offshore introduces a variety of new man-agement and governance issues that need to be considered. The chapter discusses how the federal government is resolving these governance issues and the role of states in managing offshore wind. The specific experiences of Massachusetts and New York are highlighted, and a review of their specific coastal policies toward offshore wind is given. The chapter con-cludes with a discussion of how the role of the states can be increased, and how individual states can better prepare for offshore wind development.

The experiences of the states in their movement toward greater reliance on sustainable sources of energy show the importance of politics, markets, and leadership in the emergence of sustainable energy as a fea-sible substitute to fossil fuels. While each story is unique, the threads of political environments, the impact of markets, and the exercise of leader-ship weave through each case. The success or failure of state sustainable energy programs hinges on how these key factors play out. States inter-ested in moving forward with sustainable energy efforts would do well to consider their impacts carefully.

1. Sustainable Energy: An Overview of Policy and Programs

Dianne Rahm
University of Texas at San Antonio

Introduction

Energy use is one of the key features of modern social organizations. Whether that organization is the household or the nation, energy use is a dominant aspect of life. Energy is needed for heating, air conditioning, transportation, refrigeration, industrial manufacturing, agricultural production, communications, and the operation of electronic equipment. Reliable and affordable sources of energy are essential to the smooth operation of modern economies and societies.

Since the Industrial Revolution, developed nations have primarily relied on fossil fuels for their energy needs. Coal, oil, and natural gas have fueled factories, provided for transport, and supplied the household needs for the nations. Fossil fuel use has its drawbacks. It contributes to environmental pollution and carbon dioxide production — a major greenhouse gas linked to global climate change. Fossil fuels are also limited in quantity and will eventually be exhausted.

Sustainable energy is energy that comes from renewable sources. Often these sources are common geological features such as sunshine, blowing wind, moving water, or heat released from the Earth. Sources of sustainable energy can be grown when agricultural production is used for energy crops. Waste can be converted into fuel when agricultural and forest wastes (corn stalks and woody plant material) or landfill gas is burned.

Advanced technologies, such as wind turbines and photovoltaic (PV) panels, can be brought to bear to provide sustainable energy. Experimental technologies, such as hydrogen fuel cells, drawing on hydrogen produced from renewable sources, are under development.

Conservation and energy efficiency have a huge role to play in the movement toward a sustainable energy society. Green building designs that drastically reduce the need for heating and air conditioning, advanced designs for transport including vehicles designed to run partially or totally on ethanol or gasoline-electric hybrid designs that vastly increase mileage, as well as energy efficient appliances and lighting are all of enormous value. The more conservation and energy efficiency are brought into play, the easier it will be to provide for remaining energy needs using renewables.

Shifting to a society that relies primarily on sustainable sources of energy makes logical sense for environmental, security, and long-term viability reasons but actually making the transition is not easy. The fossil fuel economy and infrastructure are well entrenched. Diffusion of new technologies and processes takes time and often requires assistance to get over the barriers of initial adoption. This is where public policy plays a crucial role. While energy is and will remain a private sector industry, the public sector does play a role in helping sustainable energy gain a foothold in the economy.

By any estimation, the current use of renewable sources of energy is small. Consumption of all forms of energy in the U.S. in 2003 was 98.22 quadrillion BTUs (Quads).[1] Of this about 40 percent was consumption of energy from petroleum products, 23 percent natural gas, 23 percent coal, 8 percent nuclear power, and 6 percent renewable energy (Energy Information Administration 2005a). Of that 6 percent, 1 percent was from solar, 47 percent was from biomass, 5 percent was from geothermal, 45 percent was from hydroelectric, and 2 percent was from wind (Energy Information Administration 2004). In 2003, of the 3,883 billion kilowatthours (kWh) of electricity generated in the United States, about 71 percent came from fossil fuels, 20 percent from nuclear power, 7 percent from hydroelectric plants, and the remaining 2 percent from non-hydro renewables. Of that 2 percent, 71 percent was derived from biomass, 16 percent from geothermal, 13 percent from wind, and less than 1 percent from solar and photovoltaics (Energy Information Administration 2005b).

This chapter explores the variety of public policies and programs currently in place that address the needs of the emerging sustainable energy sector. After discussing the federal policy framework, largely defined by the National Energy Act of 1978 and the Energy Policy Acts of 1992 and 2005, the chapter turns to a discussion of the state programs and policies.

Drawing on data gathered from a survey of government program managers in the 50 states, the variety of financial incentives, programs, and policies at the state level are examined. The chapter concludes with a discussion of the perceived effectiveness of government efforts.

Federal Policy Framework

The main thrust of federal energy policy since the Second World War has been to assure a safe and reliable supply of cheap and abundant energy. To that end, the federal government has largely supported the interests of the private sector fossil fuel industry, although providing a regulatory framework to those sectors perceived as monopolies. Another role that the federal government has played in energy policy is in the subsidy of nuclear power. In the aftermath of the invention of nuclear weaponry, the federal government played a major role in promoting the peaceful use of that technology — nuclear power.

Federal policies have provided energy efficiency standards for appliances, electronic equipment, and vehicles although some would suggest that the performance demands have been rather lax. The federal policies that do exist to promote renewable energy include financial incentives, regulatory policies, and R&D programs supported by the Department of Energy and the national laboratories. Many of these incentives and policies were codified into law by three statutes: the National Energy Act of 1978, the Energy Policy Act of 1992, and the Energy Policy Act of 2005.

THE NATIONAL ENERGY ACT OF 1978 (NEA)

Passed in the wake of the oil shock of the early 1970s, NEA focused on decreasing dependence on foreign oil importation and increasing conservation and energy efficiency. The Public Utilities Regulatory Policies Act (PURPA) was a part of NEA. PURPA sought to improve energy conservation and efficiency in the utilities sector and had important impacts on the development of renewable energy (Energy Information Administration 2005b). Electrical power generation and delivery, since its 19th century origins, had been dominated by large companies who owned both power production facilities and the transmission lines. In this monopoly situation, the federal government provided regulatory controls until deregulation was introduced in 1978 with PURPA. PURPA initiated partial competition in the generation of electricity by requiring that monopoly utilities compare the cost of purchasing energy from other vendors rather than producing it themselves. This allowed the entrance of some independent producers into the previously monopoly controlled market. PURPA required that utilities purchase energy from small independent producers with the price to be set at the "avoided cost"—the cost the utilities would have to pay if they expanded their facilities to generate the added energy (Hinricks and Kleinbach 2002). Avoided cost calculations were to be set by each state. Some states, like California and New York, set their avoided cost calculations high so that renewables would be favorably impacted. In 1995, however, the Federal Energy Regulatory Commission (FERC) took responsibility for determining avoided cost. This change resulted in lower avoided cost scales than those in states that had written their calculations to be favorable to renewables (Energy Information Administration 2005b).

The Energy Tax Act of 1978, also part of NEA, created a series of financial incentives to promote renewables. It included a 30 percent investment tax credit for residential consumers for solar and wind energy equipment and a 10 percent investment tax credit for businesses for the installation of solar, wind, or geothermal equipment. These credits changed over time and expired in 1985 (Energy Information Administration 2005b).

THE ENERGY POLICY ACT OF 1992

The 1992 Energy Policy Act (EPAct), Public Law 102–486, was the most important energy bill of the 1990s, albeit the only major one, for the promotion of renewables. It expanded PURPA to include a wider range of electricity generators, effectively creating a deregulated market for electricity across the United States. This law allowed independent power producers from any geographical region to sell electricity to industry or utilities in other regions of the country. Transmission lines were opened to allow a competitive market (Hinricks and Kleinbach 2002). In addition, the EPAct provided a 10-year 1.5 cent per kilowatt hour (kWh) production tax credit (PTC) for investor owned wind turbines and biomass plants for plants brought into production between 1994 and 1999 (Energy Information Administration 2005b). While this incentive has undoubtedly provided a huge incentive to the development of renewables, several problems were associated with it. First, the PTC repeatedly expired and was subsequently reinstated by Congress. It was most recently reinstated by the Energy Policy Act of 2005, discussed more fully below. The result of this instability fueled a boom and bust cycle economy that dominated (and to a large extent continues to dominate) the investor owned renewable energy sector. Also, the PTC was initially restricted to wind and biomass. This had an averse affect on the emergence of other renewables until the rules were widened to allow them.

Titles III and V of EPAct contained provisions to promote the use of alternative fuels, that is, fuels that are not derived from petroleum. The goal was to reduce dependence on foreign oil. Congress established requirements under EPAct to build a fleet of alternative fuel vehicles (AFVs) to be used in large urban areas. The law gave the Department of Energy (DOE) the authority to manage requirements for federal, state, local, and private programs for fleet acquisition. DOE never implemented mandated controls for local or private fleets. Federal AFV fleet requirements set by EPAct required that beginning in FY 2000, 75 percent of light-duty vehicles be AFVs. Vehicles other than light duty vehicles— those weighing 8,500 pounds or more — were not covered by the law. Law enforcement, emergency, and military vehicles were also excepted. The DOE manages this AFV requirement by using a complex system of credits granted to various vehicle types and alternate fuel use. The EPAct also required that a fixed percentage of state fleet vehicles be AFV if the state operates more than 50 light duty vehicles in its fleet. The exceptions for federal fleets also apply to state fleets, however, state fleets are also excepted for a variety of additional reasons (U.S. Department of Energy 2004).

THE ENERGY POLICY ACT OF 2005

After four years in the making, the Energy Policy Act of 2005 was passed in August of 2005. While largely a law designed to support fossil fuel producers and nuclear energy, the energy bill included a number of initiatives designed to promote renewable energy.

The law provided several financial incentives. It extended the PTC through 2007 for wind, biomass, geothermal, small irrigation power facilities, landfill gas and trash combustion facilities. A new category of tax credit bonds were created by the law. These bonds, known as Clean Renewable Energy Bonds (CREBs), can be issued by governmental bodies, tribal governments, and cooperative electrical companies, to finance capital expenditure for renewable energy facilities. To support energy efficiency and conservation, the law added biodiesel fuel credits of 10 cents a gallon for up to 15 million gallons of agri-biodeisel produced before December 31, 2008. Taxpayers are permitted to claim a 30 percent credit for the cost of installing clean-fuel vehicle refueling properties. Clean fuels are defined by the law as those containing at least 85 percent volume of ethanol, natural gas, compressed natural gas, liquefied natural gas, liquefied petroleum gas and hydrogen and any mix of diesel and biodiesel that contains at least

20 percent biodiesel. This credit is allowed through January 1, 2010. The law also provides a credit for business installation (by 2008) of fuel cells, stationary microturbine power plants, and solar arrays (Perkins Coie LLP and Affiliates 2005).

To help create a market for some of this newly generated renewable energy, the law created federal procurement requirements. By 2013 the federal government is required to purchase 7.5 percent of its power needs from renewable sources, increasing from 3 percent in 2007 (Neff 2005).

Building standards were affected by the law as well. Contractors receive a tax credit for the construction of energy efficient homes purchased between 2005 and 2008. Energy efficient commercial buildings also qualify for a tax credit. Appliance manufacturers become eligible for a tax credit for engineering more energy efficient appliances and the law requires some new products to achieve new efficiency standards. Homeowners who install solar energy systems are allowed to claim a tax credit (Perkins 2005).

In terms of vehicles, the Act offers incentives for consumers to purchase energy-efficient hybrid, clean diesel, and fuel cell vehicles (White House 2005). While not increasing the corporate average fuel economy (CAFE) standards, the law directs the Department of Transportation to study the impact of new fuel efficiency standards (Neff 2005). The Energy Policy Act provides a financial incentive for alternative fuel vehicles equal to the percentage of any additional cost of placing such a vehicle in service. AFVs covered in the Act include compressed natural gas, liquefied natural gas, liquefied petroleum gas, hydrogen and other liquid at least 85 percent ethanol. The law mandates the annual use of 7.5 billion gallons of ethanol by 2012 and provides refiners, blenders and importers of gasoline a credit for any fuel that replaces or reduces the quantity of fossil fuel present in the fuel mixture (Perkins Coie LLP and Affiliates 2005).

After its passage, the Energy Policy Act of 2005 was widely criticized for its weak provisions in regard to conservation, energy efficiency, and renewables. Despite its nearly 2,000 pages of text, the law failed to address two major concerns for energy policy — the contribution of fossil fuel use to global climate change and the national security implications of continued dependence on oil importation (Crook 2005) and domestic facility locations. The Act has also been criticized for the priority it gives to building new fossil fuel and nuclear plants as well as for the authority it gives FERC to locate highly volatile liquid-natural gas ports, all potential terrorist targets, even over the opposition of state and local governments (Clarke 2005).

The States: Policies and Programs

The states have, over the course of the last several decades, established an array of programs to advance renewable energy, conservation, and energy efficiency. Although the programs established by the states differ from one state to the next, most states have put in place an array of financial incentives, regulations, and subsidies to support renewable energy, conservation, and energy efficiency.[2]

FINANCIAL INCENTIVES

States use a variety of financial incentives to encourage the development and use of renewable energy. For states that tax businesses and corporations, corporate tax credits or deductions for investment in renewable energy equipment are often provided. For instance, New Mexico provides a tax credit to corporations (to be applied to their corporate income tax) of one cent per kWh for companies that generate electricity from wind (New Mexico Energy, Minerals, and Natural Resources Department 2005). Other states with corporate tax incentives include California, Hawaii, Maryland, Massachusetts, Missouri, Montana, Mew Mexico, New York, North Carolina, North Dakota, Ohio, Oklahoma, Oregon, Texas, Utah, and West Virginia (Interstate Renewable Energy Council 2004).

Some states permit direct renewable energy equipment sales by utilities to customers as part of a buy-down, low-income assistance, or lease program. For instance, the City of Santa Clara, California offers a solar water heating service whereby the Water and Sewer Utilities Department sells, installs, and maintains solar water heating systems for residents and businesses. The city also leases solar hot water heating units for swimming pools and hot water heaters. Renters pay an initial fee for installation and subsequently are charged a monthly rate on their utility bill (City of Santa Clara 2005).

Many states offer a variety of grant programs for renewable energy equipment purchase or installation. For example, Connecticut's Clean Energy Fund, the states public benefit fund (discussed below), provides grants to commercial, industrial, and institutional buildings to install photovoltaics to provide power (Connecticut Clean Energy Fund 2005). Maine provides grants through the Maine Technology Institute under their Renewable Resources Matching Fund, a creation of the state's public benefits funds. The fund supports renewable research and development (R&D) as well as demonstration projects (Maine Technology Institute 2005). More than half of the states have some form of grant program in operation (Interstate Renewable Energy Council 2004).

Economic development efforts are sometimes linked with renewable energy promotion efforts. Seven states have industrial recruitment incentive programs to encourage renewable energy equipment manufacturers to locate or relocate in their state (Interstate Renewable Energy Council 2004). Hawaii, for instance, provides a tax credit that can be taken over five years for investment in a qualified high tech business. One of the definitions of such a business is one that conducts more than half of its activities in qualified research, including a large variety of renewable energy technologies. The credit, capped at 2 million dollars ($700,000 in the year the investment is made to $200,000 in the last year) is thought substantial enough to lure firms to the state (Hawaii Department of Taxation 2005).

For states with customers located a far distance from the grid, providing renewable energy technology leasing and lease purchase programs makes sense. Remotely located customers, for whom connection to the grid would require expensive line extension, can rent or rent-to-own stand alone renewable systems. One such program is run by Wyoming's Carbon Power and Light. Their PV leasing program offers a cost-effective option used mostly for water pumping for livestock. Carbon Power and Light pays for all construction costs for a PV system that cost less than line extension would. The leasing period is set to either five or ten years (Wyoming Carbon Power and Light 2005).

Many states provide loan programs for renewable energy equipment purchase or installation. The Missouri Department of Natural Resources, for instance, offers loans to public schools, local governments, and public colleges and universities for energy efficiency improvements (Missouri Department of Natural Resources 2005). Minnesota provides an agricultural loan program for installation of wind turbines or anaerobic digestion facilities on farms (Minnesota Department of Agriculture 2005).

Personal income tax credits or deductions to cover the cost of purchasing or installing renewable energy equipment are commonly allowed by states that tax income. Arizona's solar and wind energy credits are a good example of this type of program. Arizona permits a personal tax credit for up to 25 percent of the cost of a residential solar, or PV technology (with a cap of $1,000) (Arizona Department of Revenue 2005). Rhode Island provides a 25 percent income tax credit for homeowners who install renewable energy systems including solar water heaters, solar space heaters, PV systems, geothermal, and wind systems (Rhode Island State Energy Office 2005).

Most states have some form of production incentives in place. For instance, residents and businesses in all states have access to the Mainstay renewable energy certificate (green tag) purchase program. Mainstay is a private company that buys and sells renewable energy certificates (RECs). Once a renewable energy facility is certified, owners can sell their RECs to Mainstay for cash (Mainstay Energy 2005). Some states have state-run production incentive programs that provide owners of renewable equipment or fuels with cash payments for electricity production. New Jersey, for example, has the Solar Renewable Energy Certificate Program. This program allows owners of solar equipment to register themselves with the program. The program tracks their renewable energy production and awards a solar renewable energy certificate (SREC) to them for each 1 megawatt hour (MWh) of electricity produced. SRECs are required by New Jersey's renewables portfolio standard (discussed below), facilitating the sale of these certificates (New Jersey Clean Energy Program 2005).

Several states have put in place property tax incentives that reduce taxes based on the cost of renewable energy equipment on site. North Carolina, for instance, has a property tax exemption for active solar heating and cooling systems so that they will not be assessed at more than the value of a conventional heating or cooling system for property tax purposes (Data Base of State Incentive for Renewable Energy 2005).

Rebate programs that offset the cost of purchasing and installing renewable energy equipment are available in a number of states. New York's Long Island Power Authority, for example, has the Solar Pioneer Program which provides homeowners and businesses $4 per watt of PV systems installed. This rebate is estimated to save homeowners and businesses about half the cost of a new PV system. An additional rebate of $1 per watt is provided to schools, governments, and nonprofits (Long Island Power Authority 2005).

Sixteen states have in effect a sales tax exemption from state sales tax for the cost of renewable energy equipment. A case in point is Florida, which provides a very broad sales and use tax exemption for all solar energy systems without restriction. Any solar system that replaces the use of fossil fuel is allowed (Florida Department of Revenue 2005). Other states, such as Maryland, have more restricted sales tax exemptions that exempt only one type of fuel such as wood from taxation (Interstate Renewable Energy Council 2004).

REGULATIONS AND POLICIES

States have designed a variety of regulations and policies to encourage sustainable energy development and use. Construction and design policies, including construction regulations, green building programs, and energy codes are uses in some states. Madison, Wisconsin for instance, as part of its Climate Protection Plan, has put in place green building designs and energy efficiency standards. The goal is to reduce greenhouse gas emissions. Madison targeted the number one cause of such emissions—fossil fuel use—to achieve its goal (City of Madison 2002).

A few states have licensing regulations for renewable energy contractors. The goal is to ensure proper equipment installation. Nevada requires solar systems installers to be licensed (Nevada State Contractors Board 2005) as does Michigan (Michigan Department of Labor and Economic Growth 2005).

Five states have regulations requiring renewable energy equipment certifications to ensure consumer protection. These include Arizona, Arkansas, Louisiana, Maine, and Minnesota (Interstate Renewable Energy Council 2004).

One of the more popular and powerful policy tools are disclosure rules that require utilities to provide customers with information on monthly bills about the fuel mix of energy they are supplying and related emissions. Ohio has a leading disclosure policy. Ohio requires that electricity providers divulge to customers on their billing statement the fuel mix and the environmental consequences of that mix. Electric providers are required to identify sources of power including biomass power, coal-fired power, hydro power, natural gas fired power, nuclear power, oil fired power, wind power, solar power, and unknown sources of purchased power using a standardized format of a pie chart with specific colors for each power source specified. In so doing the competitive market in Ohio allows customers to determine from which provider they wish to purchase energy (Public Utility Commission of Ohio 1999).

Ohio also has rules that encourage green power purchasing through community choice aggregation policies. These rules in Ohio specify that the load of multiple electrical customers can be combined and as a whole be used to negotiate a contract for services from a provider. The local government often acts as aggregator and contract negotiator. This enables communities to be attractive to green power producers and to negotiate good rates. Individual customers are automatically included in the aggregate unless they specifically opt out (Public Utility Commission of Ohio 1999). Several cities also have green purchasing programs in place. Portland Oregon's Energy Division, for example, just before Earth Day 2000, made a commitment to purchase green energy for the city's residential houses. The Energy Division also encourages local businesses and city offices to purchase green power (City of Portland 2000).

Line extension analysis that provides remotely located customers a comparison of the costs for line extension or an on-site renewable system is another policy that states and localities use to encourage the development of renewables. Only four states currently make use of this policy, though. These include Arizona, Colorado, New Mexico, and Texas (Interstate Renewable Energy Council 2004).

Net metering is a policy that has been widely adopted by the states. Net metering rules allow customers with their own electricity generating capability to sell excess production. Net metering also lets small producers of renewable energy to sell their power back to the grid, making the installation of renewable energy technologies more affordable. The buy-back rate is determined by the each state but is commonly set at the retail electricity rate. As of September 2004, net metering was available in 32 states (Energy Information Agency 2005).

Public benefits funds that support renewable energy resources, renewable energy R&D, energy efficiency initiatives, and low-income support programs have been established in fifteen states. These funds are usually financed by some sort of general tax on all consumers. The money thus made available can be used to subsidize renewable energy technologies and energy efficiency initiatives (Interstate Renewable Energy Council 2004). The Delaware Energy Office is a typical example of the use of public benefit funds. It provides cash grants to customers who purchase or lease renewable energy technologies. Delaware also provides grants for technology demonstration programs for 25 percent of the cost of the programs (Delaware Energy Office 2005).

Among one of the most important policies to promote the development of renewable energy is the renewables portfolio standard (RPS). RPSs require utilities to produce a certain percentage of the total electricity production from renewables. The percentage increases over time, thus generating a stable market in which renewables can develop. Twenty one states have some form of RPS in place (Interstate Renewable Energy Council 2004). It is interesting to note that a national RPS was widely discussed as part of the Energy Policy Act of 2005 negotiations but was not included in that legislation.

A few states have regulations that mandate utilities to provide customers with a green power purchase option. Iowa enacted such a program in 2004. All electric utilities operating in Iowa must allow customers to purchase green power if they decide to do so (Iowa Department of Natural Resources 2003).

Most states have in place access laws such as solar and wind easements. These laws provide a mechanism by which a property owner can assure access to a renewable resource such as sunshine or wind if a neighbor develops in such a way that might deny access (Interstate Renewable Energy Council 2004). For example, Montana allows property owners to negotiate with neighboring property owners to create solar and wind easements for unrestricted access to sunlight and wind (Montana Department of Environmental Quality 2005).

Energy efficiency home or workplace audits, compact fluorescent light bulb rebate programs, and Energy Star appliance rebate programs are commonly employed policies to encourage energy efficiency. These programs are frequently put in place by local utilities with the encouragement of the states.

Renewable Energy Programs and Policies:
An Assessment

To assess the value of the number of financial incentive, regulations, and policies discussed above, a survey was sent to managers of energy programs in the states. Three hundred nineteen surveys were sent in the summer of 2005. One hundred forty nine completed surveys were returned yielding a response rate of 47 percent. Of the respondents, 77 percent said their program was involved with solar, 85 percent photovoltaics, 77 percent wind, 45 percent geothermal, 38 percent hydroelectric, 46 percent alternative fuels, and 63 percent biomass. Seventy three percent of program managers said that their programs involved energy efficiency.

FINANCIAL INCENTIVES

On a scale of 1 to 10, where 1 represents not at all useful and 10 represents highly useful, respondents were asked to rate the usefulness of the variety of financial incentives discussed earlier in this chapter. Table 1 presents an overview of the financial incentives and their rankings.

Those financial incentives ranked useful to highly useful (by scoring them 8 or above) included corporate tax credits, grant programs for renewable energy equipment purchases, personal income tax credits or deductions, production incentives providing owners of renewable equipment or fuels with cash payments for electricity production, and rebate programs.

Corporate tax credits or deductions for investment in renewable energy equipment were rated as useful or highly useful by 71 percent of respondents. Grant programs for renewable energy equipment purchase or instal-

Table 1: Financial Incentives (Ranked by Energy Program Managers)			
	Little or No Use	*Moderately Useful*	*Useful or Highly Useful*
Corporate tax credit	11%	19%	71%
Equipment sales	24	43	33
Equip. purchase grants	5	30	62
Industrial recruitment	18	50	32
Equip. leasing and purchasing for remote customers	21	48	30
Loans	19	47	35
Personal income tax credit or deduction	7	36	57
Production incentives	5	26	68
Property tax incentives	23	32	45
Rebates	5	21	71
Sales tax exemption	10	39	42

Source: Authors survey data. Percentages may not add to 100% due to rounding. Little or no use scored 1–4, moderately useful scored 5–7, useful or highly useful scored 8–10.

lation were generally seen positively as well. Twenty one percent of respondents rated these incentives as highly useful and 62 percent of those responding ranked such programs 8 or above. Personal income tax credits or deductions to cover the cost of purchasing or installing renewable energy equipment were ranked by 57 percent of respondents as useful or highly useful, and by 36 percent as moderately useful. Production incentives providing owners of renewable equipment or fuels with cash payments for electricity production were highly ranked. Sixty eight percent of those responding found production incentives to be useful or highly useful and 26 percent ranked them as moderately useful. Rebate programs that offset the cost of purchasing and installing renewable energy equipment were ranked useful or highly useful by 71 percent and moderately useful by another 21 percent.

Those financial incentives ranked as moderately useful (by scoring them between 5 and 7) included direct energy equipment sales by utilities to customers, industrial recruitment incentives, leasing and lease purchase programs for remotely located customers, loan programs for renewable energy equipment purchase or installation, property tax incentives that reduce taxes based on the cost of renewable energy equipment on site, and sales tax exemption from state sales tax for the cost of renewable energy equipment.

Opinions on the utility of direct renewable energy equipment sales by utilities to customers as part of a buy-down, low-income assistance, or lease program were somewhat mixed. Only 9 percent of respondents found them to be highly useful and only about one fourth ranked them 8 or above. Forty three percent of those responding ranked direct equipment sales as moderately useful while another 25 percent found them of little or no use. Industrial recruitment incentives to encourage renewable energy equipment manufacturers to locate in the state were scored by half of respondents as moderately useful, while 33 percent of respondents found them useful or highly useful. Nineteen percent of respondents found them of little or no use. Renewable technology leasing and lease purchase programs for remotely located customers for whom connection to the grid would require expensive line extension was scored as moderately useful by 48 percent of those answering the question, highly useful or useful by 30 percent, and of little or no use by 21 percent. Loan programs for renewable energy equipment purchase or installation were ranked by 47 percent as moderately useful, by 35 percent as useful or highly useful, and by 19 percent as of little or no use. Property tax incentives that reduce taxes based on the cost of renewable energy equipment on site were ranked by 32 percent of respondents as moderately useful, by 45 percent as useful or highly useful but by 23 percent as of little or no use. Sales tax exemption from state sales tax for the cost of renewable energy equipment was considered moderately useful by 39 percent of those responding while 42 percent ranked it useful or highly useful.

As Table 1 shows, four types of incentives were ranked rather poorly by a substantial number of respondents. Direct renewable energy equipment sales, industrial recruitment incentives, leasing and lease purchase agreements for remote customers, loan programs, and property tax incentives each fall in this category.

REGULATIONS AND POLICIES

Table 2 shows the variety of regulations and policies as ranked by energy program managers. Those regulations and policies rated useful or highly useful include construction and design policies, renewable energy equipment certifications, green power purchasing with community choice aggregation policies, net metering rules, public benefit funds, renewables portfolio standards, a required green power purchase option for customers, and energy efficiency measures.

Table 2: Regulations and Policies (Ranked by Energy Program Managers)			
	Little or No Use	*Moderately Useful*	*Useful or Highly Useful*
Construction and design policies	12%	30%	63%
Contractor licensing	10	46	45
Required equipment certification	10	40	50
Required fuel mix disclosure	27	44	29
Green power purchase w/community choice aggregation	13	39	47
Line extension analysis	23	36	23
Net metering rules	8	27	66
Public benefit funds	6	20	74
Renewables portfolio standard	7	22	71
Required green power purchase option	20	35	46
Solar and wind easements	20	43	37
Energy efficiency home audits	15	38	47
Compact fluorescent bulb rebates	18	39	44
Energy Star appliance rebates	12	33	55

Source: Authors survey data. Percentages may not add to 100% due to rounding. Little or no use scored 1–4, moderately useful scored 5–7, useful or highly useful scored 8–10.

Construction and design policies including state construction regulations, green building programs, and energy codes were ranked by 63 percent of respondents as useful or highly useful, although 30 percent found them only moderately useful and 12 percent of little or no use. Regulations requiring renewable energy equipment certifications to ensure consumer protection were found to be useful or highly useful by half of the respondents. An additional 40 percent saw these regulations as moderately useful. Green power purchasing with community choice aggregation policies that require or encourage the purchase of renewable energy was rated of use or highly useful by 47 percent of those answering. An additional 39 percent found these policies to be of moderate use. Net metering rules allowing customers with their own electricity generating capability to sell excess production were highly regarded by the overwhelming number of respondents. Sixty six percent of them found net metering rules useful or highly useful while another 27 percent reported them as moderately useful. Similarly, public benefits funds that support renewable energy resources, R&D, energy efficiency initiatives, and low-income support programs were reported by 74 percent of respondents as useful or highly useful. Renewables portfolio standards that require utilities to produce a certain percentage of the total electricity production from renewables were seen by 71 percent of respondents as useful or highly useful. Another 22 percent of respondents reported them as moderately useful. A required green power purchase option for customers was found useful or highly useful by 46 percent of respondents while 35 percent found it moderately useful. Twenty percent of respondents, however, ranked this policy as of little or no use.

Energy efficiency home or workplace audits, compact fluorescent light bulb rebate programs, and Energy Star appliance rebate programs were each ranked by respondents as being useful or highly useful by 47 percent, 44 percent, and 55 percent respectively.

Those regulations and policies rated moderately useful include renewable energy contractor licensing regulations, fuel mix disclose requirements, line extension analysis, and solar and wind easements and access laws.

Renewable energy contractor licensing regulations that ensure proper equipment installation were found by 46 percent of respondents to be of moderate usefulness while another 45 percent of respondents found them to be useful or highly useful. Disclosure rules that require utilities to provide customers with information on monthly bills about the fuel mix of energy they are supplying and related emissions were ranked by 44 percent of respondents as moderately useful. Another 29 percent found these regulations to be useful or highly useful while 27 percent ranked them as of little or no use. Line extension analysis that provides remotely located customers a comparison of the costs for line extension or an on-site renewable system was reported by 36 percent of respondents as being of moderate use with another 23 percent saying it is useful or highly useful. However, 23 percent also reported line extension analysis to be of little or no use. Solar and wind easements and access laws were found to be moderately useful by 43 percent of respondents. An additional 37 percent of respondents thought them useful or highly useful.

Several policies and regulations were ranked by a relatively large number of respondents (more than 20 percent) as being of little or no use. These include fuel mix disclosure rules and related emissions, line extension analysis, a required green power purchase option for customers, solar and wind easements.

Major Barriers and Facilitators

The survey provided respondents with several open ended questions and asked them to express their opinion. The first of these was "In your opinion, what are the major barriers to widespread use of sustainable energy?" The second was "In your opinion, what is the major driving force behind the movement for sustainable energy?" Content analysis was done on these responses to provide a ranked list of each.

The most commonly cited barrier to the widespread use of sustainable energy was cost. The presence of cheap fossil fuels, in comparison to more expensive renewable energy was listed by 61 percent of respondents as being the most important barrier. The second most commonly stated barrier was lack of public awareness of sustainable energy technologies, their capacity, and their viability. Twenty two percent of those responding referred to this issue as a major difficulty. Thirteen percent of those responding listed government subsidies to fossil fuel and nuclear industries as a prominent obstacle to the widespread use of renewables. Ten percent of respondents said renewable energy technologies were not yet technologically ripe. Another 10 percent of respondents mentioned resistance coming from utilities to the use of renewables as a hurdle that needs to be overcome. Nearly 10 percent of respondents saw the fact that society generally ignores the negative externalities and risks associated with fossil fuel use as a major barrier to the more widespread use of renewables. Environmental and health issues were raised in this regard. About 8 percent of respondents blamed the lack of a stable federal production tax credit and other federal policies for retarding the use of renewables. Other factors listed included lack of political will to support the industry, the political power of the fossil fuel lobby, permitting and regulatory barriers, difficulties in obtaining financing, the lack of federal net metering requirements, lack of federal leadership, lack of appropriate incentives, transmission barriers, high connection costs, lack of long range planning in cities for green building, policies that require lowest cost energy for consumers, NIMBY siting issues, and lack of full life cycle cost analysis before purchase decisions are made.

Energy program managers responding to the question concerning the major driving force behind the movement for sustainable energy listed the environment as the primary factor. Forty two percent of respondents spoke about global warming, the risks of fossil fuel use, and other environmental issues. The second most stated driving force was the rising cost of fossil fuel. Twenty three percent of respondents mentioned that factor. Nearly 20 percent mentioned security and defense needs for energy independence. Twelve percent of those responding to the question spoke of the awareness that business as usual was not sustainable as a major driving force. Slightly over 10 percent of respondents listed renewables portfolio standards, production tax credits and other government policies. The other factors mentioned included the unstable supply of fossil fuels, grass roots efforts, the sustainable energy lobby, economic development, and potential job creation.

Respondents were asked to speculate what laws or regulations might more fully encourage the emergence of sustainable energy. Over one quarter of those answering the question suggested the creation of a federal renewables portfolio standard. Fifteen percent said they would put in place a federal income tax credit for renewable purchases. Twelve percent argued for a stable federal production tax credit. Other suggestions included mandatory national green building standards, a federal carbon tax, the end of fossil fuel subsidies, requiring net metering for all utilities, a renewables R&D tax credit, feed-in tariffs, increasing CAFE standards, appliance energy efficiency standards that increase annually, federal public benefits funds, mandatory federal government renewables purchasing, federal educational efforts, standard interconnection and net metering protocols, and a massive "Manhattan Project" effort.

Conclusion

This chapter has provided an overview of the variety of public policies and programs currently in place that address the needs of the emerging sustainable energy sector. The federal policy framework, largely defined by the National Energy Act of 1978 and the Energy Policy Acts of 1992 and 2005, is limited. The states, however, have developed a variety of state programs and policies to promote the development of the renewable energy sector. Most of these programs can be categorized as financial incentives, regulatory mechanisms, or promotion policies.

Energy program managers in the states tend to believe that corporate tax credits, grant programs for renewable energy equipment purchase, personal income tax credits or deductions, production incentives providing owners of renewable equipment or fuels with cash payments for electricity production, and rebate programs are highly effective. Program managers also highly rate construction and design policies, renewable energy equipment certifications, green power purchasing with community choice aggregation policies, net metering rules, public benefit funds, renewables portfolio standards, a required green power purchase option for customers, and energy efficiency measures.

Energy program managers find less effective but still of value direct energy equipment sales by utilities to customers, industrial recruitment incentives, leasing and lease purchase programs for remotely located customers, loan programs for renewable energy equipment purchase or installation, property tax incentives that reduce taxes based on the cost of renewable energy equipment on site, sales tax exemption from state sales tax for the cost of renewable energy equipment, renewable energy contractor licensing regulations, fuel mix disclose requirements, line extension analysis, and solar and wind easements and access laws.

A number of barriers to the full emergence of the renewable energy sector exist, however energy program managers in the states cite cost as the most significant barrier to the widespread use of sustainable energy. The presence of cheap fossil fuels, in comparison to more expensive renewable energy, is the fundamental obstacle. Other noteworthy barriers include lack of public awareness of sustainable energy technologies, government subsidies to fossil fuel and nuclear industries, the immaturity of renewable energy technologies, and the lack of appreciation of the environmental consequences associated with fossil fuel use. Aside from the rising cost of fossil fuels, the link between fossil fuel use and environmental damage is what many energy program managers in the states see as the major driving force behind the renewable energy sector.

Notes

1. The Quad is the standard measurement used to depict energy use. A Quad is equal to 10^{15} BTUs. One BTU is the amount of energy it takes to raise the temperature of a pound of water from 39 to 40 degrees F.

2. The Interstate Renewable Energy Council maintains the Database of State Incentives for Renewable Energy (DSIRE). This excellent resource provides detail on each of the program established in the states.

References

Arizona Department of Revenue. 2005. Solar Tax Credit. Available at *http://www.revenue. state.az.us/brochure/543.pdf.* Accessed October 12, 2005.
City of Madison. 2002. Climate Protection Plan. Available at *http://www.ci.madison.wi.us/ environment/ccp_2002.pdf.* Accessed October 12, 2005.

City of Portland. 2000. City Energy Challenge. Available at *http://www.sustainableportland. org/energy_gov_challenge.html*. Accessed October 15, 2005.

City of Santa Clara. 2005. Water and Sewer Utilities. Available at *http://cho.ci.santa-clara. ca.us/pub_utility/ws_dept.html*. Accessed October 11, 2005.

Clarke, Richard A. 2005. Things Left Undone *The Atlantic Monthly* 296(4): 37–38 .

Connecticut Clean Energy Fund. 2005. Photovoltaic Program for Solar PV Installations on Commercial, Industrial and Institutional Buildings. Available at *http://www.ctcleanenergy. com/documents/CIIPVRFP91504V2.pdf*. Accessed on October 11, 2005.

Crook, Clive. 2005. Does Oil Have a Future? *The Atlantic Monthly* 296(3): 31–32 .

Data Base of State Incentives for Renewable Energy. 2005. North Carolina Incentives for Renewable Energy. Available at *http://www.dsireusa.org/library/includes/incentive2.cfm? Incentive_Code=NC09F&state=NC&CurrentPageID=1*. Accessed October 12, 2005.

Delaware Energy Office. 2005. Delaware Energy Programs. Available at *http://www.delaware-energy.com/programs.htm*. Accessed October 15, 2005.

Energy Information Administration. 2004. *Renewable Energy Trends with Preliminary Data for 2003*. U.S. Department of Energy.

_____. 2005a. *Annual Energy Outlook 2005*. U.S. Department of Energy, DOE/EIA-0383 (2005). Also available at *http://www.eia.doe.gov/oiaf/aeo/*. Accessed October 3, 2005.

_____. 2005b. *Policies to Promote Non-hydro Renewable Energy in the United States and Selected Countries*. U.S. Department of Energy. Available at *http://www.eia.doe.gov/fuel renewable.html*. Accessed October 3, 2005.

Florida Department of Revenue. 2005. Tax Information Publication. Available at http://sun6. dms.state.fl.us/dor/tips/tip05a01–05.html. Accessed October 12, 2005.

Hawaii Department of Taxation. 2005. Department of Taxation Announcement No 2005-xx. Available at *http://www.state.hi.us/tax/temp/anndraft_act215.pdf*. Accessed on October 11, 2005.

Hinricks, R. A. and M. Kleinbach. 2002. *Energy: Its Use and the Environment*. Fort Worth: Harcourt.

Interstate Renewable Energy Council. 2004. Database of State Incentives for Renewable Energy. Available at *http://www.dsireusa.org*. Accessed October 11, 2005.

Iowa Department of Natural Resources. 2003. Green Power Requirement Takes Effect January 1, 2004. *Iowa Energy Bulletin* 30(2): 4. Available at *http://www.iowadnr.com/energy/ news/ebulletin/03winter.pdf*. Accessed October 15, 2005.

Long Island Power Authority. 2005. Solar Pioneer Program. Available at http://www. lipower.org/cei/solar.incentives.html. Accessed October 12, 2005.

Maine Technology Institute. 2005. Renewable Resources Matching Fund Program. Available at *http://www.mainetechnology.com*. Accessed October 11, 2005.

Mainstay Energy. 2005. Meet Mainstay Energy and Efficiency Tracking. Available at http://mainstayenergy.com/. Accessed October 11, 2005.

Michigan Department of Labor and Economic Growth. 2005. Mechanical Examination, Licensing Information, and Applications. Available at *http://www.michigan.gov/cis/0,1607, +7–154–10401–45140—,00.html*. Accessed October 12, 2005.

Minnesota Department of Agriculture. 2005. Agricultural Improvement Loan Program. Available at *http://www.mda.state.mn.us/agfinance/improvement.html*. Accessed October 11, 2005.

Missouri Department of Natural Resources. 2005. Energy Revolving Fund. Available at *http://www.dnr.mo.gov/energy/financial/loan.htm*. Accessed October 11, 2005.

Montana Department of Environmental Quality. 2005. Net Metering and Easements. Available at *http://www.deq.state.mt.us/energy/renewable/netmeterrenew.asp*. Accessed October 15, 2005.

Neff, Shirley. 2005. Review of the Energy Policy Act of 2005 — Summary. Center for Energy, Marine Transportation and Public Policy, Columbia University, August 2, 2005.

Nevada State Contractors Board. 2005. Contractor Information. Available at *http://nscb. state.nv.us/main_contractor.htm*. Accessed October 12, 2005.

New Jersey Clean Energy Program. 2005. New Jersey Solar Renewable Energy Certificate Program. Available at *http://www.njcep.com/srec/.* Accessed October 11, 2005.

New Mexico Energy, Minerals, and Natural Resources Department. 2005. Wind Energy. Available at *http://www.emnrd.state.nm.us/ecmd/html/wind.htm.* Accessed October 11, 2005.

Perkins, Broderick. 2005. Energy Policy Act of 2005. *Realty Times,* August 9, 2005. Available at *http://realtytimes.com/printrtpages/20050809_energypolicy.htm.* Accessed October 3, 2005.

Perkins Coie LLP and Affiliates. 2005. Summary of the Energy Policy Act of 2005. Available at *http://www.perkinscoie.com/content/ren/updates/energy/080105.htm.* Accessed October 3, 2005.

Public Utility Commission of Ohio. 1999. Environmental Disclosure Rules 4901: 1–21–09. Available at *http://www.puco.ohio.gov/emplibrary/Case991611Sec490120030529.pdf.* Accessed October 15, 2005.

Rhode Island State Energy Office. 2005. Renewable Energy Incentives. Available at *http://www.riseo.state.ri.us/programs/rei.html.* Accessed October 12, 2005.

U.S. Department of Energy. 2004. FreedomCAR & Vehicle Technologies Program: Energy Policy Act (EPAct). Available at *http://www.eere.energy.gove/vehiclesandfuels/epact/about/index.shtml.* Accessed October 3, 2005.

White House. 2005. The Energy Bill: Good for Consumers, the Economy, and the Environment. Available at *http://www.whitehouse.gove/news/releases/2005/07/200050529–9.html.* Accessed October 3, 2005.

Wyoming Carbon Power and Light. 2005. Photovoltaic Leasing Program. Available at *http://www.carbonpower.com/memberservices.htm.* Accessed October 3, 2005.

2. Governing Energy Innovation: The Case of New York State

W. Henry Lambright,
Sarah Pralle, and Jessica Boscarino
Syracuse University, The Maxwell School
of Citizenship and Public Affairs

Introduction

In November 1996, New York State residents voted to approve a $1.75 billion environmental bond fund. Called the Clean Water/Clean Air Bond Act, the measure funded myriad environmental protection and restoration projects. Its focus was environment, but many of the specific provisions in the Act reflected the recognition that environmental impacts could be mitigated in part by changing energy supply. The provision of such a large amount of public funding for environmental activities was monumental, and the Bond Act's progenitor, Governor George Pataki, proclaimed it as such, noting in 1997, "One hundred years ago, New York's Governor, Teddy Roosevelt, led the modern conservation movement. Last year, our people went to the polls and rekindled that proud tradition of environmental leadership... New York is again poised to the lead the nation" (Pataki 1997).

The Bond Act was only the biggest of a sequence of actions that gradually brought less polluting energy to the forefront of state priorities. In June 2001, for example, Governor Pataki issued an executive order directing all state-owned facilities to purchase 10 percent of their electricity from renewable sources by 2005 and 20 percent by 2010. Three years later, the state Public Service Commission enacted a Renewables Portfolio Standard (RPS) which required that 25 percent of the state's electricity come from renewable sources by 2013. At present, eighteen other states have a similar policy, and only Maine requires that a larger percentage of electricity is derived from renewables.[1] In April 2003, Governor Pataki reached beyond the state level when he invited governors from the Northeast to begin planning for a regional response to climate change. Pataki pledged that New York State would act unilaterally if necessary, but emphasized the importance of addressing the climate change issue on at least a regional scale.

State innovation and leadership in environmental policy is not new, of course: given the relative lack of leadership at the federal level in recent years on myriad environmental issues, states have taken the lead in tackling problems that are typically seen as national or international in scope (Rabe 2004).

Even so, the case of policy innovation in New York State is noteworthy because of the considerable evolution and amplification of energy policy that has occurred in recent years. This chapter seeks to explain this evolution in energy policy. It will argue that the success of renewable energy legislation in New York can be attributed to three key factors: 1) the support and encouragement of environmental groups and private developer interests at the local level combined with the absence (thus far) of sustained opposition by affected publics; 2) the existence of facilitative regulation as well as bureaucratic capacity and support for energy research and development and; 3) the political will and policy entrepreneurship of the Pataki administration. This combination of factors has resulted in ambitious state energy policy, making New York an important case study in energy policy innovation in the contemporary era.

Federalism, Policy Innovation, and Policy Entrepreneurs

The environmental movement of the 1960s and 1970s led to the enactment of a wide array of environmental statutes at the national level governing everything from landfills to water pollutants to endangered species. This explosion in federal regulation reflected environmental advocates' lack of faith in the willingness and ability of states and localities to address serious environmental problems such as air and water pollution (Crenson 1971).

Cities and states were seen as sympathetic to local industry at best and entangled in an inevitable "race to the bottom" with other jurisdictions at worst, a structural feature of federalism that allegedly prevented states from being leaders and innovators in environmental policy.[2] Advocates of national regulation argued that the mobility of capital and the inability of states to control the flow of capital across state borders meant that states would be in competition with each other to provide a "business friendly" environment, resulting in a lack of progressive environmental policies at the state level. Federal regulation was necessary, it was argued, to provide a minimum floor below which states could not fall.

More recently, "race to the bottom" theories have been challenged on both theoretical and empirical grounds. Scholars of environmental federalism have noted that states often go above and beyond national minimum standards; some have even dubbed states the "new heroes" of American federalism (Rabe 2006). These scholars note that local and state governments may face "upward" pressures to strengthen environmental regulations from citizens and interest groups, not just "downward" pressures from anti-regulatory forces. States have also built their administrative capacity to address complex environmental problems. With increased incentives and capacity to address environmental problems, and with a network of environmental policy professionals who act as entrepreneurs for innovative policy ideas, new environmental programs can rapidly diffuse across state borders.

Acknowledging the potential for state leadership and innovation in environmental policy does not explain why any particular state assumes leadership around an individual issue or set of issues, however. In general, we should expect that the severity of the environmental problem, the partisanship of state leaders, and the degree of public mobilization and support for environmental policies will shape a state's response to environmental problems. Beyond these broad contextual factors, the unique features of a state political environment can encourage innovation: we focus in particular on the presence of policy entrepreneurs. As Kingdon (1984) notes in his study of agenda setting, policy entrepreneurs in and outside government play a large role in bringing attention to issues, in "coupling" policy problems with solutions, and in identifying and taking advantage of "windows of opportunity" to push policy proposals to the next stage of the policy process. In other words, policy entrepreneurs move the policy process along from one stage to another, often overcoming the opposition or indifference of others. The actor that plays this role may change over time; in the agenda setting phase, an interest group might take the lead, while during implementation, a government bureaucrat might be the main policy entrepreneur. But unless some entity fills the role of policy entrepreneur — someone who is willing to invest personal resources such as time, material resources and political capital into an issue — the policy often stalls at some stage in the process.

Successful policy entrepreneurs seek solutions that are technically feasible and compatible with public values and the values of policy specialists (Kingdon 1984). The criterion of technical feasibility means that the current state of technology can limit the type of solutions advocated by policy entrepreneurs. But as the cases of energy policy innovation below illustrate, policy change can beget technological change. In New York State, the 1996 Environmental Bond Act funded research and development into green energy technologies while the Renewables Portfolio Standard was designed to provide a market for renewable energy. Both policies have encouraged the development of technologies based on renewable sources of energy rather than fossil fuels, suggesting that "technical feasibility" is itself shaped by public policy. With respect to Kingdon's second criteria, the solutions promoted by Governor Pataki and others in his administration are generally compatible with the values of the public and policy specialists. None of the policy changes outlined in the following cases require significant sacrifices on the part of the public. Moreover, the largely market-based solutions advocated by Pataki have blunted potential opposition from industry; in the case of the New York City bus system, the Governor has managed to support a nascent industry in the state, leading to financial gains for that sector. Put differently, his policies have supported native businesses while helping to decrease the state's reliance on out-of-state energy sources.

The next section provides some background material to understand the political context for energy policymaking in New York State. Following this, examination of three cases of energy innovation in the state. The first is the transition from diesel fuels in the urban (especially New York City) bus system. The second is the deployment of wind energy technology in rural regions of the state. The third is the still-developing case of the Regional Greenhouse Gas Initiative through which New York seeks to institute regional climate change policy with sister states. The bus and wind cases have lengthy histories and are well into the implementation stage. The climate change policy innovation case is at the policy formulation stage.

The New York State Energy Policy Setting

NEW YORK STATE'S ENERGY INFRASTRUCTURE

New York State government is characterized by a strong governor, who wields a great deal of power over state policy and expenditures (New York State Senate 1988). The executive branch drafts the state budget and, while the legislature considers the budget and suggests changes, the executive has the ability to veto these changes line-by-line. In order to override the veto, the legislature must garner widespread support in both houses. This support is very difficult to obtain because of the nature of New York State's legislature. The State Assembly is composed of 150 representatives and is heavily Democratic and skewed in the downstate (New York City) direction. The Senate, with equal representation for state districts, leans in the direction of upstate — and Republican — majorities. Stalemates between the two houses mean that little happens in Albany unless the New York governor plays an energetic role in policy.

Below Governor Pataki sits the state Energy Planning Board, which has jurisdiction over all energy policy in New York. Created by Pataki in 1998, the Board consists of the leaders of the major public administrative units of government for energy. They are the New York State Energy Research and Development Authority (NYSERDA), the State Department of Transportation (DOT), the Department of Environmental Conservation (DEC), the Department of Economic Development, and the NY State Public Service Commission (PSC). Pataki appoints the heads of NYSERDA, DOT, DEC, PSC, and the Economic Development office. Thus, the governor is able to place like-minded individuals on the Board. This leadership is important because the Board has responsibility for drafting the State Energy Plan, a set of recommendations for energy policy in New York. The first Energy Plan was written in 1977 and the document is drafted every four years, most recently in 2002.

Perhaps the most important governmental body that contributes to New York's energy infrastructure—from a standpoint of technological innovation — is NYSERDA. This authority, which is dedicated entirely to energy research and development (R&D), sets New York apart from most other states. NYSERDA was established in 1975 during the energy crisis of that decade. It was created as a public benefits corporation, funding research into energy supply and efficiency, as well as energy-related environmental issues. It derives its funding from an assessment on the interstate sales of New York State's investor-owned electric and gas utilities, federal grants, and voluntary annual contributions by the New York Power

Authority and Long Island Power Authority (two public-sector utilities). This structure means that NYSERDA employees are not civil servants, and its basic budget has historically not come from the New York State budget. This fact has given NYSERDA both a measure of political insulation and organizational resilience.

This quasi-private, quasi-public organization was small in budget and personnel when it was first formed, and therefore NYSERDA found it was most effective when it "leveraged" projects that were already underway with other sources of funds. When deregulation reduced the amount of mandatory R&D being conducted by the utilities, Governor Pataki took note of the shortfall and began enlarging the budget of NYSERDA so it could take on some of the functions previously sponsored by the private sector. From 1975 to 2005, the budget of NYSERDA grew from approximately $15 million to approximately $220 million, with substantial gains in the Pataki era. NYSERDA maintains a leveraging, market-oriented approach today. It usually does not make available grants for the full cost of research and development, but rather provides researchers with a financial incentive sufficient to proceed with a project they wish to pursue and for which they need additional funding.

Another state agency that has traditionally been an important actor in terms of energy is the Public Service Commission. The Commission regulates the state's electric, gas, steam, telecommunications, and water utilities. In the past, the Commission required electric utilities to devote a certain percentage of funds towards energy research and development, fostering technological innovation. After deregulation of the energy industry, most utilities ceased funding R&D, which is now an optional activity. However, the Public Service Commission continues to be a relevant organization in energy. In 2004, acting upon a directive by Governor Pataki and the recommendations of the Energy Planning Board, the Commission enacted a Renewables Portfolio Standard. This ambitious and significant policy will stimulate the generation of electricity from renewable sources and provide a market for its sale.

Energy policy and technology is also influenced at the regional and local levels. The Department of Transportation's municipal arm in New York City, the Metropolitan Transit Authority (MTA), has been very active in promoting clean-fuel buses in the city. By connecting with state government and, ultimately, other municipal agencies across the region, the Metropolitan Transit Authority has spearheaded the introduction of hybrid electric buses for commercial transportation.

Another significant state organization operating at the regional level is the New York Power Authority. This is a not-for-profit, state-owned

utility, which "anchors much of the state's existing renewable power supply with large hydroelectric projects on the Niagara and St. Lawrence rivers,
as well as other waterpower facilities" (Ciminelli 2004, A19). Some 19 percent of New York's current energy supply for power comes from hydroelectric sources.

Pataki as a Policy Entrepreneur

Since his election in 1994, George Pataki has chosen to use the powers of the governor to move the state energy infrastructure in a "greener"
direction. Pataki was born in 1945 and grew up on his family's farm in
Peekskill, New York, a rural area of Westchester county. He received his
Bachelor's degree from Yale University in 1967 and a law degree from
Columbia in 1970. In 1981, he successfully ran for Mayor of Peekskill. After
serving two terms as mayor, Pataki was elected to the New York Assembly, where he served four terms before winning a seat in the State Senate
in 1992. Two years later, he ran for governor and defeated three-term incum-
bent Mario Cuomo. Pataki was re-elected in 1998 and again in 2002.

A Republican, Pataki looked to Theodore Roosevelt as a model leader.
He once said, "TR understood the difference between an activist government that helps the people and an overbearing government that diminishes their freedom... Government can do great things for the American
people if it limits its role to doing a few things and doing them well"
(Friends of Pataki 2003, 2). Pataki has been an activist governor in the fields
he has selected, one of which is the environment, an issue that he clearly
cares deeply about. His energy policy has largely stemmed from this environmental activism.

Pataki says that he owes his interest in the environment to his youth,
growing up along the banks of the Hudson River. His admiration for Theodore Roosevelt is revealed not only in Pataki's public actions, but in his
naming of one of his four children Teddy. His closest aide, Chief of Staff
John Cahill, is a former director of the state Department of Environmental Conservation. He has surrounded himself with appointees in key envi-
ronmental/energy positions in his administration who share his values.
To be sure, he has to deal with the host of contentious issues any governor must face — such as rising health care costs, economic disparities, and
constant struggles to balance the budget — and is harshly criticized for
actions in these areas. However, he is most at home dealing with policies
that involve environmental issues, and increasingly, renewable energy; in
this realm has won plaudits, although detractors remain in the environmental community.[3]

New Technology for NYC Buses

The transportation industry accounts for fully 32 percent of U.S. carbon dioxide emissions (Rocky Mountain Institute 2005). Mass-transit vehicles such as buses are often some of the worst offenders given their frequent stops and long idle times. New York City has taken significant steps to reduce the impact of commercial vehicles on air pollution and climate change. NYSERDA has supported research and development in this area, and in 1996, the governor promoted and citizens of New York passed a bond act that provided funds for various environmental improvements. Among the programs thereby established was one for the purchase of alternative fuel vehicles. This innovation is well into the implementation stage and may reach institutionalization in the future.

Beginning in 1993, the Natural Resources Defense Council and a group of other environmental advocacy organizations began a campaign to inform the public about the health risks of diesel emissions and to convince government to invest in alternative technologies. The "Dump Dirty Diesel" campaign sought the complete phase-out of all diesel vehicles. They argued for a short-term switch to natural gas, to be eventually replaced with alternative vehicles, such as hybrid electrics. The groups ran a high profile campaign, purchasing advertising space on New York City buses that read "Standing behind this bus could be more dangerous than standing in front of it."

Although these actions got the attention of New York leaders, the state was already very active in clean-fuel transportation by this time. In 1990, NYSERDA became interested in the potential of hybrid electric buses for commercial service. An Ontario, Canada-based company, Bus Industries of America (later Orion Industries) successfully bid to receive NYSERDA funding to develop a hybrid electric drive train for buses. A host of other entities also offered funding for the project, which cost $1.25 million in total. Out of this effort came a small commercial bus that utilized a hybrid natural gas-electric engine, and used 30–40 percent less energy and emitted 70 percent fewer pollutants than standard diesel engines. It was the first commercial hybrid system in the United States.

This bus showed so much promise throughout the testing period that NYSERDA got involved in an effort to develop a full-size commercial vehicle. The consortium included the Metropolitan Transit Authority, the NYC Transit Authority, and Con Edison. The group received $2.5 million from the Federal Transit Authority, to be administered by NYSERDA. In 1995, General Electric was selected by NYSERDA to develop a hybrid electric drive train for a forty-foot bus for which Orion Industries would supply the bus hardware. The entire process of developing, producing, and testing the vehicle cost approximately $5–$6 million. However, the project screeched to a halt when disagreements arose among General Electric, the Metropolitan Transit Authority, and the Federal Transit Authority over procurement of the buses. The price that General Electric proposed for manufacturing the buses was far greater than the Metropolitan Transit Authority was willing to spend, and all of the groups involved became very frustrated.

NYSERDA was forced to find a new supplier, who would repeat the development, production, and testing process once again. Lockheed Martin (later BAE Systems) showed interest in supplying the hybrid technology; however, the firm insisted upon securing a purchase agreement from the Metropolitan Transit Authority before it would develop the buses. The Authority was aware of impending EPA emissions standards that mandated the use of only low-sulfur diesel fuel by June of 2006.[4] In addition, they recognized the potential cost savings to be realized through the use of hybrid buses. Therefore, the MTA agreed to purchase twenty-five of Lockheed's vehicles, an amount to be increased after six months of problem-free operation. NYSERDA provided Lockheed with approximately $1–2 million and the company contributed an additional $20 million of its own funds to the project. By 1998, a pilot fleet of ten hybrid buses were integrated into regular revenue service on the streets of New York.

Clearly, hybrid electric bus technology was being developed out of the public spotlight for several years. However, the development and deployment of these alternative vehicles accelerated dramatically when the governor became involved. With the passage of the Clean Water/Clean Air Bond Act in 1996, the state provided $230 million for clean air projects, including the development and purchase of clean fuel buses. In Pataki's 1997 State of the State Address, he pledged to replace old diesel buses with alternative fuels and technology through the "Clean-Fuel Bus Program." He released funds from the Bond Act (in conjunction with other state and federal money) for the procurement of emerging hybrid electric technology.

Subsequently, Pataki has released rounds of funding from the Clean Water/Clean Air Bond Act for clean bus technology. Each time, the funding has been split between compressed natural gas and hybrid electric vehicles and infrastructure. The program soon expanded beyond New York City to the city of Syracuse and to Tompkins, Westchester, and Broome counties. In 2000, Pataki announced an expansion of the Clean-Fuel Bus Program and estimated that by 2006, there will be three hundred and eighty-five hybrid buses in use across the state. As of September 2004,

Pataki has released seven rounds of funding under the program, totaling $28 million.

The Clean-Fuel Bus Program moved quickly through the policy process stages, from agenda setting activities conducted by both the Metropolitan Transit Authority and environmental advocacy groups, to formulation, adoption, and implementation. Bond Act funds are now largely disbursed, and continued hybrid electric development may need to rely on private sector funds in the future. There is good reason to believe that such a transition will not hamper the technology's deployment, however. When the Bond Act was passed in 1996, NYSERDA, the Metropolitan Transit Authority, and developers had already demonstrated a successful, commercial hybrid electric bus. Before they were aware that state funding would become available for the procurement of these buses, the Metropolitan Transit Authority agreed to purchase them from Lockheed Martin. Thus, the Bond Act is better understood as a piece of legislation that accelerated the diffusion of this technology rather than stimulated it in the R&D stage. In the words of one NYSERDA official, "without Bond Act funding, the technology still would have moved, but much more slowly... it is responsible for the hybrids being as successful as they are, but it wasn't necessarily critical" (Drake 2005). Given that hybrid buses can cost up to $125,000 more per bus than standard diesel buses do, how can it be explained why New York City's Metropolitan Transit Authority so enthusiastically adopted the technology?

There are three closely related factors that contributed to this decision. The first reason is that Metropolitan Transit Authority officials realized that they would eventually be required to reconfigure their fleet in order to comply with federal Environmental Protection Agency standards mandating the phase-out of all standard diesel fuels beginning in 2006. This left the Authority with three options: low-sulfur diesel fuel, compressed natural gas (CNG), or hybrid electrics. When considering emissions standards, hybrid technology is far superior to the other two options. Hybrids emit 50 percent less nitrogen oxides than low-sulfur diesel and CNG buses, 75 percent less carbon dioxide than low-sulfur diesel buses, and 90 percent less carbon dioxide than CNG buses (Walsh 2004). Thus, as the Chief Maintenance Officer of the Metropolitan Transit Authority articulated, the organization views hybrid electrics as "The Bus of the Future" (Walsh 2005).

Secondly, apart from statutory requirements, the Metropolitan Transit Authority was driven by environmental considerations. A commitment to minimal environmental impact permeated the organization. Two top Authority leaders, Chief Maintenance Officer John Walsh and Director of

Equipment Maintenance Dana Leavy, were key individuals in imparting and acting upon this pledge. In addition, the Metropolitan Transit Authority had outside forces campaigning for environmentally-friendly business practices. A group of environmental organizations, including the Natural Resources Defense Council and West Harlem Environmental Action, launched an initiative to push the Authority into phasing out the use of pollutant-heavy diesel fuels. These groups became involved with the planning of the Clean-Fuel Bus Program, and played a large role in Pataki's decision to commit to having the cleanest fleet in North America. One official reflected that environmentalists served as "advocates for forcing us to move forward" (Walsh 2005). The depth of MTA's environmental commitment, influenced by both internal and external forces, is illustrated in the fact that the New York City Metropolitan Transit Authority was the first transit agency in the country to purchase and operate hybrid electric buses.

Lastly, and most importantly, the Metropolitan Transit Authority recognized that they could reap significant financial benefits by increasing their fleet of hybrid electric buses. The engines used in hybrid vehicles are not fuel-specific. Therefore, depending on the availability and cost of various fuels, hybrid buses can use standard or low-sulfur diesel, or natural gas. Furthermore, many different forms of energy storage can be utilized in the vehicles, including batteries and hydrogen fuel cells. This flexibility means that transportation authorities can adapt to future needs without incurring large costs to update technology. Whereas natural gas vehicles require retro-fitting of bus depots to handle maintenance issues, no additional infrastructure is required to service hybrid buses. In addition, hybrids are 35 percent more fuel efficient than standard diesel engines. The average standard diesel bus uses 13,000 gallons of fuel per year, as opposed to 8,800 gallons used by hybrids. At a gas price of $2.00/gallon, this amounts to a yearly price differential of $8,400 per bus (Walsh 2004).

As is illustrated above, hybrid electric bus technology was initiated by bureaucratic government — namely, NYSERDA and the New York City Metropolitan Transit Authority. It was pursued for both environmental and economic reasons. However, it likely would have remained a small program that proceeded at a leisurely pace without the involvement of Governor Pataki. The Clean Air/Clean Water Bond Act provided millions in funding for transit authorities across the state to purchase hybrid buses, helping to reduce procurement costs. Pataki's 2000 Executive Order directing the Metropolitan Transit Authority to commit to achieving the cleanest vehicle fleet provided an additional impetus.

Pataki's interest in hybrid vehicles stems from both his environmental activism and his desire to improve New York's economy. The buses are manufactured at two New York plants—Orion Bus Industries in Oriskany, and Nova Bus in Schenectady. Phasing out the use of diesel vehicles that are manufactured elsewhere and shipped in-state in favor of locally produced buses brings additional revenue into New York. In Pataki's own words, "In addition to cleaning up our air, these buses represent the future of New York's economy" (New York State Office of the Governor 2000, 1).

Indeed, hybrid electrics appear to be the mass-transit vehicle of choice for the future. Their use continues to grow at an increasing rate. In 2003, the Metropolitan Transit Authority had 10 forty-foot buses in use; by 2004, this number jumped to 131 and at the end of 2005, estimates suggest that the fleet will increase to 325 (Walsh 2004). Although hybrids are still more expensive to produce than standard diesels, the savings to be reaped from fuel efficiency will prove to make the buses increasingly affordable. If gas prices continue to rise, the amount of time before transit authorities begin to see a return on investment will shrink, making them more and more desirable. At a price of $2.00/gallon, hybrid buses can reap a $100,000 savings over diesels within twelve years. If this price increases to $3.00/gallon, the twelve-year price differential between diesel and hybrid electric buses is more than $125,000 (Walsh 2004).

Wind Energy for Rural New York

Policy surrounding wind energy development in New York is entering the implementation stage. The Renewables Portfolio Standard (RPS) of 2004 represents a significant policy action, both in scope and impact. If New York achieves the 25 percent production rates for renewable energy set out by the RPS, its proportional generation of renewables will be second only to Maine.[5] By requiring that a percentage of overall energy production come from renewable energy sources, the legislation will serve to make wind energy an economically competitive energy source in New York. Moreover, environmental groups estimate that increasing renewable energy production will reduce emissions of nitrogen oxides, sulfur dioxide and carbon dioxide by 5 to 7 percent and improve air quality (Environmental Advocates of New York 2005). However, implementing the RPS will be challenging because it is a very ambitious policy. The relatively short timeframe until compliance and its emphasis on new wind development places a premium on expediting the process of siting, permitting, and construction, which has delayed many existing projects.

Wind energy development dates to before the adoption of the RPS, and its burgeoning success can be attributed to many actors, including developers, NYSERDA, the Public Service Commission, and Governor Pataki. In 1981, California became home to the first commercial wind farm in the United States. Initial excitement over the potential of wind-generated electricity led to a proliferation of the technology that lasted until the mid–1980s. By the end of the decade, however, these early turbine models proved to be relatively inefficient and petroleum prices slid to record low levels, causing enthusiasm for wind energy to wane. With the inception of the federal Production Tax Credit (PTC) as a part of the 1992 Energy Policy Act, wind development increased once again. The PTC provided a tax credit of 1.5 cents per kilowatt hour (kWh) (increased annually thereafter) for electricity generated by wind for the first ten years of a project's operation. The credit was set to expire in June 1999, and a flurry of activity preceded this event as developers attempted to get their turbines online before the expiration date.

During the early days of wind technology, very little activity was occurring in New York. When Pataki took office as Governor in 1995 as a strong proponent of the environment, however, developers began to take notice. In fact, the history of wind power in New York details a technology that was initiated by industry, threatened by lack of federal support, and rescued by state government. During the late 1990s, developers began to look closely at New York as a promising market for producing and selling wind energy. New York State has enough natural potential to produce 62 billion kWh of wind-generated electricity per year (American Wind Energy Association 2005), an amount that would power approximately 5.8 million homes.[6] Many areas of New York that are rich in wind resources are relatively sparsely populated. Unlike some communities in popular tourist areas such as Cape Cod, New York residents are generally receptive to the installation of wind farms.[7] Additionally, and perhaps most importantly, under George Pataki, New York State government has been very supportive of wind energy development.

The existence of NYSERDA and the funding it provides for the development of wind farms is crucial to attracting developers. Currently, NYSERDA has pledged $20 million in grants to defray the development and construction costs of four proposed wind farm projects across the state, in addition to funding already provided to the three commercial wind farms in existence. Additionally, Pataki's support of wind energy was an important draw for industry. Developers noted that Pataki was willing to work with state regulators to facilitate the lengthy regulatory process involved with wind farm siting so as to prevent unnecessary delays (Moore 2005). Wind developers identified in New York a promising natural landscape, receptive public, and a state government that would serve as a valuable ally.

In 1999, PG&E Generating announced plans to construct New York's first large-scale, commercial wind plant on the farms of upstate Madison County. The project was developed by Atlantic Renewable Energy Corporation, a Virginia-based company that has projects all across the Eastern United States. The Madison plant went online in September 2000. At the same time, Western NY Wind Corporation was working on a project in Wyoming County, which would produce roughly half the amount of electricity of the Madison plant. This plant, in Wethersfield, NY, went online one month after the turbines began spinning at Madison.

By this time, the federal Production Tax Credit had expired, resulting in a nation-wide decrease in wind development from 575 MW of new capacity in 1999 to 43 MW in 2000 (Union of Concerned Scientists 2005). Atlantic Renewable and Western NY Wind Corporation recognized an opportunity in New York, however. New York residents supported renewable energy, and the belief at the time was that wind power would "clearly sell in New York — that's not even debatable" (Knauss 1999). The fact that New York was one of only a few states that had a body like NYSERDA made it even more attractive. The Madison plant received $2 million in NYSERDA funding. Bill Moore of Atlantic Renewable, who developed the Madison plant, believes "developers would not have come here without NYSERDA support" (2005).

The initial success of the Madison and Wethersfield plants led to the construction of a third merchant plant in upstate New York. Atlantic Renewable constructed the Fenner wind farm in the same area as the Madison plant. Fenner was designed on a completely different scale, however, and, at the time it was built, was the largest wind farm in the Eastern United States, producing 300 MW of electricity per year, enough to power approximately 90,000 homes.[8]

Wind developers were initially drawn to New York for its natural potential and welcoming public and government. However, they have experienced several challenges. As mentioned above, the Production Tax Credit for wind energy has expired and been reinstated several times since its inception in 1992. This lack of stability in federal support has caused a great deal of market uncertainty, no doubt resulting in lowered rates of wind energy development. Although wind energy is the cheapest "clean" renewable energy, it is nonetheless relatively expensive when compared to subsidized oil and coal. Without financial incentives that place wind energy on a more even playing field with fossil fuels, renewables development remains stalled.

While the vast majority of communities are welcoming to wind development, the new technology does encounter some resistance. As all existing wind farms in New York are located in rural areas, most residents appreciate the installation of turbines on local land as a new source of revenue. Others recognize the environmental benefits of wind power. However, developers are increasingly coming up against residents that complain about the aesthetic impact of tall turbines, the noise associated with the blades, and the potential harm posed to bird populations (Poetz 2004). These reactions rarely prevent the siting of a wind farm in any specific area, but do significantly slow the process while developers seek to reassure inhabitants and try to mitigate the effects of misinformation.

Perhaps the largest single barrier to wind energy generally has been the lack of a guaranteed market for green energy. In the absence of buying agreements from utilities or power producers, investors have been very resistant to fund wind energy development. While these challenges continue to prevent the wide-scale adoption of wind energy technology elsewhere in the nation, New York has addressed these barriers directly. Funding provided by NYSERDA for wind energy development has reduced the capital costs associated with siting and constructing a wind farm. In the absence of the Production Tax Credit, this money has been essential. That it was provided was due in part to Governor Pataki, who took a personal interest in pushing renewables. In addition to NYSERDA's filling a "federal money gap," the governor pushed on another front. The adoption by the Public Service Commission of the state Renewables Portfolio Standard in fall 2004 has been instrumental in providing a market for renewables. By requiring utilities to provide 25 percent of their electricity from renewable sources, wind developers have secured a buyer for their product. This makes the acquisition of loans more accessible, as lenders are more willing to provide funds.

After a several-year lull, wind energy is once again growing in New York. Five facilities produce 48 MW of electricity annually, and currently proposed projects would bring the total to 637 MW per year. In the greater U.S., the country's wind energy generation increased by 30 percent last year (Clemence 2004). If the planned Flat Rock Wind Power site is completed in northern Lewis County, it will be the largest wind farm in the Eastern United States, dwarfing the existing New York plants.

The governor's interest in renewables grew out of his environmental priorities initially, but was greatly reinforced by the events of September 11th, 2001. The terrorist attacks heightened his awareness of New York's energy dependence and vulnerability, as reflected in his remarks during the 2002 "State of the State" address: "I will also introduce a program to improve our environment and reduce our dependence on foreign imported energy by leading the nation in the development and deployment of renewable energy resources.... By doing so we can not only clean our air, but also ... increase our security" (Pataki 2002, 11). The Energy Planning Board agreed with Pataki's sentiments and pushed for greater renewables development to increase energy security (New York State Energy Planning Board 2002).

New York and Regional Climate Change Partnerships

Whereas the other cases discussed in this chapter detail policy innovation that was initiated by private industry or government agencies and subsequently supported by high-level policy adopted by the governor, climate change policy seems to have originated at the top. Governor Pataki is leading an effort to tackle the problem of climate change at the regional level, and his commitment to the issue has moved the policy into the formulation stage. The involvement of ten other states means that policy adoption and implementation will be both very difficult and potentially very rewarding.

The Regional Greenhouse Gas Initiative (RGGI) is the culmination of increasing gubernatorial interest in climate change. In June 2001, Pataki formed a Greenhouse Gas (GHG) Task Force to advise him on policy recommendations and strategies for reducing New York's greenhouse gas emissions. In addition, as a member state of the Northeast States for Coordinated Air Use Management, an organization dedicated to regulating air quality in the Northeast, New York has been involved with climate change initiatives pursued under the Conference of New England Governors and Eastern Canadian Premiers. The Conference's Climate Change Action Plan, adopted in June 2001, called for the establishment of a greenhouse gas registry to create baseline emissions assessments. New York participated in the formation of the Regional Greenhouse Gas Registry, which was launched in October 2003.

On April 25, 2003, Governor Pataki sent a letter to ten governors of Northeastern and Mid-Atlantic states, asking them to join New York in a regional effort to reduce greenhouse gas emissions. He proposed a regional cap-and-trade program regulating carbon dioxide emissions released by power plants. The program would involve a cooperative process to establish a maximum emissions level, allocate emissions allowances among the source plants, and design a system of allowance trading. By July, Pataki received positive responses from the governors of Connecticut, Delaware, Maine, Massachusetts, New Hampshire, New Jersey, Rhode Island and Vermont. Maryland and Pennsylvania declined to join the partnership, but agreed to participate in the process as observers. In addition, the Premiers of the Eastern Canadian Provinces and the Province of New Brunswick are observers to the effort.

Based upon the cap-and-trade program regulating nitrogen oxides and sulfur dioxide in the 1990 Clean Air Act amendments, the Regional Greenhouse Gas uses a market-based approach. The goal of the initiative is to reduce carbon dioxide emissions while maintaining energy affordability and reliability. To this end, Pataki identified the states that comprise the three major electricity systems in the region. By securing cooperation from these states, the program can ensure that regulations do not interfere with interstate electricity sales.

The Regional Greenhouse Gas Initiative builds off of existing state commitments to reduce greenhouse gas emissions. For example, New York's energy plan calls for a 5 percent emissions reduction from 1990 levels by 2010, to be reduced even further by 2020. Similarly, New Jersey pledged to reduce emissions to 3.5 percent below 1990 levels by 2005. The conference of the New England Governors and Eastern Canadian Premiers, another regional alliance, called for a 10 percent reduction in greenhouse gases from 1990 levels by 2010 (Regional Greenhouse Gas Initiative 2003). Pataki hoped to harness these individual commitments and improve their effectiveness by pursuing a harmonized approach. As he noted when he sent his letter inviting the states to join, "Today, we are pursuing a course of cooperation and we are confident that this will achieve meaningful reductions in harmful emissions without disrupting electricity markets" (New York State Office of the Governor 2003a, 1).

The Initiative is designed to be executed in stages. The first stage, the learning phase, was completed in March 2004. The primary purpose was to create a forum where the states could begin to come together. This would facilitate not only early talks as to which experts to pull into the process and what legal mechanisms the states preferred, but also to share experiences regarding carbon dioxide emissions regulation. Next, the Initiative proceeded into the first development phase, begun in October 2003. During this stage, states decided upon the core design of the cap-and-trade program through the use of data collection, modeling, and cost-benefit analysis. A draft proposal for the program design was released at the end of August 2005. Now, the process will move into the second development phase. This effort focuses on establishing offset mechanisms for surplus emissions reductions outside of the electricity sector.

These two development phases can best be understood as policy formulation, the stage at which the process is currently operating. During formulation, member states are designing policy goals and mechanisms for the initiative. After planning is complete, the initiative will move into policy adoption, where it will be seen whether or not the states agree to the Initiative as it has been proposed by the state representatives. If adopted, it will move into implementation. After implementation of the initial carbon dioxide cap-and-trade program, the states will consider whether or not to expand the initiative to cover non-power plant sources of carbon dioxide, or to include other greenhouse gases.

Each of the tasks within the phases is coordinated by a state-led Subgroup. For instance, Connecticut is the lead Subgroup for data gathering and technical analysis in the first development phase. Representatives from other states also participate in the tasks. In addition to the Subgroups, the entire process is overseen by a Steering Committee that consists of representatives from three states that are appointed for six-month terms. The initiative allows for a stakeholder process, whereby selected stakeholder groups from the energy and environmental sectors in each state can attend meetings and submit comments on the effort.[9]

This initiative is distinctive for many reasons. To begin with, the program has fostered bi-partisan cooperation. Of the participating states, six of them have Republican governors and four have Democrats in office. This cross-party collaboration builds off of a long history of multi-state environmental initiatives. As observers to the Conference of New England Governors and Eastern Canadian Premiers, New York has been very active in regional actions to reduce acid rain and mercury. New York also participates in the Ozone Transport Commission, a body created by the 1990 Clean Air Act amendments.

Although a regional coalition may seem ineffective in the face of a global problem such as climate change, the member states are home to one-fifth of the nation's population. Therefore, the Regional Greenhouse Gas Initiative has the potential to make a serious contribution to climate change mitigation. Moreover, the initiative could serve as a model to other states, the nation, and the world as a whole. As the advocacy group Environmental Defense noted, the Initiative sets a "critical national precedent as to how to deal with global warming" (New York State Office of the Governor 2003b, 1).

Conclusion

While environmentalists were once skeptical about the ability and willingness of states to be leaders in environmental policy, some are now heralding them as the last best hope for environmental progress. As Barry Rabe (2006) notes, "According to this line of argument, states are consistently at the cutting edge of policy innovation, eager to find creative solutions to environmental problems" (35). The performance of states in environmental policy is uneven at best, and a substantial role still exists for the federal government: indeed, significant progress in moving toward a sustainable energy policy in the United States will require massive federal investment in alternative energy research and technology. Nevertheless, not all state governments are waiting for the federal government to act but are taking the lead in energy policy innovation. As this chapter has shown, New York State is one of the leaders in this area: among other innovations, it has encouraged the growth of wind energy and hybrid electric buses, and it is spearheading a regional effort to combat climate change. What or who is responsible for advancements to date? It has been argued that three factors are at work; together they have caused the beginning of what can be called policy amplification — the convergence of various policy streams adding up to a general, discernable energy transition away from fossil fuels.

The first factor in this process of transition is interest at the local level on the part of governmental and nongovernmental actors. In the case of hybrid electric buses, there was interest in hybrid electrics from environmental groups such as West Harlem Environmental Action and the regional bus enterprise, the Metropolitan Transportation Authority. These organizations wanted cleaner-burning fuels and had a regulatory impetus owing to clean air standards. In wind energy, there was pressure for change at the local level by private developers and residents who perceived economic development opportunities. Support at the state and local level for these innovations, in other words, was quite high while opposition to them was relatively weak. The relative lack of opposition to these proposals may be due to the skill of policy entrepreneurs, who chose locations for wind farms where support was generally high. It is also important to note that pressure on utilities for wind energy innovation has been modest thus far. Pataki has set a goal of 25 percent of New York's energy sources coming from renewables by 2013. If it takes a heavier state hand to reach that goal than thus far, the utilities may protest. But up to now, their response has been accepting of change. Similarly, the other states that Pataki has sought to enlist in his climate change initiative have not yet been asked to do more than meet, plan, and formulate options. The policy adoption stage will be a greater test of commitment to strong, coordinated goals, much less implementation.

The second factor responsible for the transition to more renewable energy is the state government bureaucracy. The New York State Energy

Research and Development Agency (NYSERDA), Public Service Commission, and Department of Transportation were prominent in the bus and wind cases. NYSERDA is a unique state agency in that it promotes energy technology innovation through R&D funding; most states do not have such a body. The Public Service Commission, as regulator, set the Renewables Portfolio Standard rules that provided a market pull from the utilities. The Department of Transportation encouraged change at the New York City level through the organization's local arm, the Metropolitan Transit Authority. And the various agencies are coordinated via a state Energy Planning Board and given general direction through an Energy Plan. This collection of state agencies has provided forward motion in promoting alternative energy sources, although the process has been somewhat piecemeal.

The third factor, the governor's political will, pulled the agencies together and accelerated and amplified policy innovation. Pataki's philosophy is to put the governor's power behind a few areas of policy, and environment/energy has been one to which he has given major priority. The Bond Act was his early spur to the whole process in that it provided financial resources for change. The Renewables Portfolio Standard exists because of Pataki's interest in renewable energy, an interest spurred by his experience with the September 11th terrorist attacks. The Renewables Portfolio Standard jump-started wind energy innovation. Pataki strengthened NYSERDA financially and helped speed regulatory action to ease wind energy's introduction. Pataki's influence also led to the regional climate change initiative. It is possible all these innovations might have progressed without the governor's intervention, but he clearly was a catalyst for accelerating the process.

In sum, New York State serves as an interesting model in state leadership and gubernatorial policy entrepreneurship around the issue of energy technology and policy. The case of New York State suggests a pattern of policy amplification, whereby one policy innovation leads to more innovation, adding up to significant policy change. This process exemplifies what is required if a true energy transition away from fossil fuels is to occur in the 21st century.

Notes

1. Maine's RPS requires that 30% of electricity generation come from renewable sources by 2000 ("State Clean Energy Maps and Graphs" Union of Concerned Scientists, http://www. ucsusa.org/clean_energy/renewable_energy/page.cfm?pageID=895. Load date: 03/07/05). When the RPS was enacted, more than 30% of the state's electricity was already being generated by renewables. The regulation was designed to ensure that these sources continued to be utilized.

2. For a review and critique of this literature, see Richard Revesz, Rehabilitating Interstate Competition: Rethinking 'Race-to-the-Bottom' Rationale for Federal Environmental Regulation. *New York University Law Review* 67: 1210–1254.

3. Pataki has received several awards from environmental organizations throughout his tenure. In June 2002, Scenic Hudson Inc. awarded Pataki the "Spirit of the River Award" for his work restoring the Hudson River estuary. In March 2004, Pataki received Audubon New York's William Hoyt Environmental Leadership award. On April 1, 2005, Pataki was awarded the Sol Feinstone Environmental Award from the State University of New York — School of Environmental Science and Forestry.

4. In January 2001, the EPA passed regulation on heavy-duty engines using diesel fuel. The standards require a 97 percent reduction in the sulfur content of diesel fuel. See *Heavy-Duty Engines and Vehicle Standards and Highway Diesel Sulfur Control Requirements*, U.S. Environmental Protection Agency, 40 CFR Parts 69, 80, and 86.

5. Under its Renewables Portfolio Standard, 30% of Maine's electricity is produced through renewable energy.

6. In 2001, 107 million U.S. households consumed 1,140 billion kWh of electricity (Department of Energy. 2005. U.S. Household Electricity Report. Available at http://www.eia.doe.gov/emeu/reps/enduse/er01_us.html#Electricity). At this rate, 62 billion kWh of wind-generated electricity would power approximately 5.8 billion homes.

7. Support of wind farms is not universal, however, and opposition is growing. Tom Golisano, a billionaire living in the Rochester, NY region, started a nonprofit organization dedicated to limiting the number of wind projects in upstate New York. See Michelle York, "Sometimes a Windmill Can Be a Lightning Rod," *New York Times*, 24 July 2005.

8. One megawatt (MW) of wind energy capacity produces enough electricity to power approximately 300 homes (American Wind Energy Association. 2004. U.S. Wind Energy Industry Rankings. Available at: http://www.awea.org/pubs/factsheets/USwindindustry rankings2004.pdf. Accessed November 8, 2005).

9. These organizations include the Conservation Law Foundation, the Public Interest Research Group, the Union of Concerned Scientists, Constellation Energy, Entergy, and Dominion Energy. For a complete list, see http://www.rggi.org/stakeholder_member.htm.

References

American Wind Energy Association. 2001. *Wind Group Applauds New York Commitment to Renewable Energy: Wind Generation Will Benefit From Pataki Move.* Available at *http://www.awea.org/news/news010613nys.html* Accessed November 1, 2004.

Ciminelli, Louis. 2004. New York at the Forefront of Green Power Movement. *Syracuse Post-Standard.* December 10, A19.

Clemence, Sara. 2004. Change is in the Wind: As New York Turns to Renewable Energy Sources, Massive Towers and Turbines Spring up on Farms to Reap Power from Air Currents. *The Albany Times Union.* October 17, E1.

Crenson, Matthew A. 1971. *The Un-Politics of Air Pollution.* Baltimore, M.D.: The Johns Hopkins Press.

Drake, Richard. Personal interview. February 4, 2005.

Environmental Advocates of New York. 2005. *Fact Sheet: the New York Renewable Energy Portfolio.* Available at *http://www.eany.org/pressreleases/2004/pop_rps.html* Accessed September 30 2005.

Friends of Pataki. 2003. About Governor Pataki. Available at *http://georgepataki.com/gp_docs/about/index.shtml* Accessed February 23, 2005.

Knauss, Tim. 1999. Windmills of Madison County: Hunt for "Green Power" Takes to the Air. The Hilltop Farm Would Be the First Large-Scale Wind Power Station in New York. *The Syracuse Post-Standard.* July 14, A1.

Moore, Bill. Personal interview. February 22, 2005.

New York State Energy Planning Board. 2002. New York State Energy Plan and Final Environmental Impact Statement.

New York State Office of the Governor. 2000. *Governor Pataki: $3.6 Million for 72 Clean-Fueled Buses.* Available at *http://www.state.ny.us/governor/press/year00/feb04_00.htm* Accessed January 1, 2005.

_____. 2003a. *Governor Calls on Northeast States to Fight Climate Change.* Available at *http://www.state.ny.us/governor/press/year03/april25_2_03.htm* Accessed March 24, 2005.

_____. 2003b. *Governor Announces Cooperation on Clean Air Initiative.* Available at *http://www.state.ny.us/governor/press/year03/july24_03.htm* Accessed March 24, 2005.

New York State Senate. 1988. *A Guide to New York State's Government.* Available at *http://www.senate.state.ny.us/sws/aboutsenate/branches_gov.html* Accessed March 28, 2005.

Pataki, George. 1997. New York State of the State Address. Available at *http://www.state.ny.us/governor/keydocs/sos97.html* Accessed November 5, 2004.

_____. 2002. New York State of the State Address. Available at *http://www.state.ny.us/governor/keydocs/sos02.html* Accessed November 5, 2004.

Poetz, Elmer. 2004. Meeting Wind Resistance: Turbine Projects In WNY are at a Standstill Due to Concerns over Risk to Birds. *The Buffalo News.* July 8, A1.

Rabe, Barry. 2004. *Statehouse and Greenhouse: The Emerging Politics of American Climate Change Policy.* Washington, D.C.: Brookings Institution Press.

_____. 2006. Power to the States: The Promises and Pitfalls of Decentralization. In *Environmental Policy: New Directions for the Twenty-First Century,* edited by Norman J. Vig and Michael E. Kraft, 34–56. Washington, D.C.: CQ Press.

Regional Greenhouse Gas Initiative. 2003. About RGGI. Available at: *http://www.rggi.org/about.htm.* Accessed October 21, 2004.

Revesz, Richard. 1992. Rehabilitating Interstate Competition: Rethinking 'Race-to-the-Bottom' Rationale for Federal Environmental Regulation *New York University Law Review* 67: 1210–1254.

Rocky Mountain Institute. 2005. *Transportation Greenhouse Gas Emissions.* Available at *http://www.rmi.org/sitepages/pid342.php* Accessed March 28, 2005.

Union of Concerned Scientists. 2005. *Renewable Energy Tax Credit Saved Once Again, but Boom-Bust Cycle in Wind Industry Continues.* Available at *http://www.ucsusa.org/clean_energy/clean_energy_policies/update-on-production-tax-credit-for-renewable-energy.html* Accessed September 30, 2005.

Walsh, John. 2004. NYCT Operating Experience with Hybrid Buses. Presented at the New York City Transit Department of Buses, November 30, New York, New York.

_____. Personal interview. February 14, 2005.

York, Michelle. 2005. Sometimes a Windmill Can Be a Lightning Rod. *New York Times.* July 24, 1.28.

3. Renewable Energy in Texas: The Role of the Renewables Portfolio Standard

Dianne Rahm
University of Texas at San Antonio

Introduction

When hurricane Rita hit the Gulf Coast of Texas in September of 2005, following the destruction caused by hurricane Katrina less than a month earlier, an awareness of the fragility of the fossil fuel industry sank in among the public. Texans, and perhaps most Americans, were shocked by the number of refineries that were shut down and the impact of these twin natural disasters on the ability of Texas and other Gulf Coast states to deliver oil, natural gas, and refined petroleum products to the market. It is not surprising that the potential of renewables as sources of energy once again became a central topic of interest.

Renewable energy comes from ordinary sources including sunshine, wind, the movement of water, the heat of the earth, and the growth of plants and animals. These sources of energy were used almost exclusively prior to the Industrial Revolution when the shift to fossil fuel use occurred. Coal, oil, and natural gas continue today to provide most of the energy used in the developed world. Fossil fuel use, however, poses problems. While there is controversy regarding when fossil fuel depletion will occur, there is agreement that these fuels will eventually be exhausted. There is a growing awareness that fossil fuel use produces greenhouse gases associated with global climate change as well as other environmental pollutants. For both of these reasons, the search for alternative fuel sources is essential.

Finding sources of renewable energy is only one part of the equation. A legal and regulatory framework must be established to provide for the viability of renewables within the context of an already well established and embedded system of fossil fuel use. Texas was an early adopter of one such framework — the renewables portfolio standard (RPS).

After briefly discussing the renewable energy capacity of Texas, this chapter explores the RPS initially established by Texas, discusses its provisions, how it was implemented, and the problems it faced. The chapter closes with a discussion of the recently passed amendment to the initial law which seems to address many of the problems associated with the initial legislation and regulatory framework.

Texas Renewable Energy Capacity

Due to its size and diverse climate, Texas has a great potential to generate nonpolluting renewable energy. Texas' renewable energy capacity can be estimated by focusing on the renewable resource bases: solar, wind, biomass, water, and geothermal. These resources are generally abundant but variable based on location within the state. For instance, winds blow stronger at higher elevations and in certain locations, sunshine varies from sunny locations versus cloudy ones, biomass grows more profusely in fertile areas than in infertile ones, and water resources are spatially distributed across the state. The key to developing Texas' renewable resources lies in developing technologies and infrastructure that can utilize these resources in an economical way as well as in setting up a regulatory regime that makes investment in technology and infrastructure commercially viable (State Energy Conservation Office nd_a).

Being a generally sunny state, the solar power potential in Texas is good. Solar energy is available throughout the state in enough concentration to power distributed solar energy systems such as hot water heaters and photovoltaic (PV) panels and in some locations commercial grade solar projects. Solar power can be used in a variety of ways. Solar water heaters, both passive systems requiring no moving parts and active systems with some moving parts, transfer the heat of the sun to water to partially or totally offset the need to use other sources of power to heat water. In a state with many swimming pools, the use of solar water heaters is a very practical application of renewable energy. The other primary use of solar power is in the form of PVs, which offer a cost effective alternative to off-grid and small power applications. PVs are commonly used in telecommunications equipment, small consumer equipment, water pumps, gate openers, and solar lighting (State Energy Conservation Office nd_b). Solar energy is most concentrated in the western part of the state, so applications that might involve commercial solar power plants would be most cost effective if located there (Virtus 1995).

Texas has long been a user of wind power. Eighty thousand rugged old windmills are still in use in Texas pumping water for residences and livestock. Commercial wind energy though, requires the use of large turbines, rated at 500 kilowatts or higher capacity. Studies have shown that the annual capturable wind power in Texas is approximately 250,000 MW (State Energy Conservation Office nd_c). Wind energy capacity is rated on a scale of 1 to 6 where 3 is marginal, 4 is considered good, 5 is very good, and 6 is excellent. (A rating of 3 indicates that wind speeds average 12 mph at 33 feet of elevation while a rating of 5 indicates average wind speeds of 14 mph at the same altitude.) While the Gulf Coast region south of Galveston and the northwestern part of the state rank marginal to good, the best sources for wind power in Texas are in the west. The mountain passes and ridge tops of the Trans-Pecos have the highest average wind speeds in Texas, making them quite suitable for commercial wind farms (Virtus 1995).

Biomass, the use of plants and animals for energy, has been used since prehistory. Today, innovative technologies tailored for the use of biomass allow for its use in applications ranging from heating homes to fueling cars and running electrical equipment (State Energy Conservation Office nd_d). Texas biomass comes from a variety of sources including agriculture, forests, brackish water ponds, and urban areas. Agricultural biomass for Texas includes harvest residues, process wastes, and energy crops such as corn. Forest biomass includes logging residues, mill residues, and woody energy crops. Urban biomass includes municipal solid waste, sewage, landfill gas, and used cooking oils. Saline water technologies make use of the brackish water common across Texas. This salty water grows algae prolifically and these algae can be harvested to extract biodiesel feedstocks, a form of biomass that can be used to produce energy. Texas is a major biomass producer, with waste being the leading resource in the state (Virtus 1995). For instance, the average Texan discards about of ton of trash per year, most of which ends up in municipal solid waste landfills. This 22 million tons, when buried in a landfill, breaks down and generates landfill gas (LFG — a mixture of methane and carbon dioxide). The 70 billion cubic feet of methane created can be captured and used for fuel. It is estimated that if the 70 largest landfills in Texas were developed for energy use, the LFG recovered could provide the energy needs for 100,000 Texas homes (State Energy Conservation Office nd_e).

Texas water resources are limited in terms of what can be applied to energy production. Hydroelectric energy potential is poor due to the level terrain and low rainfall. Washington state, for instance, has the potential to produce 75 percent more energy from water than does Texas. Texas ranks 43 out of the 50 states in hydroelectric potential. That said, there are a number of rivers and streams that could be tapped for hydroelectric power that are currently not utilized. Other water potential consists of tidal wave power of the Gulf Coast and saline water technologies. In particular, abundant Texas brackish water can be used to create solar ponds which store solar thermal energy efficiently (Virtus 1995).

Geothermal energy comes from the heat at the Earth's magma interior. In some places the heat transfers to rock and water close to the Earth's surface and this source can be drawn upon for its energy. While most of the Earth's geothermal resources are in the Pacific Rim, the U.S. base of geothermal resources are in the West. California, Alaska, and Hawaii hold the overwhelming majority of these resources for the U.S. Texas, however, does have some low-temperature geothermal resources that can be of restricted use. The central Texas hydrothermal aquifers range from 90 to 160 degrees Fahrenheit that can be used for some limited applications including space heating, aquaculture, desalinization, and resort spas. Texas does not have access to a high-temperature hydrothermal resource that could be used for electricity generation (Virtus 1995).

As the above discussion points out, the primary renewable resources available in Texas are wind, solar, and biomass. To better understand how Texas has attempted to utilize these renewable resources, and the barriers faced in the process, it is necessary to begin with a discussion of the Texas fossil fuel industry.

Renewables Portfolio Standard — Some Background

With the discovery of oil early in its history, Texas became a lead player in the fossil fuel industry. With a large store of resources, Texas was a net energy exporter of the oil and natural gas that fueled the nation's growing economy in the 19th and 20th Centuries. In 1992, however, Texas hit a turning point when it began to consume more oil and gas than it produced. Texas became an energy importer. This situation motivated state officials to look for an alternative to energy importation (Sloan 2005). Then Governor Ann Richards, in March of 1993, created the Sustainable Energy

Development Council to develop a strategic plan to exploit the state's renewable energy resources. An initial study of Texas renewable energy potential capacity, done in support of the strategic plan, concluded that if developed and promoted, renewable sources of energy offered Texas an option of energy independence (Virtus 1995).

The national deregulation of the electric industry also had a role to play in Texas' move toward increased use of renewables. Electricity generation in Texas, like the rest of the United States since its beginnings with Thomas Edison's 1882 New York City plant, had been characterized by large centralized power plants. Giant utilities serving large geographic regions were vertically integrated. Their monopoly ownership of production equipment, transmission lines, and control over retail delivery resulted in strict government regulation. This highly regulated structure came under scrutiny during the general policy discussions that emerged in the 1970s and 1980s regarding the value of deregulation for the transportation and communications sectors. The central idea behind the deregulatory movement was that the introduction of competition would decrease prices. Electric deregulation also brought the opportunity for states to address the issue of energy dependence by reexamining the mix of fuels used for electricity generation.

The national restructuring of the electricity industry, which began in 1978 with the passage of the Public Utilities Regulatory Policies Act (PURPA), provided an opportunity for greater use of non-polluting fuels in electricity generation. PURPA, passed in the years of the OPEC oil price shocks, required utilities to compare the costs of adding new capacity (termed "avoided cost") with the cost of purchasing electricity from independent power producers using renewable energy or cogeneration (producing heat as well as electricity) and to select the least expensive option. States were given the authority to set the avoided cost level and to determine the point at which mandatory renewable energy purchases would be required. The 1992 Energy Policy Act expanded PURPA to include a wider range of electricity generators, effectively creating a deregulated wholesale market for electricity across the United States. This law allowed independent power producers from any geographical region to sell electricity to industry or utilities in other regions of the country. Transmission lines were opened to facilitate such a market (Hinricks and Kleinbach 2002).

The restructuring of the wholesale market for electricity was accompanied, to a certain extent, by restructuring of the retail market as well. The decision of whether to allow consumers a choice in their purchase of electricity is one of the ways states restructured their retail markets. Several states put in place programs that required retailers to disclose the energy mix used to produce electricity and to permit customers to select a renewable (green) energy option. Some states also moved toward restructuring their retail markets by introducing competition between providers, including Texas, Arizona, California (briefly), Illinois, Michigan, Ohio, Pennsylvania, Virginia, New York, New Jersey, Delaware, Connecticut, Massachusetts, New Hampshire, and Maine (Brennan, Palmer, and Martinez 2001).

A number of states took advantage of the window opened by deregulation to address the issue of increasing the amount of renewable energy in their overall electricity generating energy portfolio. A variety of different policy mechanisms were tried. For example, in 1998 California put in place the use of production incentives to encourage the use of renewable energy. A series of subsidies paying a fixed rate per kilowatt hour (kWh) of electricity produced from renewables were offered. Pennsylvania, in 2000, put in place a program adapted from the California model but tailored it to supporting wind power alone (Bolinger and Wiser 2002). Minnesota, in 2002, provided $9 million to support the development of commercial biomass and wind power (Wiser 2002). California, Pennsylvania, and Massachusetts each initiated buy-down programs for photovoltaics— that is, providing customers rebates or tax credits for a percentage of the cost for the purchase and installation of PV systems. The California program merely returned a percentage of the capital cost for installed capacity. Pennsylvania and Massachusetts returned a higher percentage of capital cost based upon the performance efficiency of the PV installed (Bolinger and Wiser 2002). Several states experimented with putting a renewables portfolio standard in place at the time of retail restructuring (Connecticut, Maine, Massachusetts, Nevada, New Jersey, Pennsylvania and Texas) and others considered it (Arizona, Iowa, Vermont and Wisconsin) (American Wind Energy Association 1999). A RPS is a legal requirement that some of the energy provided in the electricity market come from renewable energy sources, thus ensuring a minimum market for renewable energy (Bolinger and Wiser 2002; Drabic 2003).

RPS designs vary. Either retail suppliers or generators of electric power may be required to purchase renewable energy. RPS are generally implemented using a system of tradable Renewable Energy Certificates (RECs) to track renewable energy purchases and to assure compliance. Using tradable RECs can make an RPS flexible and reduce the administrative overhead necessary for enforcement. With tradable RECs, the retailer or generator of electricity must obtain credits equal to their RPS obligation. This obligation can be determined by requiring a fixed percentage of total Megawatts (MW) produced or sold to be from renewables (Bolinger and Wiser 2002).

To meet these requirements, retail suppliers or generators can either construct and operate their own facilities using renewables, purchase RECs packaged with renewable power from independent renewable energy providers, or purchase RECs from a private credit market (without purchasing the energy itself). The RECs set up several desirable features. By providing compliance flexibility, they reduce the overall cost of the RPS. Also, the use of tradable RECs assures that the cheapest sources of renewables will be developed first, thus lowering the cost of renewable energy overall. With the use of RECs retailers or generators do not have to develop their own sources of renewables if they do not want to because they can purchase credits to fulfill their obligations on the open market (American Wind Energy Association 1999).

The Initial Texas Renewables Portfolio Standard

As part of its deregulation of electric utilities and restructuring efforts, Texas established a renewables portfolio standard in 1999 with the passage of the Texas Public Utility Regulatory Act (PURA). Shortly thereafter the Texas Public Utilities Commission (PUC) provided detailed RPS regulations (PUC Substantive Rules §25.173 Related to Goal for Renewable Energy). These regulations required that utilities in the competitive market reduce the environmental impacts of power production by phasing in the use of renewable energy. The rules were also developed to contribute to rural economic development by encouraging renewable energy businesses in rural areas as well as to assist farmers who could easily continue to farm or ranch while leasing a small portion of their land to the owner of a wind turbine or solar array.

PURA and its rules flowed directly from the Integrated Resource Planning (IRP) process adopted by the State Legislature in 1995. The IRP required that renewable resources and conservation be considered for inclusion in the Texas resource mix. The IRP process focused on meeting the growing needs and increasing demand for electricity in a rapidly growing state with cost-effective, reliable, and environmentally sound resources.

The IRP process obligated utilities to assess customer values and preferences and consider these in their resource planning. Between 1996 and 1998 eight of the nine investor-owned utilities in Texas (representing two thirds of electric customers in the state) polled their customers to determine public support for renewables and energy efficiency. The results of the IRP customer evaluation showed that Texans clearly preferred better air quality and were willing to purchase electricity (even at a higher cost) that was generated by renewable resources to get it. When the Texas legislature considered electric restructuring in 1999, the consumer choices for renewables revealed by the IRP exercise, along with intensive pressure by the renewable energy industry, assured that renewables were given serious consideration. These preferences were reflected in PURA and the rule-making associated with its implementation (Sloan 2005).

The Public Utilities Commission regulation stated that beginning in 2002, retail energy providers selling electricity in the competitive areas of the state (80 percent of the total Texas load) were required to include in their portfolios an increasing percentage of renewable energy sources including wind, biomass (specifically landfill gas), hydropower, and solar. The regulations phased in 400 MW of renewables by 2003, 850 MW by 2005, 1400 MW by 2007, and 2000 MW by 2009 and continuing through 2019. These phase-ins were to add to the already existing 880 MW of renewable energy already online. By 2019, these levels were to represent about 3 percent of the overall portfolio for energy providers located within Texas or delivering to the Texas grid (up from 1 percent in 1999) (Wiser and Langniss 2001).

While this is a rather modest increase, at the time of adoption it represented one of the most ambitious state plans for the inclusion of renewables. A 1,000 MW utility generates enough electricity for a city of a million people or about 580,000 typical U.S. homes. If fired by coal, such a plant requires 9,000 tons of coal each day. If fired by oil, the plant uses 40,000 barrels a day or one tanker each week (Hinrichs and Kleinback 2002; Schimmoller 2004). By adding 2,000 MW, therefore, the initial Texas plan had potential for impact. That said, given the overall renewable potential capacity of Texas, these initial target goals were modest, and as history would show, were reached far earlier than the law required.

The PUC required electricity retailers in the state to demonstrate that they had met their yearly renewable energy obligation by presenting renewable energy certificates to the regulating authority (the trading program administrator) each year. Tradable RECs were issued for each MW of power generated using renewable sources within Texas or delivered to the Texas grid. RECs were restricted to facilities built after 1999 thus encouraging the development of new renewable power generating facilities (although offsets were provided for use of pre–1999 renewable energy power generating facilities). Failure to submit the required RECs resulted in significant penalties. The penalties were assessed as the lesser of $50 per MWh or 200 percent of the average market value of credits for that compliance period.

Retailers were responsible for conducting sufficient advance planning to acquire enough RECs to meet their obligation (PUC Substantive Rules §25.173 Related to Goal for Renewable Energy).

The PUC rules required that the administrator of the trading program submit an annual report to the Texas Public Utilities Commission. Beginning with the program's first compliance period of 2002, the program administrator was required to submit a report to the commissioner on or before April 15 of each calendar year. These reports contained information pertinent to renewable energy power generators and competitive retailers. The reports were to provide "the amount of existing and new renewable energy capacity in MW installed in the state by technology type, the owner/operator of each facility, the date each facility began to produce energy, the amount of energy generated in megawatt-hours each quarter for all capacity participating in the trading program or that was retired from service" as well as "a listing of all competitive retailers participating in the trading program, each competitive retailer's renewable energy credit requirement, the number of offsets used by each competitive retailer, the number of credits retired by each competitive retailer, a listing of all competitive retailers that were in compliance with the REC requirement, a listing of all competitive retailers that failed to retire sufficient REC requirement, and the deficiency of each competitive retailer that failed to retire sufficient RECs to meet its REC requirement" (PUC Substantive Rules §25.173 Related to Goal for Renewable Energy).

Enactment of the Texas RPS set off a surge of renewable energy power development within the state. Between 1999 and 2001 more than 10 wind projects totaling over 930 MW had been built, 12 new landfill gas projects added another 44 MW to the portfolio, and another 50 MW of hydropower renovations entered the planning stage. By 2001, 2650 MW of wind projects had applied for grid access indicating that growth projections were exceeding targets (Wiser and Langniss 2001).

By 2002, Texas had become one of the country's largest renewable energy markets. This growth continued. The January 2003 report of the Texas Public Utilities Commission to the 78th Texas Legislature reported that the construction of renewable energy facilities has proceeded significantly quicker than the mandates in PURA. The mandates required that 400 MW of new renewable capacity be installed in Texas by 2003. As of October 1, 2002, approximately 1,000 MW had been installed and by 2005 it had become apparent that the full mandate of 2,000 MW, required to be installed by 2009, would actually be met much earlier (Texas Public Utilities Commission 2003).

Texas RPS Design and Implementation Features

Several design and implementation features of the initial Texas RPS help explain some of the success of the program. First, the Texas RPS did not restrict projects to one technology. Wind, solar, biomass, landfill gas, hydro, and geothermal were all encouraged. In fact, the openness of the RPS in not targeting a specific technology relied on market forces to determine which technologies were appropriate. Since wind was the closest to market ready in the state, and was favored by a federal tax subsidy, the initial RPS worked heavily to favor wind. The Texas RPS did not work at odds with federal incentive programs, such as the Production Tax Credit (PTC) for renewable power. As long as a federal PTC remained in effect, Texas retailers could benefit from the PTC without impacting their obligations under the RPS.

Some other features seem worth discussing. The Texas RPS tried to create incentives for at least some electricity suppliers to sign long-term contracts for RECs, with the hope of stabilizing the market for prospective renewable energy providers and encouraging entry into the market. Finally, in May of 2001, the Texas RPS developed a web-based process for the administration of the RECs that enabled issuance, registration, trade, and retirement of RECs (Wiser and Langniss 2001).

The RPS allowed each competitive electricity retailer to acquire sufficient RECs to meet their obligations. These requirements were set in proportion to the percent of the overall statewide competitive market they control. RECs could only be obtained from renewable generation sources certified by the state. Electricity retailers not in compliance were fined up to $50/MWh (5 cents/kWh) (Database of State Incentives for Renewable Energy 2004).

Since the RPS was set up to encourage new renewable power capacity, a design issue involved how to treat already existing renewable capacity. The Texas RPS handled this issue by allowing older sources of renewable energy to be given "REC offsets" which would be issued on a MWh basis and counted as part of the mandate for RECs for the retailer who is supplied by an older renewable energy facility. REC offsets, however, were not tradable on the REC market (Sloan 2005).

The Texas RPS included several mechanisms that were designed to help with successful implementation by creating greater flexibility. First, to assure that the system was sufficiently supplied with RECs at the beginning of the implementation of the law, the Texas RPS provided for 'early banking' of RECs. That is to say, RECs were generated up to six months in advance of the first compliance year to be sure there would be adequate supply. Also, the rules allowed a small REC 'deficit allowance' of up to 10 percent for electricity retailers in the first two compliance years before penalties were applied. Finally, the Texas RPS provided for two-year banking so that RECs could be held over from one year to the next (Sloan 2005).

There are a few complicating factors associated with the implementation of the RPS. For instance, because the law specified clear MW target goals for added capacity, it used a capacity conversion factor (CCF) to translate MW goals into Megawatt-hour requirements that could be tracked by RECs (Database of State Incentives for Renewable Energy, 2004). This proved to be contentious as those selling RECs wanted the CCF to be high while those buying RECs wanted the CCF to be low (Sloan 2005).

The initial Texas RPS emphasized the development of the most available renewables for the least costs. This design feature worked to the advantage of wind but to the disadvantage of other technologies. Importantly, technologies that could provide generation offsets, such as solar water heaters and geothermal heat pumps, were not included in the REC system at the time of its creation (Sloan 2005).

The Problem of Transmission

One of the major obstacles associated with the rapid increase in renewable generating capacity is getting it to the grid so it can be used. This is particularly an issue in the West Texas plateau area surrounding the town of McCamey. By the end of 2001, the area had installed wind turbines with a generating capacity of 755 MW. Unfortunately, the transmission system in that year was capable of transmitting only 330 MW. The problem was made worse by the fact that to upgrade a line, the lines have to be taken out of service while being upgraded. By mid–2005 the McCamey area was estimated to be able to export 600–700 MW, however, the upgrades caused challenges.

Electric Reliability Council of Texas (ERCOT) rules specified that transmission costs should be spread among all customers by virtue of uniform pricing regardless of distance to the load. This developer-friendly system caused problems because transmission capacity takes longer to build than generation capacity. New lines take five to seven years for design, permitting, and construction while new wind turbines can be up and running in two. The cost of building transmission lines, while sensible for the long run, affect the short-term bottom line in a highly competitive market. Without PUC authority to order line enhancements, transmission owners in Texas needed assurances that they would recoup their investment before proceeding on a project. Without this guarantee, infrastructure improvement in Texas would not move forward as needed. This situation proved thorny because before wind producers could get bank loans to develop more capacity, they needed to be able to show bankers that the transmission lines were in place to deliver the product (Sloan 2005).

Although the initial RPS encouraged the construction of renewable energy projects, it failed to address the key issue — expanding the use of renewable energy from West Texas demanded the ability of the transmission system to move power from generation sources to customers at a reasonable cost (Texas Renewable Energy Industry Association 2005).

The Role of the Federal Production Tax Credit

One other factor, not under the control of the initial Texas RPS, was the instability of the federal PTC for renewable energy. One of the most significant federal policies to promote the growth of renewable energy has been the federal production tax credit (PTC). The PTC was first enacted as part of the 1992 Energy Policy Act. It provided a 1.8-cent per kilowatt-hour benefit for the first ten years of a facility's operation. This incentive proved to be considerable in moving the development of renewable energy forward. There have been, however, two fundamental problems with the federal PTC: instability and applicability.

The most important problem is that Congress has allowed the PTC to expire repeatedly before reinstating it. It was originally put in place for only seven years. The original legislation specified that the credit would sunset in June of 1999. However, in December of 1999 it was revived and extended until the end of 2001. It lapsed until March 2002, when it was reinstated for a second time until December of 2003. It remained lapsed through 2003 and most of 2004. In October of 2004 it was revived and extended through December 2005 and applied retroactively to January 2004. The Energy Policy Act of 2005 extended the production tax credit through December 31, 2007 (Neff 2005). The second major problem with the PTC has to do with ambiguities regarding to which technologies it applies. Originally, it was applied only to wind technologies but in 2004 it was expanded to include geothermal, solar, biomass, and municipal solid waste (Union of Concerned Scientists 2004). In early years, therefore, the subsidy went only to wind but was later expanded to other renewables.

Despite the problems of instability and applicability, the PTC has had demonstrated impacts on the development of renewable energy. Looking just at wind power installations nationally (for the dates that numbers are available), while the PTC was in force, many wind capacity additions took place. For instance, in the years 1999, 2001, 2003, and 2005 (estimates) 575, 1,714, 1,689, and 2,500 MW of additional wind generating capacity were installed, respectively. However, in the years when the PTC had lapsed (2000, 2002, 2004) only 43, 410, and 480 MW were installed, respectively. Clearly the lack of stability of the PTC has created a substantial boom and bust cycle (Union of Concerned Scientists 2004).

In Texas, anticipation of the expiration of the PTC at the end of 2003 sparked a rush to install new wind farm capacity in West Texas where 758 MW was installed by January 2003 with another 300 MW to be in service by the time of anticipated PTC expiration. This boom in turn created a problem because the West Texas transmission network was not designed to handle this load. These transmission constraints created an interesting secondary dilemma. The extension of the PTC in October of 2004 through the end of 2005 created another boom cycle for wind. Additional capacity of 486 MW was announced in response to the extension (Texas Renewable Energy Industries Association 2005). The passage of the Energy Policy Act of 2005 in August of that year, with its extension of the PTC through 2007 will undoubtedly serve as a continuing incentive.

Results of the Initial Texas RPS

As mentioned earlier, addition of renewable capacity after the passage of the Texas RPS out paced the mandatory minimum requirements by a considerable amount. For instance, actual installation by January 1, 2006 is anticipated to be between 2,500 MW and 3,000 MW, exceeding by as much as 50 percent the amounts mandated. Much of this added capacity has been in wind, and to a lesser extent, in landfill gas. The RPS has not, however, forced significant capacity additions in PVs or solar, despite the fact that Texas lists among the states with the greatest solar potential (Dioun 2004). In Texas, wind currently accounts for 96 percent of renewable generating capacity added since the passage of the RPS (TREIA 2005a).

This is probably the case because wind and landfill gas are closer to being market efficient in comparison to solar or PVs. Wind clearly benefited as a result of the federal PTC, which for some time was targeted only at wind. In addition, it is important to note that wind power development has taken place in regions of western Texas and the Panhandle that exhibit high wind power potential. For instance, some of the mountain passes and ridge tops of the Trans-Pecos in western Texas are classified as wind power class 6 (the highest) with excellent potential for commercial viability (Virtus 1995). Most Texas wind generators are currently located in Crane, Crockett, Pecos and Upton counties in West Texas. The bulk of the new and future planned projects are in a corridor about 100 miles wide along I-20 from Abilene to Odessa (TREIA 2005a). With exceptional wind sites (Dioun 2004) and high energy demand, Texas has been fertile ground for the wind industry. Texas has added some of the largest (up to 280 MW) and lowest-cost (under 3 cents/kWh, with federal incentives) wind projects in the world (Sloan 2005).

While it was thought that the RPS would encourage a large number of electricity retailers to enter into long-term contracts with renewable energy providers to guarantee their ability to comply with the RPS mandate, not many did. A few of the largest retail providers entered into long-term agreements with renewable providers but most electricity retail providers continue to rely on the secondary REC market to meet their compliance requirements. That is, they are purchasing RECs on the spot market. Because the RPS allows for two-year banking of RECs, some of those dependent on the spot market would like to have the multi-year banking provision removed from the law arguing that it causes hording of RECs and thus increases the prices (Sloan 2005).

The ease of trading RECs also resulted in the rise of a voluntary green power market in Texas. Austin Energy's Green Choice program has become one of the nation's largest voluntary renewable energy programs. Green Mountain Energy, located in Texas, is the nation's largest competitive retailer of renewable energy. The voluntary green market retired nearly 800,000 RECs in 2003 up from 231,000 in 2002 (Sloan 2005).

Conclusion

In July of 2005 the 79th Legislature passed an amendment of the initial RPS law that addresses the three major problems with the original legislation. The amendment was signed into law by Governor Perry in September of 2005 (TREIA 2005b). Section 3 of the amendment increased the RPS goal from 2,880 MW by 2009 to 5,880 MW by 2015, and established a target of 10,000 MW by 2025. This change effectively dealt with the problem of the low MW goals set by the initial RPS.

The initial RPS favored least expensive technologies. This feature made wind the most likely technology to take advantage of the rules. But other potential renewables with enormous potential can emerge as part of the REC system. The amendment addresses this problem by earmarking 500 MW for non-wind producing renewables. This provision will undoubtedly provide a boost to biomass (agricultural and waste) projects for the Panhandle region, forest trimmings and sawmill waste in East Texas, and for solar energy use across the state. The fact that the law carved out a piece for non-wind, however, reverses some of the logic of the initial legislation which allowed market forces to be the primary driver of the choice of renewable source.

One other important change was incorporated into the amendment. Under the initial RPS law, transmission lines were a problem. Lenders would not provide loans to generators without such lines in place but lines were slow to be built due to constraints on transmission line owners. For this circular problem to be solved, a detailed plan had to be laid out by the PUC for further line development and the PUC needed enforcement capability. The amendment to the RPS law addresses this issue. It provides for transmission planning and construction, thus removing the problem with the initial RPS of wind turbine construction outstripping transmission capacity. The PUC is authorized by the amendment to require a utility to "construct or enlarge facilities to ensure safe and reliable service for the state's electric markets and to reduce transmission constraints within ERCOT..." (Section 2, Senate Bill 20, enrolled version, 2005). Only time will tell if these provisions are powerful enough to bring the necessary transmission to the state.

With the major barriers to continued development of renewables in Texas addressed in the new legislation and regulatory powers given to the PUC, the future for growth of renewables in Texas again looks hopeful. Whether the changes brought to the regulatory climate by the amendment will succeed in achieving maximum growth of renewables in the state, however, is questionable. Given the overall renewable capacity of Texas, the amended goals remain modest. Even if 10,000 MW are achieved by 2025, it begs the question of how much more could be brought online if more aggressive targets were established.

References

American Wind Energy Association. 1999. How a National Renewables Portfolio Standard Would Affect Utilities. *American Wind Energy Association*, June 30.

Bolinger, M. and R. Wiser. 2002. Production Incentive Auctions to Support Large-Scale Renewables Projects in Pennsylvania and California, *Ernest Orlando Berkeley National Laboratory.*

_____. 2002. The Use of Capital- and Performance-Based Buy-Down Programs for PV in California, Pennsylvania, and Massachusetts, *Ernest Orlando Berkeley National Laboratory.*

Brennan, T. J., K. Palmer, and S. Martinez. 2001. Implementing Electricity Restructuring: Policies, Potholes, and Prospects, Resources for the Future. Discussion Paper 01–62.

Database of State Incentives for Renewable Energy. 2004. Texas Incentives for Renewable Energy. Available at *www.dsireusa.org*

Dioun, Mina. 2004. Texas Energy: The Next Generation. The Role of Renewables in Generating Electricity. *Texas Business Review* August.

Drabic, J.R. 2003. State Policies Set Mandates for Renewable Energy. *BioCycle Energy* October 38–40.

Hinricks, R. A. and M. Kleinbach. 2002. *Energy: Its Use and the Environment*. Forth Worth, TX: Harcourt.

Neff, Shirley. 2005. Review of the Energy Policy Act of 2005. *Report of the Center for Energy, Marine Transportation and Public Policy* August 2 Columbia University, New York, New York.

Schimmoller, Brian K., 2004. Renewable Energy Enters Commercial Era. *Power Engineering*, April: 38–44.

Sloan, Mike. 2005. The Texas RPS. *Renewable Energy World* January-February: 30–41.

State Energy Conservation Office. Renewable Energy Resources for Texas, *State Energy Conservation Office*, SECO Fact Sheet No. 8, nd_a.

_____. Solar Electricity Works for Texas. *State Energy Conservation Office*, SECO Fact Sheet No. 12, nd_b.

_____. Roping the Texas Breezes. *State Energy Conservation Office*, SECO Fact Sheet No. 14, nd_c.

_____. Biomass: Nature's Most Flexible Energy Resource. *State Energy Conservation Office*, SECO Fact Sheet No. 15, nd_d.

_____. Clean Energy from Texas Landfills. *State Energy Conservation Office*, SECO Fact Sheet No. 16, nd_e.

Texas Public Utility Commission. 2003. Report to the 78th Legislature. Scope of Competition in Electric Markets in Texas, January.

TREIA, Texas Renewable Energy Industries Association. 2005a. New Law Will Increase Texas Renewable Energy. Available at *http://www.treia.org/news.php*. Accessed August 2005.

_____. 2005b.Texas to hit Renewable Goal Early. Available at *http://www.treia.org/news.php*. Accessed August 2005.

Union of Concerned Scientists. 2004. Renewable Energy Tax Credit Saved Once Again, but Boom-Bust Cycle in Wind Industry Continues. Available at *http://www.ucsusa.org/clean_energy/renewable_energy/page.cfm?pageID=121*, last updated December 2004. Accessed December 2004.

Virtus Energy Research Associates. 1995. Texas Renewable Energy Resource Assessment: Survey, Overview, and Recommendations. July.

Wiser, R. and O. Langniss. 2001. The Renewables Portfolio Standard in Texas: An Early Assessment. Ernest Orlando Berkeley National Laboratory, LBNL-49107, November.

Wiser, R., 2002. An Open-Ended Renewables RFP in Minnesota Funds Biomass and Innovative Wind Applications. Ernest Orlando Berkeley National Laboratory.

4. California and the Implementation of Renewable Energy Technologies

Catherine Horiuchi
University of San Francisco

Introduction

On September 12, 2002, Governor Gray Davis signed into law Senate Bill 1078, the California Renewables Portfolio Standard. One of numerous energy-related measures enacted in the wake of the 2001 collapse of the state's partial restructuring of the electric system regulation, SB 1078 establishes an aggressive mandate for increased use of renewable energy. The most aggressive renewables standard in the nation when enacted, this legislation requires the state's utilities to increase the proportion of overall generation of renewable energies by one percent of total consumption per year, reaching 20 percent in 2017. The California renewables portfolio standard offers several years of implementation history for consideration by other states contemplating similar legislation.

This chapter describes the California strategy on renewables and questions whether legislation such as SB 1078 may negatively affect generation source sustainability and electric system robustness. It provides background on the state's early endorsements of alternative energy sources and the missteps related to 2001's so-called energy crisis. It then continues with an overview of state leadership's commitment to preventing another energy shortfall, and the passage of SB 1078. Steps taken to implement SB

1078 are described. Problems with the funding model for the portfolio and issues around incentives follow, and possible solutions proposed to resolve these problems. Implementation activities are measured against progress toward the goal of the portfolio standard: a reduction of dependence on fossil fuels and an increase in sustainability through the promotion of renewable alternatives. The chapter concludes with a capsule summary of the argument.

Background on California's Commitment to Renewable Energy

California's energy history provides essential background for understanding the state's renewables portfolio standard (RPS) strategy. Motivation to invest in renewable energy has several sources. Slowing the consumption of non-renewable fuels, mainly fossil fuels such coal and natural gas, is one driver. Limiting hazardous waste products from nuclear plants is another. Adding to the earlier issue of acid rain are concerns about the contribution of greenhouse gases produced in electric generation from fossil fuels to global warming of the atmosphere.

Two aspects of this history are described here. The first is the state's strong advocacy for environmental protection of its famous coastline and the Sierra Nevada watershed in light of the pressures on land use, water consumption and air quality from its high population. The second is its electric system restructuring failure, where a leading edge partial deregulation model produced blackouts and the total collapse of its novel market design rather than anticipated energy savings and system stability.

ENSURING ENVIRONMENTAL SUSTAINABILITY DESPITE OVERALL SYSTEM GROWTH

The state and people of California have a long history of institutional leadership in environment-friendly energy policy. Retail consumers receive electricity on a non-competitive, highly regulated basis from either public power agencies or investor-owned utilities. Legislative and California Public Utility Commission (CPUC) mandates also encourage alternative energy development, principally affecting only investor-owned utilities. Public power or municipal utilities are active in renewable energy initiatives on a voluntary basis, focused primarily on value to ratepayers who buy a commodity with few available substitutes in a monopolistic service environment, and secondarily on taxpayers who are subject to whims of political expediency. SB 1078 directly impacts only investor-owned utilities, but for over 30 years all utilities have looked to the state's Energy Commission for forecasting, facilities siting, and special programs management. Its decisions can affect public power and investor-owned utilities alike.

Following the Arab oil embargo, the national energy crisis it triggered in the 1970s, and the 1978 passage of the Public Utility Regulatory Policies Act (PURPA), California developed a robust regulatory setting for independent power producers using traditional fossil, hydroelectric, and nontraditional fuels technologies. These independent power producers could assure their product would be part of the energy mix, thanks to CPUC decisions creating "standard offer" contracts. Contracts between the independents and the investor-owned utilities reflected costs avoided by the utilities whenever independents produced electricity for resale. These reduced utilities' need to construct additional regulated assets. The avoided costs model resulted in favorable terms and a high response from qualifying independent power facilities, and saved ratepayers money as well, since utilities receive a fixed rate of return based on total operating and capital costs.

For decades, California has led the nation in environmental activism through battles over water, air, and land use. A leader in developing and adopting energy conservation practices, the state employs wide ranging strategies to responsibly use constrained resources. The consumed kilowatt-hour is identical regardless of the energy source, so there are limits on what can be done on a retail level to assure cost-effective and efficient energy use. Building codes provide one mechanism to achieve environmental improvements. These include durable structural standards for new or retrofit buildings and highly adaptable radio-dispatched load management. Title 24, Part 6 of the California Code of Regulations established in 1978 energy efficiency standards to reduce consumption in all buildings. These strategies resulted in substantial if incremental improvements in energy efficiency throughout the 1980's after the first energy shock. The wave of legislative responses to the failure of the restructuring plan in 2001 augmented these decades-old efforts.

Increasing use of renewable resources as part of an overall balanced energy system requires concerted and focused action, as illustrated by an example from the Sacramento Municipal Utility District. Following years of rate increases derived from operational problems at the Rancho Seco nuclear plant, ratepayers voted in 1989 to advise shutting down the nuclear power plant, creating an immediate need for 900 megawatts of consistent electric power. The District responded with short-term contracts for power, and the nation's largest energy efficiency and load management program, augmented with renewable energy projects using wind, geothermal, and photovoltaic sources.

The District's many innovative projects included a popular residential photovoltaic rooftop program, and it continues to expand the world's largest utility photovoltaic system. In 2001 it added more than 100 sites providing two megawatts of new generation, bringing the total amount of photovoltaics on its system to approximately 10 megawatts—enough to serve nearly 3,400 homes (Sacramento Municipal Utility District nd).

Investor-owned utilities follow a regulatory mandate to set aside a public goods charge of 2.85 percent of total revenues. Historically, this has been used for low income programs, energy efficiency initiatives, and support for development of advanced and renewable technologies. This last category has included all types of sustainable energy projects.

Sustainability also has been and continues to be advocated through state government initiatives and standards. For example, the California Integrated Waste Management Board as part of its zero waste strategic target maintains a "green building" design and construction website. The governor in 2004 issued an executive order to increase by 20 percent the energy efficiency of all state facilities. The state's long interest in energy-related policy translated to an early adoption of a restructured electric system, discussed in the next section.

Failed Restructuring Effort, Increased Interest in Renewables

When the Federal Energy Regulatory Commission (FERC) developed open access rules in the 1980s, both public and private power companies participated in planning committees around possible rules or legislation. Assembly Bill 1890 (AB 1890) created in 1996 the partial deregulation model that failed in 2001. In two legislative special sessions, and with the state of emergency resulting in extraordinary gubernatorial powers, numerous rules were enacted and bills passed to address the financial and operational crisis and underlying market flaws. Through these means, the state's leadership sought to prevent any recurrence of the electricity market collapse.

California's partial restructuring of the electric system disrupted the progressive electric generation and consumption strategies in widespread use throughout the 1980s. AB 1890 changed incentives for independent power producers, the utilities and their customers through the divestiture of fossil fuel assets from the investor-owned utilities, and the establishment of two mandatory electricity markets. Since all accepted power bids into the day ahead market received the same market-clearing price per megawatt-hour, bidders maximized their returns by selling the cheapest power. Utilities saved money by buying cheap fossil power rather than generating expensive alternative power. The utilities increased revenue further by selling more kilowatt-hours of cheaply procured power at tiered consumer rates that rise sharply when more than a baseline amount of electricity is consumed. The price per kilowatt-hour had been further augmented with a surcharge to capture the "stranded costs" of regulatory assets which also increased utility incentives to sell more power, accelerating stranded costs collection. Utilities scaled back consumer incentives to reduce power during summer peaks substantially, since initial bidding for power pushed prices to near zero in mid–1999.

Market conditions reversed in 2000 as sophisticated gamesmanship emerged. The dramatic shock of blackouts in early 2001 was followed in the fall by the collapse of aggressive utility and energy trading firm Enron. Reports abounded throughout 2002 of its accounting irregularities and market manipulations through vividly named "Fat Boy" and "Death Star" strategies (McLean and Elkind 2003). The California energy crisis has been the subject of state and federal hearings, government and think tank reports (Waere 2003), broadcast documentaries (Chandler and Bergman 2001), countless mass media and newspaper articles, and several books (Sweeney 2002; Timney 2004).

Committed to Sustainablity:
Enacting the Renewables Portfolio

In the overheated environment of the energy crisis, Senate Bill 1078 (Sher) was enacted. As a companion, SB 1038 (Sher) was passed, providing a funding mechanism and additional specification on generation that is eligible for Supplemental Energy Payments (SEP) funds. In SB 1078, the state committed itself to sustainability of the state's high quality of life despite continuing population growth and uncertainty about fuel supplies through the enactment of the renewables portfolio standard (RPS).

Legislating the Renewables Portfolio Standard

SB 1078 (Sher) requires California's investor-owned utilities to increase procurement of electricity from defined renewable resources one percent per year reaching a minimum of 20 percent of total generation from renewables in 2017. The legislation assigns the Energy Commission to certify eligible facilities as eligible for supplemental energy payments (also known as SEPs), to allocate these payments, and to develop a unified accounting system to verify compliance statewide. In order to determine the amount of the supplemental energy payments, the bill tasked the Energy Commission to create and periodically reset a Market Price Referent.

The legislation creates a renewable energy target and the basic outline of a method to reach the target. It requires annual increases in megawatt-hours generated from renewable sources, reaching 20 percent of total consumption no later than 2017. Investor-owned utilities are not required to construct or own these generating facilities, rather they must follow a Least Cost Best Fit annual bid process, monitored by the Energy Commission. Supplemental energy payments buy down the average price per kilowatt-hour of renewable energy, making these sources more competitive with the best current technology fossil fuel generation, the combined cycle gas turbine.

Byron Sher's bill directed the CPUC to implement the RPS for electrical portfolio, "if funds are made available as described." With SB 1078 and 1038, the state committed to fostering in-state renewable energy generation, limiting plants eligible for supplemental payments to those inside the state or at the borders.

As in most cases where new funding supports are created, those who own existing sources hoped to be included in some way. The legislation created eligibility for ten years of SEP payments for "repowered" existing generation, if investment equals 80 percent of the value of existing facilities; the bill language excludes utilities, both investor-owned and public power. Eligibility for repowering payments requires replacement of:

- Wind: the turbine and generator, any gearbox, nacelle, and blades
- Biomass: the boiler using either stoker or fluidized bed technology
- Geothermal: the steam generator, including turbine rotors, shaft, and gear assemblies
- Small hydro: the turbine and supporting structures
- Solid waste: the conversion gasifier and combustion turbine
- Landfill gas: the internal combustion engine or combustion turbine
- Digester gas: the digester unit and internal combustion engine or turbine

A CHANGE IN EXECUTIVE LEADERSHIP

On October 7, 2003, California voters elected to remove Governor Gray Davis from office. The people's displeasure developed over time in part from belief that he mismanaged the energy crisis, later compounded with budgetary problems that resulted in state bonds dropping to near junk bond rating. The new governor, political neophyte Arnold Schwarzenegger, came to Sacramento with a promise to change the way the state operates. One of his first acts created the California Performance Review. Collapsing the number of energy-related boards and commissions was among ideas to improve energy system management, but his "blow up the boxes" strategy to streamline energy planning faces constitutional challenges to shifting rate-setting authority away from the CPUC (Lifsher 2005).

In this unstable setting, energy policy ideas have been instantiated in an Energy Action Plan (EAP) and an Integrated Energy Policy Report (IEPR). The renewables portfolio standard is part of these policy initiatives. In the next section, this implementation process is described, and issues with some details are highlighted.

IMPLEMENTING THE STANDARD

To implement the standard, the Energy Commission and the CPUC held several rounds of hearings, and funded research toward establishing a workable system. The renewables portfolio standard augments existing programs for renewable energy, emerging technologies, and public goods fund management. These hearings decided such matters as defining what constitutes "new" generation. (California Energy Commission 2003a, 8).

A 2003 joint report outlined the challenges in meeting the renewable energy requirement based on existing and potential resources (California Energy Commission and California Public Utilities Commission 2003). As the RPS process was beginning in 2002, the state generated a total of 28,907 gigawatt hours of renewable energy derived from 7,049 megawatts from wind, solar, small hydroelectric, biomass/waste, and geothermal renewable generation sources. Interim procurement in 2003, while the process was being developed, was estimated to push the total to 30,000 gigawatt hours. By 2010, the modified target date for reaching 20 percent, it was estimated over 50,000 gigawatt hours of renewable generation would be required. Maintaining the 20 percent level under load growth from 2010 to 2017 would require an additional 11,000 gigawatt hours in annual procurement. The 60,980 gigawatt hours required in 2017 were estimated at less than a quarter of the technically feasible in-state potential renewable generation. However, funding and political challenges would not be trivial.

The enacted renewables portfolio standard differs from the state's past efforts to develop sustainable energy sources. Those efforts focused on creating new electric generation from renewable sources at a cost roughly equivalent to that generated from fossil resources, and increased renewable energy capacity with limited price supports. SB 1078 contrasts in its concentration on consumption, rather than capacity. Rather than measuring success by the total megawatts available from renewable resources, it mandates increases in the consumption of renewables. This is a strategic difference, as it intends to shift consumption away from fossil resources to renewables, with limited regard to cost differentials which would be resolved through price supports. In past efforts, if renewable energy was available, but cheaper power could be attained from fossil fueled assets, the decision was frequently made to consume the fossil fuel, reducing the average cost per kilowatt-hour.

Funding for the RPS initially derived from the rate component allocated for public goods programs, a sum of approximately $135 million annually. In 2003, 55 percent of this fund — formerly subsidizing low income customers, energy conservation programs, and research and development — was allocated instead to support RPS payments. To supplement these further, SB 1038 extends a rate surcharge on consumption originally tasked to support a renewable market between 1998 and 2002 as part of the original restructuring legislation, AB 1890. This extension of the surcharge and changes in allocations increases available funds for supplemental energy payments.

An early review of the renewables portfolio standard (Golden 2003) lists three hurdles in implementation: a workable benchmark pricing methodology, preemption under PURPA, and effective enforcement. PURPA's focus on avoided cost impedes development of renewables resources that might have higher costs than traditional plants while offering other important advantages. These can range from diversification of sources, fewer externalities, and possibly longer plant life.

Changed Focus from Generation to Consumption; Setting the Value of Capacity

Focus on generation, rather than adequate marginal capacity for all hours, contributed to the gamesmanship and collapse of the state's partial restructuring of the electric system. Following the energy crisis, marginal capacity received more attention. The RPS similarly does not focus on capacity, rather its target is a percentage of total consumption. Since renewable energy sources do not have the same operating profile as fossil fuel plants, an evaluation of the capacity equivalence of these sustainable sources was included in the PIER-funded study (California Energy Commission 2004).

Under the old model, vertically integrated utilities overbuilt as allowed by the CPUC; under cost-plus pricing, all costs were bundled and all received a "fair rate of return" currently close to 10 percent. Under the new model of individually owned generation, rather than the old avoided cost model, each individual project takes the risk of not selling output. Firm contracts for baseload power require firm output. Wind power has unpredictable intermittent output, and solar has mostly predictable intermittent output. This intermittent nature make them generally unsuitable as baseload units, but power may be purchased either as peak load (solar on hot summer days, for example), as-available load, or as on-call capacity.

A 2004 Public Interest Energy Research (PIER) capacity study, prepared for the California Energy Commission (CEC) by the California Wind Energy Collaborative as part of PIER's $62 million in annual research support, describes integrations costs for intermittent energy sources (California Energy Commission 2004). Costs of the California Independent System Operator (CAISO) hour-ahead energy market are not included in initial integration costs, since the CAISO settles the costs related to imbalance between scheduled energy and the actual demand with its existing system. Balancing Energy and Ex-Post Pricing (BEEP) costs are allocated to the generator who deviates from the schedule without dispatch instructions, with specific rules in place for both controlled and intermittent generation. The cost of managing transmission with a large increase in intermittent sources and more transmission ties becomes an issue for later legislation. Similarly, this exclusion fails to acknowledge that the CAISO cannot "schedule" wind, in the absence of secondary, backup power.

Capacity credit for intermittent renewables can be compared to the reference case, gas turbine spinning reserve with its guaranteed instant on. With capacity payments, the generator is paid as if the energy is needed, even if it is not. To use a capacity payment model for renewables, the state needs to establish an agreed upon value that will allow for payments other than precise hours used. The wind industry argues that all generation is offline sometimes, theirs is just offline more, so the way base case gas turbine generation is valued as capacity can be translated to wind, and suggests that wind be rated based on simulation models. The measure for this is called effective load carrying capacity (ELCC), where 100 percent ELCC means guaranteed availability (California Energy Commission 2004). Using this measure under simulation, the model yields 83 percent ELCC for geothermal production, 90 percent for solar energy, and 23 percent to

25 percent for wind, depending on location. This means that four times as many megawatts of wind power need to be built to be approximately equivalent to nameplate capacity of gas turbine spinning reserve.

PROGRESS IN PROCUREMENT

Between 2002 and 2005, changes in procurement have occurred in California's investor owned utilities (Wiser 2005). San Diego Gas and Electric has increased from 1 percent renewables to 4.5 percent in three years, through new contracts totaling 275 megawatts. Southern California Edison increased from an already-substantial 17 percent to 18.2 percent in 2004, and is in the process of repowering four wind projects. Pacific Gas and Electric increased from 10.4 percent to 12.4 percent but then fell back to 11.7 percent with a bad hydroelectric season in 2004.

Southern California Edison in March 2005 submitted for CPUC review six long-term renewable power contracts (Regional Business News 2005). The firms for this set of contracts from its second requests for bid include wind power with Coram Energy, SeaWest, and Western Wind; biomass power from Silvan Biomass and Imperial Valley Biomass, geothermal from Vulcan Power, and biofuels from McCarthy Farms. These figures and contracts indicate early success in procurement under the RPS.

ISSUES IN IMPLEMENTING THE
RENEWABLES PORTFOLIO STANDARD

Despite the increases in renewables achieved in the first years, some issues have emerged as the legislation has been implemented. Table 1 summarizes the legislated conditions and initial effects in early activity toward meeting the procurement target.

Another challenge relates to the difficulty of measuring the effects of the RPS on overall system reliability. The increased connection of small generating source require rich data, more detailed than the existing one-minute incremental system-wide load (California Energy Commission 2004). Beyond total load and generation source, the data that would be needed to measure reliability effects include:

- Total generation
- Net actual imports/exports
- Net scheduled imports/exports
- Area control errors
- Frequency deviations

Table 1: Implementation Details of Early RPS Implementation

Legislated Conditions	Early Outcomes
Investor-owned utilities face 1% per annum procurement requirement	Publicly-owned utilities develop voluntary programs. Some lobby for mandated municipal utility programs.
Supplemental energy payments to producers authorized	Above-market costs of renewable energy paid from public goods charge, masking true costs.
	Preference for lowest initial cost of renewable power (e.g., wind, small hydro) reduces diversification.
Least cost best fit selection standard	Existing low cost power results in renewables failing "avoided cost" test.
	Proposal to reprice low cost power at market price, and end cost-plus pricing for hydropower.
No inclusion of transmission effects	Free rider problem; first source bears full cost of connection to grid

The costs to create this level of granularity in data are not known. The CAISO has been plagued by complaints of high costs, and is undergoing a downsizing under new executive leadership. It is not clear when or if this data will begin to be collected.

Two other issues challenging successful implementation of the renewables portfolio standard are described at greater length here. First, structural and regulatory constraints affect the funding model for the portfolio. Second, the supplemental energy payments result in consumption incentives that could increase the state's dependence on fossil fuels. These are described below.

ISSUES WITH THE FUNDING MODEL

A non-bypassable rate component allocated for public goods programs funds most supplemental energy payments. Core values of equity and sustainability are affected by this funding mechanism.

Seeking renewables that can produce electricity at near-market prices results in the prevalence of wind power and small hydropower projects. Supplemental energy payments for more expensive renewables, such as solar, would necessarily be higher, resulting in fewer renewable megawatts procured. Supplemental energy payments do not change the actual project costs. SEPs cannot make most renewables projects directly competitive with traditional fossil fuel projects or existing hydroelectric and nuclear plants whose initial capital construction costs have been paid, where only ongoing fuel, operating, and maintenance expenses are incurred. SEPs mask the full cost of the switch in power sources through indirection; the public, as ratepayers and taxpayers, pays the full cost as they fund these subsidies. The retail pricing per kilowatt hour metric does not reflect surcharges, so the fully-loaded price per kilowatt hour is obscured. Consumers notice higher bills, but are uncertain how to reduce electric costs to prior levels, unless they are eligible for a reduced-price rate class. The number of customers eligible for low income, medical necessity, senior, and similar rate classes is much higher than enrolled, so the potential for customer rate shifting is high. This shifts costs to the remaining customers.

In addition to the basic inequalities in rates and subsidies, the location of generation projects collides with a newly emerging area of public management interest, environmental justice. As a result, legislators are adding language establishing preferences for projects benefiting the poor and communities of color. To meet some of these alternative goals, caps on SEPs are under consideration.

SKEWED INCENTIVES FOR RENEWABLES GENERATION

Fuel diversification was one driver for the renewables portfolio. In the divestiture of fossil fuel generation in the late 1990s as part of the state's electric system restructuring, new owners immediately tore out the capability of fossil fuel plants to run on fuel oil. The investor-owned utilities had installed this capacity previously, when regulatory rules required that plants be equipped to run on more than one fuel source. The new owners did not inherit this regulatory requirement, and removal of fuel oil capacity reduced their costs with a reduced parts inventory, narrower workforce skill sets, and less maintenance required. This course of action, combined with construction of additional natural gas plants in the wake of the energy crisis, resulted in an immediate over-dependence on natural gas in the state. The price of natural gas has risen more than 50 percent following this change, including brief periods where it spikes for weeks or months at twice the average price. Dependence on natural gas for electric generation is projected to increase from 25 percent of total generation twenty years ago to 35 percent in 2003 and 44 percent in 2013, despite the renewables portfolio standard (California Energy Commission 2003b).

The increase in transaction costs related to intermittent energy sources that will occur with their increase in use statewide has not been considered part of the costs of implementing the RPS. Using this model in assigning integration costs for renewables in assessing bids means that 10 intermittent sources statewide will receive an equal ranking as one large intermittent source, even though the connection and management costs of using ten sources rather than one will be much higher. This increases renewables costs indirectly through the CAISO settlement charge process, and leaves the implication that the source of the costs is the CAISO, not the choice of generation.

STRATEGIES TO RESOLVE IMPLEMENTATION ISSUES

The issues California faces in implementing the renewables portfolio standing can be addressed. Success will take concerted action on several fronts, some with potential for negative political consequences.

Change the Regulated Pricing Model for Existing Energy Sources. One strategy to make renewables more competitive is to artificially raise the price of hydropower, fossil fuel power, and nuclear power so that neither traditional independent power producers nor new fossil plants are preferred in meeting the "avoided cost" standard. The George W. Bush administration has considered this type of "market pricing" to advocate new fossil and nuclear plants in lieu of traditionally cheap hydropower. The CPUC could set the "avoided cost" to match prices that can be met using renewable sources. However, federal preemption on rates may trump California's RPS, if this strategy is adopted by the CPUC to foster renewables.

Revisit Baseline Consumption and Tiered Rates. Baseline consumption refers to a specified amount of energy that is considered reasonable consumption for a household. Absent from public discourse on renewables is consideration of the reasonableness standard. Despite efforts to increase efficiency, average household consumption has risen. A rule of thumb now suggests only 750 households can be supported on one megawatt of new capacity, rather than the 1,000 households per megawatt estimate of ten years ago. General consumption trends in California finds its residents living in larger houses, driving larger cars, even being larger citizens. Baseline users are shielded from paying full costs of energy consumption.

Acknowledge Necessity and Inevitability of Political Expediency. Elected officials must receive the majority of votes to stay in office. This affects interest and ability to act on cold, scientific reporting of energy information. In the earliest days of the California energy crisis, one of the first pieces of legislation enacted protected the majority of constituents in every district from directly shouldering the inflated energy costs. For rate-payers consuming up to 130 percent of baseline, no rate increases were allowed. This means over 50 percent of Californians continue to be insulated from direct awareness of the actual cost of the energy they consume. In the absence of meaningful price signals, consumer behavior is predictable.

Similarly, when accounting fraud and other criminal business practices at Enron came to light, legislators and the governor held special hearings and press conferences, diverting attention from the actions and choices they were making on pricing and purchases. Collateral effects of political acts can endure for decades, as in the case of California's long-term, above-market, take-or-pay energy contracts.

Accepting the inevitability of political actors behaving politically is essential to sound energy policy.

FUTURE TRENDS

Trends include revisions to the Integrated Energy Policy Report and the Energy Action Plan. Changes in energy governance appear less likely. The research community will continue to strongly advocate for inclusion of its advanced and renewable technologies as some portion of overall renewables funding. Less clear are the future plans of the oil companies, the outcome of pending legislation, and the success of leading edge renewables projects. These are discussed below.

Differing Strategies of Major Oil Companies on the Future of Fossil Fuels. If the development of renewable sources challenges fossil fuel providers, it should be reflected in their strategic market plans. The companies vary in their approach to the multiple challenges in proven reserves, global warming, and government efforts to respond to the 1997 Kyoto Protocol.

Royal Dutch Shell, in a recent analysis of strengths, weaknesses, opportunities and threats, considers the trend toward renewables as an opportunity. The company has begun acquisition of wind farms, including in 2002 the purchase of Whitewater Hill, a 60 megawatt "wind park" in California. The use of hydrogen in the biomass-to-energy process provides a new market for a fuel that is included in many advanced technologies programs and eligible for price supports. This categorization persists despite most hydrogen being derived through petro-chemical refinement (Royal Dutch Shell 2003).

In contrast, the Wall Street Journal noted Exxon Mobil's opinion remains that solar and wind energy will provide less than 1 percent of the world's energy supply, even as late as 2025 (Ball 2005). Rather than branching out to alternative energy sources, the world's largest oil company is focusing on increased energy efficiency in its own operations, improving the efficiency of internal combustion engines for cars and trucks, developing hydrogen extraction from fossil fuels, and considering how to make carbon sequestration cost effective.

While these firms differ in their response to the scientific consensus on global warming, the industry's forecast for fossil fuel remains positive. Natural gas and petroleum prices are near record highs, whether due to political instabilities in oil-producing regions such as Iraq, or increased demand supporting economic growth. China seeks to purchase the U.S. firm Unocal for its Asian oil reserves. Australian BHP Billiton among others seeks state approval for an offshore liquefied natural gas terminal off the California coast in Ventura County. These suggest that despite the high percentage of renewable energy consumption targeted with the RPS, no reduction in fossil fuel requirements is expected anytime soon in the state of California.

New Legislation. The 2005 legislative session saw the introduction of SB 107 (Simitian and Perata), a bill to fix some of the issues observed in the initial implementation of the RPS. Out-of-state and out-of-country generation would be eligible for SEPs. It would accelerate the procurement target to 20 percent by 2010, pre-date eligible renewables from 2006 to 2003, and study the feasibility of increasing the renewable procurement to 33 percent by 2020.

The End of the Power Authority. In 2001 and 2002, the California Power Authority had $6 billion in bonding authority to initiate renewables projects. However, rapid natural gas plant construction in 2001 and the signing of long term take-or-pay contracts made these projects fiscally and operationally infeasible. In the 2004 budget bill, all funding for the Power Authority was diverted into the general fund. Work on an updated Energy Action Plan is being carried out by its partners for the initial plan, the CEC and the CPUC.

The RPS Effect on Proposed Projects. Several forward-looking technology projects have been certified. These include one biodiesel (51 megawatts), one biomass/digester gas combination (107 megawatts), two municipal solid waste (MSW) conversion projects (23 megawatts), three existing photovoltaic sites (less than 1 megawatt total), and one solar thermal project (101 megawatts).

Due to the enactment of the RPS, projects as large as or much larger than all earlier ones are being proposed and certified. For instance, the California Central Power has proposed a biomass/digester gas facility which will come online in late 2007. This facility is twice as large as any biomass project in the state and 25 times larger than the largest digester gas facility. The solar thermal project dwarfs all other solar thermal production facilities. These projects, their cost profiles, actual production profiles and transmission implications have to be considered speculative.

Conclusion

The renewables portfolio standard adds to a continuing series of energy policy innovations in California. Some of these initiatives have gone very well: the development of independent power producers and codified energy efficient construction standards among them. Others have turned out badly: most spectacularly the collapse of the restructured energy markets and the short-lived Consumer Power and Conservation Financing Authority. The RPS is succeeding in its effort to add renewable energy sources, but at the cost of reduced funding for energy efficiency, conservation, and low-income customer supports. This is resulting in a counterintuitive increase in commitment to and use of non-renewable fossil fuels. Fundamentally, in California all energy policy has an interest politics orientation. For good or ill, ratepayers and taxpayers shoulder the bundled costs of these policy choices.

References

Ball, Jeffrey. 2005. Digging In: Exxon Chief Makes a Cold Calculation on Global Warming. *Wall Street Journal*, June 14, A1.

California Energy Commission. 2001. *Investing in Renewable Electricity Generation in California.* 500-00-022 June.

_____. 2003. *Renewables Portfolio Standard: Decision on Phase 2 Implementation Issues: Final Committee Draft.* 500-03-049FD August.

_____. 2003. *Electricity and Natural Gas Assessment Report — Final Commission Report (includes Appendices).* 100-03-014F.

_____. 2004. *California Renewables Portfolio Standard Renewable Generation Integration Cost Analysis Phase III: Recommendations For Implementation.* 500-04-054 July.

_____ and California Public Utilities Commission. 2003. *Overview: Renewables and California's RPS.* Sacramento.

California Wind Energy Collaborative. 2004. *California Renewables Portfolio Standard Renewable Generation Integration Cost Analysis: Phase III: Recommendations.* California Energy Commission Public Interest Energy Research Program. P500-04-054 July.

Chandler, Michael and Lowell Bergman. 2001. Frontline: Blackout! PBS Broadcast June 5. Available at *http://www.pbs.org/wgbh/pages/frontline/shows/blackout.* Accessed May 30, 2005.

Business CustomWire. 2005. $53 Billion in New Investment Required to Meet U.S. Renewable State Standards. March 15.

Golden, Kevin S. 2003. Senate Bill 1078: The Renewable Portfolio Standard — California Asserts Its Renewable Energy Leadership. *Ecology Law Journal* 30: 693–713.

Lifsher, Marc. 2005. Energy Plan Hits a Legal Hurdle. *Los Angeles Times*. June 23.

McLean, Bethany and Peter Elkind. 2003. *The Smartest Guys in the Room: The Amazing Rise and Scandalous Fall of Enron*. New York: Portfolio.

Phillips, Kathryn. 2003. Public Utilities and Renewable Energy in the Central Valley: Increasing the Voluntary Commitment. The Center for Energy Efficiency and Renewable Technologies. November.

Regional Business News. 2005. SCE signs six new renewable power contracts. Available at *http://search.epnet.com/login.aspx?direct=true&db=bwh&an=CX2005068X2972*. Accessed April 1, 2005.

Royal Dutch Petroleum Company. 2003. *Royal Dutch Petroleum: SWOT Analysis*. Datamonitor.

Sacramento Municipal Utility District. nd. 2001 Public Goods Annual Report. Sacramento.

State of California. 2005. *Draft Energy Action Plan II: Implementation Road Map for Energy Policies. Sacramento: Energy Resources Conservation and Development Commission and Public Utilities Commission*. June 8.

Sweeney, James L. 2002. *The California Energy Crisis*. Stanford: Hoover Institution Press.

Timney, Mary M. 2004. *Power for the People: Protecting States' Energy Policy Interests in an Era of Deregulation*. Armonk, NY: M.E. Sharpe.

Waere, Christopher. 2003. The California Electricity Crisis: Causes and Policy Options. Available at http://www.ppic.org/content/pubs/R_103CWR.pdf. Accessed June 20, 2005.

Wiser, Ryan, Porter, Kevin, and Mark Bollinger. 2005. *Preliminary Stakeholder Evaluation of the California Renewables Portfolio Standard — Consultant Report, Publication No. CEC-300-2005-011*. Available at *http://www.energy.ca.gov/2005publications/CEC-300-2005-011/CEC-300-2005-011.PDF*. Accessed June 20, 2005.

_____, _____, Grace, Robert and Chase Kappel. 2003. *Evaluating State Renewable Portfolio Standards: A Focus on Geothermal Energy. National Geothermal Collaborative*. Available at *http://www.geocollaborative.org/publications/RPS.pdf*. Accessed March 1, 2005.

5. Renewable Energy Development Policies in the Upper Midwest

Justin R. Barnes and
Barry D. Solomon
Michigan Technical University

Introduction

The successful development of renewable energy in the U.S. hinges on many interrelated factors. Foremost among these is the size and availability of the different potential resources, which can be highly variable even at small scales. Economics (in the form of major drivers of the local, state, or national economy) as well as the cost-effectiveness of various technologies also play a major role. Connected to these factors are localized issues that arise from the environmental and economic ramifications of pursuing different forms of renewable energy. Because of the inherently site-specific nature of potential resources and the vast number of stakeholders, formulating national energy policy is intensely problematic. At the same time, working only at local levels seriously limits the potential for major progress. In the U.S. states have thus emerged as major players in renewable energy policy. State governments have the ability to optimize policy to suit the particular needs of their residents as well as offer the potential for appreciable increases in renewable energy utilization.

This chapter summarizes the renewable energy policies of three states in the Upper Midwest: Minnesota, Iowa, and Michigan, with an emphasis on the goals and effects of specific policies. While all of these states have vast renewable energy potential, their commitments and approaches to addressing barriers to renewable energy are quite different. It is important to keep in mind that policy instruments can help to overcome barriers to renewable energy use. While states may not be able to change the nature of their renewable resource base, they have the power to affect the economic and social factors that inhibit the adoption of a more sustainable energy future. This said they have considerable freedom in doing so and a variety of policy options with which to work with. Thus, policies are sometimes complex, interconnected, and only applicable to different sectors and technologies. The chapter is divided into sections organized by state. Each section begins with a brief description of recent trends in electricity production (Table 1 contains profiles for all three states), and proceeds through a summary of policies for the development of renewable sources of electricity and fuels. Following this are sections discussing the major policy differences and what we can conclude from comparing these state policies. First, however, we begin with a short overview of the major renewable energy resources in the Upper Midwest.

Renewable Energy Potential in the Upper Midwest

The renewable energy potential in the Upper Midwest is largely comprised of wind and biomass resources. Other energy technologies such as hydropower, solar, and methane recovery offer some potential, but even with maximum exploitation their contribution to the overall energy profile of most states is likely to be small. In the following sections, we have attempted to provide estimates of how much energy might be obtained from several sources of renewable energy in this region. In addition, some potential barriers to specific resource categories are outlined to give the reader a basic understanding of what stands in the way of their adoption as large contributors to energy production.

WIND

The states of the Upper Midwestern U.S. have some of the best wind energy potentials of any region of the country, led by North and South Dakota. According to the American Wind Energy Association, Minnesota, Iowa, and Michigan rank 9th, 10th, and 14th respectively among all states with regard to overall wind energy potential. These rankings correspond to an estimated average wind power output of 75,000 MW for Minnesota, 62,900 MW for Iowa, and 7,460 MW for Michigan[1] (AWEA 2005).

Table 1: State Electric Power Industry Profiles[a]

	Minnesota	Iowa	Michigan
2002 Generating Capacity	11,287 MW	9,338 MW	29,335 MW
2002 Electricity Net Electricity Generation	52,777,966 MWh	42,528,385 MWh	117,889,087 MWh
Annual Growth Rate of Electricity Production (1993–2002)	2.0%	3.2%	1.1%
2002 Non-hydro Renewable Generating Capacity[1]	578 MW	529 MW	388 MW
2002 Non-hydro Renewable Electricity Production[1]	2,077,095 MWh	1,017,402 MWh	2,501,404 MWh
Annual Growth Rate of Non-hydro Renewable Electricity Production (1993–2002)	7.3%	48.3%	2.1%
1993 Market Share of Production for Non-hydro Renewables	2.5%	0.1%	1.9%
2002 Market Share of Production for Non-hydro Renewables	3.9%	2.4%	2.1%

[a] A comparison of maximum generating capacity and actual electricity production indicates that the renewable technologies used in Michigan (landfill gas, wood waste) have a higher capacity factor than those used in Minnesota and Iowa, which are dominated by wind energy.

Source: EIA (Energy Information Administration). 2004a. *State Electricity Profiles 2002.* DOE/EIA-0629. Washington, D.C.: U.S. Department of Energy.

Although the overall wind potential is high in this region, there can be substantial geographic and seasonal variability (12 to 33 percent) of wind resources within them in windy areas (Klink et al. 2003). For instance, much of the wind potential in Michigan is found offshore in the Great Lakes and along exposed coastlines. Most offshore areas are estimated to have at least class 5 wind potentials, with seasonal variations from class 6 in winter to class 3 (considered the minimal level for wind resource development) in summer. Wind energy potential generally diminishes quickly as you move farther inland due to the hilly terrain and extensive forest cover found in Upper Michigan and northern Lower Michigan. Some exposed ridges in inland areas however, are estimated to have class 3 and class 4 wind resources.

The best wind resources in Minnesota are found in the western and southern portions of the State. Large areas of class 4 winds are found along the western and southern margins of Minnesota, with the resource diminishing as you travel north and east. The land is predominately composed of open hills and plains with isolated ridges. These elevated ridges generally offer the best wind resources. The area of class 4 wind potential found in southern Minnesota continues into the northwestern third of Iowa, which has similar terrain and wind characteristics. Wind potential in Iowa diminishes as you travel south and east although class 3 wind resources can be found in exposed areas throughout most of the State. Winds are generally higher in winter and spring throughout both states (Elliot et al 1987). In recent years these data have been refined and more detailed maps have been created, however the general distribution of wind resources remains similar to these broad descriptions.

While this assessment of the wind resources may paint an optimistic picture of the potential of wind power development in the Upper Midwest, there are several significant obstacles. One of these is the large distances from areas with good wind resource potential to load centers such as Chicago, Milwaukee, and Minneapolis-St. Paul. This problem is aggravated by the state of the electric transmission grid in the Upper Midwest, which has been described by the U.S. Department of Energy as "generally constrained" (DOE 2004a, 2). During the last decade many wind farm developers in the region were able to use the excess capacity of the existing transmission system, allowing them to avoid the need to make expensive upgrades (MDOC 2002). Now that much of this existing capacity has been claimed, however, connecting new wind farms to the power grid will be far more difficult. While the Midwest Independent Systems Operator is exploring options for expanding the transmission system, doing so could take many years, and the question of who should pay for the expansion is unresolved (DOE 2004a).

In addition to transmission bottlenecks, the variability of wind resources causes problems for utilities. Wind energy providers cannot guarantee a fixed amount of electricity when a utility needs it, adversely affecting the reliability of the grid. One of the results of this is that utilities are reluctant to offer fixed long-term purchase contracts to wind energy providers, affecting their ability to finance the significant up-front costs of large projects. The 2003 Michigan Renewable Energy Report identifies further difficulties, including obtaining access to the grid, local ordinances that restrict turbine siting, and public concerns about wildlife impacts (MREP 2003). State policies and programs can be used to overcome some of these challenges.

Biomass

Biomass encompasses a wide range of possible fuel feedstocks from agricultural wastes to energy crops to logging residues. Some of these fuels are already used for process heating or electricity production by some businesses, such as paper manufacturers, but in most cases the potential resources have barely been tapped. Dedicated energy crops such as switchgrass or hybrid poplar are one such resource, as are agricultural wastes like corn stover and wheat chaff. Either one of these might be used directly as a fuel source in steam power plants or as a feedstock for ethanol production (DOE 2004b). Ethanol, which historically has relied on the valuable starchy portion (the kernel) of grain crops such as corn as the feedstock, could be greatly expanded through new technology that uses the cellulose residues found in the actual plant itself. Cost reductions in this process may make lignocellusoic production of ethanol commercially viable within the next decade (Lave, Griffin and MacLean 2001).

In addition to energy production, energy crops can provide other economic benefits for farmers and ecological benefits for wildlife. In 2002 the federal government began allowing farmers to plant energy crops in land set aside from normal cultivation under the Conservation Reserve Program or CRP (Iowa DNR 2002). The aim of the CRP is to enhance water quality and prevent erosion of marginal terrain by excluding it from row-crop cultivation. Farmers can place land in the CRP for 10-year periods, collect annual payments from the government, and then farm the land again at the end of the program period. Allowing farmers to cultivate energy crops on this land lets them benefit twice from the program. Also, erosion is prevented and water quality is preserved because unlike traditional crops switchgrass is perennial and provides ground cover and wildlife habitats through the year (Murray and Best 2003). In this way, normal farm output of traditional crops would not be sacrificed to grow energy crops and with new ethanol production processes these crops could be used for their original purpose, food. According to the U.S. Department of Agriculture in 2003 Minnesota had 1.7 million acres enrolled in the CRP, Iowa had 1.9 million acres, and Michigan had 300,000 acres (USDA 2004). Although it is unlikely that all of this land could be used for energy crop production, average yields of up to five tons of dried biomass annually per acre make the potential significant (Launder 2002; Lemus et al 2002, 436–37).

The potential for biomass energy development in these three states is thus substantial. In 1999, the Oak Ridge National Laboratory estimated biomass potentials in all 50 states from five feedstocks: urban wastes, mill residues, energy crops, agricultural residues, and forestry residues. The total potential electricity production was estimated at 47.7 million MWh for Iowa, 30.9 million MW for Minnesota, and 17.7 million MWh for Michigan (DOE 2005a). The estimate for Iowa actually exceeded the State's total electricity production in 2002 (EIA 2004a). At the moment, the most significant obstacle to further use of biomass as an energy feedstock is the collection cost. The largest potential resource, agricultural residues, is currently considered to be too expensive to harvest as a source of energy. The same holds true for forest residues and to a lesser extent energy crops (DOE 2005a).

OTHER TECHNOLOGIES

Included in this category are technologies such as landfill gas, solar power, anaerobic digestion, and hydropower. Of these solar power probably has the most potential, but its regional application is limited to smaller residential size systems rather than large-scale power production from solar-thermal technology. Hydropower and landfill gas production are present in all three states, but the overall resource base for these technologies is small (DOE 2005a). Anaerobic digestion of animal waste offers promise for large livestock operations, but again the resource base is small, and only cost-effective for large operations. The Minnesota Department of Commerce estimates that Minnesota, which has a larger resource base, could obtain only about 115 MW of capacity by fully exploiting its swine and dairy waste resources (MDOC 2003a).

State Policies for Supporting Renewable Energy

MINNESOTA

Overview of Electricity Production. Electricity production patterns have changed in Minnesota during the last decade. During the period of 1993–2002, total generating capacity rose from 9,549 MW to 11,287 MW, an increase of almost 2.0 percent per year. Not all fuel source categories, however, have experienced similar growth rates. The percentage share of coal as fuel for electricity production fell from 64 percent in 1993 to 52 percent in 2002 (although the total nameplate capacity for coal power plants has remained about the same). Non-hydro renewable capacity, which is dominated by wind and landfill gas, in contrast increased from 200 MW in 1993 to 578 MW in 2002, for a growth rate of 12.5 percent per year. This has corresponded to a total market share increase of 3.0 percent, from 2.1 percent in 1993 to 5.1 percent in 2002. Actual power output from non-hydro renewables grew from 1.1 million MWh in 1993 to almost 2.1 million MWh in 2002 increasing from a 2.5 percent market share to a 3.9 percent market share. This growth has occurred in both the electric utility sector (7.7 percent annual growth) and among independent power producers or IPPs (15.2 percent annual growth) who hold about 70 percent of the renewable energy capacity in Minnesota. Dual-fired and natural gas-fired plants make up most of the remaining increases in total electricity production capacity (EIA 2004a). Wind power, now exceeding 700 MW of capacity, made up the largest portion of renewable electricity production in recent years with the remaining portion composed of roughly equal contributions from hydropower and landfill gas (EIA 2004b).

Xcel Energy Mandates. Much of the recent increase in renewable energy use in Minnesota can be attributed to legislation concerning Xcel Energy. Xcel Energy (formerly Northern States Power Company) is by far the largest utility operating in Minnesota, supplying nearly 60 percent of the total utility and IPP-generated electricity in 2002 (EIA 2004a). A significant portion of this generation is supplied by the Prairie Island nuclear power plant. In the early 1990s this plant began running out of space to store its spent fuel rods and petitioned the State for permission to construct a dry cask storage facility to store the excess waste. In 1994 Minnesota passed legislation allowing this, but in return required Xcel to build or contract for at least 425 MW of wind energy capacity and 125 MW of biomass capacity (since reduced to 110 MW) by the end of 2002. In 2001, the Minnesota Public Utilities Commission (MPUC) added a requirement of 400 MW additional wind capacity to be installed by the end of 2006. Subsequent legislation in 2003 resulted in further requirements for 300 MW of wind capacity to be installed by the end of 2010, bringing the total requirement to 1125 MW. The non-profit group Minnesotans for an Energy-Efficient Economy has proposed more than twice this level of wind power in the State by 2010 (Noble and Hoffman 2002, 141). The 2003 legislation also required that 100 MW of the newest capacity be from small (< 2 MW) generators (DSIRE 2004). Xcel obtained its first wind power purchase contract in 1994 for a 25 MW wind farm in the Buffalo Ridge region owned by Kenetech Wind Power. It continued its acquisitions throughout the late 1990s and into the 21st century, contracting for more than 500 MW of wind power capacity by the end of 2003. Nearly all of the wind generating capacity installed in Minnesota, 615 MW as of April 2005 (AWEA 2005), is contracted by Xcel Energy and thus directly attributable to the Prairie Island legislation.

In addition to the wind and biomass requirements, the 1994 legislation also imposed a penalty on every dry cask stored in the new facility, to be allocated into a fund called the Xcel Renewable Development Fund. This penalty was originally set at $500,000 per cask, with the total of 17 dry casks resulting in an annual payment of $8.5 million into the fund starting in 1999. Subsequent legislation was passed in 2003 to extend the period during which Xcel is allowed to continue dry cask storage, increasing the annual payment to $16 million. This fund serves several purposes—providing grants for renewable energy production, research and development (R&D), and as a source of funds for state renewable energy production incentives.

Project funding has occurred in several phases, with the first round of 17 projects being completed in 2001. Funding for these projects totaled more than $15 million, with $6.3 million allocated to R&D and $9.8 million for renewable energy production, totaling an estimated 12 MW. One of these projects was a $1.5 million fund dedicated to providing rebates for newly installed photovoltaic (PV) systems (Xcel 2001). This program, which provides a $2,000 per kW rebate (4 kW capacity limit) for grid-connected PV systems installed after June 2002 was originally open only to customers of Xcel Energy, but was expanded in January 2004 to include all state utility customers. From July 2002 to April 2004, a total of $237,000 was given out to 43 participants with a combined capacity of 120 kW of grid-connected PV (DSIRE 2004). When combined with a State sales tax exemption (6.5 percent general sales tax rate) for wind and PV systems, the Minnesota Department of Commerce (MDOC) estimated that the cost of a PV system can be reduced by 25–35 percent (MDOC 2003b). Further cost reductions can be obtained through federal programs and solar programs offered by other Minnesota utilities. R&D projects included investigations on methods for storing energy from wind turbines, developing better biomass-coal co-firing technology, and improving the cost-effectiveness of PV cells. Applications for the second round of projects were submitted in 2004, with 25 projects totaling $23 million receiving pre-approval subject to review by the MPUC (Xcel 2005).

Renewable Energy Production Payments. The Xcel Renewable Development Fund has also been used to support State production incentives involving small-scale (< 2MW) wind power, on-farm anaerobic digesters, and new hydropower production at pre-existing dams. This production payment was enacted in July 1997 and offers a 1.5 cent/kW payment to eligible facilities for 10 years after they begin production (DSIRE 2004). Xcel is required to set aside $6 million from the RDF per year to fund this incentive, with $4.5 million slated for wind power production, and $1.5 million dedicated to supporting anaerobic digesters. Originally, the legislation specified that new wind facilities were eligible for enrollment until the end of 2006, (Minnesota Statute 216C.41 2003) but in November 2003 the incentive program was put on hold when the original goal of 200 MW of installed or planned capacity was met (De Fiebre 2005).

As of March 2005, 155 MW of small-wind energy had been installed with the remainder required to begin operation by May 2005. A total of 55 MW of planned capacity remains on the waiting list and will become eligible if the deadline is not met by facilities already enrolled in the program. Facilities on the waiting list and those who miss the production deadline are eligible to receive a smaller incentive payment of 1.0 cents/kWh (De Fiebre 2005). The effect of this incentive payment on other eligible technologies has been much less than its impact on wind energy. As of May 2004, there were only two on-farm anaerobic digesters operating in Minnesota, with four in the planning stage (Gupta 2004), and two refurbished hydroelectric facilities claiming the incentive payment (MDOC 2004a). This is most likely because of the nature of the incentive payment, which appears to be aimed at supporting smaller scale facilities not covered by federal production incentives. Consequently, only residential, commercial, and non-profit entities are eligible to receive the payment.

Non-Mandated Renewable Energy Objective. While much of the recent expansion of renewable energy in Minnesota can be attributed to mandates involving Xcel Energy, future expansion will involve all Minnesota utilities. In 2001, the Minnesota legislature codified a renewable energy objective (REO) calling for all Minnesota utilities to make a "good faith" effort to increase their production of energy from renewable sources. Goals of 1 percent renewable production by 2005 and 10 percent by 2015 were set as guidelines. An additional stipulation called for biomass energy production to reach 0.5 percent in 2005 and 1.0 percent by 2015 (DSIRE 2004). While this objective is "voluntary," in reality it is more substantive than it appears for several reasons.

First, although achievement of the renewable energy goals is not mandated, Minnesota intends to ensure that a good faith effort is made by requiring that utilities to file comprehensive plans on how they expect to meet the objective with the MPUC. Utilities are obligated to file these plans once every two years detailing what they have accomplished, their future actions, obstacles encountered, and solutions to any obstacles. These reports will then be circulated to members of the Minnesota legislature for review and approval. In light of the treatment of Xcel Energy by the legislature, it is likely that such review will keep the utilities on track, lest they invite more restrictive regulations.

Second, this objective is applicable to Xcel Energy and works in addition to the requirements under the wind and biomass mandates. As we mentioned earlier, Xcel is the largest electricity supplier in Minnesota with a market share of nearly 60 percent, hence its inclusion is very significant. By excluding the requirements Xcel must meet under the Prairie Island legislation from the objective goals, the 2015 goal of 10 percent renewable production is actually a large underestimate of the market penetration of renewable energy in Minnesota. In reality, if all the requirements and goals are met, renewable energy production in 2015 should comprise 19 percent rather than 10 percent of the market.

Related to this underestimate are the preliminary counting procedures for calculating the renewable generation of each utility. As is typical for a renewables portfolio standard (RPS), generation sold to sources outside of Minnesota is not eligible to be counted, nor is energy generated outside of Minnesota that is counted towards requirements in another state. Furthermore, energy generated from hydroelectric facilities of greater than 60 MW is excluded, as is production devoted to green-pricing programs that are required to be offered by Minnesota utilities under the same legislation.[2] In general, a utility must show that any production capacity it wants counted under the REO was constructed or contracted for the specific purpose of meeting the REO objective. Thus, production capacity installed prior to 2001 will be ineligible in most cases. The end result of these counting procedures is that while renewable resources (including hydropower) made up 11 percent of retail consumption from July 2003 to June 2004, REO-eligible generation made up only 3 percent of retail consumption (MDOC 2005a).

While the REO program is young, the results thus far are encouraging and utilities appear to be taking the program seriously. Figures from 2003–2004 indicate that out of the 13 utilities covered under the objective, nine had enough renewable generating capacity to meet their 2005 obligations, and one was less than 1 MWh short. One of these utilities, Great River Energy, issued an RFP in October 2005 that called for 120 MW of wind-generated power (Vomhof 2005). Furthermore, most of the utilities that were in a position to meet the 2005 goal had significant excess generation capacity, prompting the State to look into instituting a credit trading system, as exists in neighboring Wisconsin (Berry 2002). A similar situation has arisen with regard to the biomass generation goal, as six utilities are in a position to meet the 0.5 percent goal for 2005 and most of the rest have little or no biomass capacity. A credit trading system may help alleviate this situation as well (MDOC 2005a).

Net Metering & Interconnection Standards. Minnesota began its support for renewable energy production in 1983 by adopting a statewide net metering program. In contrast to some other states, Minnesota does not limit the total size of its program, meaning all state utilities and cooperatives are obligated to supply net metering to any customer who wants it regardless of how many net metered customers they already have. The only major restriction that Minnesota places on net metering is a size limit of 40 kW (DSIRE 2004). The number of net metered customers in Minnesota is currently the highest it has ever been at 162 (127 wind, 34 solar, and one waste-oil) producing 2,039,524 kWh of electricity in 2004. This is an increase of 37 customers and 700,000 kWh of generation from 2003 (MDOC 2004b). It is difficult to attribute this increase to any specific policy and it may have as much to do with the declining cost and increasing efficiency of renewable energy systems than with state policy. However, the PV rebate program and sales tax exemptions on wind and PV systems almost certainly played some role in expanding the number of net-metered systems. Further increases are likely in the future, as Minnesota instituted standard interconnection procedures in 2004, which should make the interconnection process easier for prospective personal generators (DSIRE 2004).

Grant & Loan Programs. Minnesota has two programs that support renewable energy development on agricultural land by offering low interest loans: the Value-Added Stock Loan setup in 1994, and the Agricultural Improvement Loan instituted in 1995 (DSIRE 2004). While the loans are similar in some respects, their purposes are different. The Agricultural Improvement Loan is designed to support projects for building or improving permanent farm structures. The Value-Added Stock Loan program is meant to provide capital to farmers wishing to buy stock in local cooperative programs including wind power projects or renewable fuel production facilities. Both loan programs are administered by the Minnesota Department of Agriculture (MDA) through the Rural Finance Authority and are available for small wind (< 1MW), anaerobic digestion, and other biomass energy projects. Each program requires that the net worth of recipients be less than $361,000 and will provide up to 45 percent of the planned project cost as a low-interest loan. The main differences between these programs are that the Agricultural Improvement Loan has a limit of $200,000 at 5 percent interest while the Value-Added Stock Loan program has a maximum loan of $40,000 at 4 percent interest. Additional loans and grants are available for the construction of anaerobic digesters as a component of sustainable agricultural practice and water quality improvement (MDA 2005).

Further financing opportunities are available for non-farm renewable energy applications under the Minnesota Energy Investment Loan Program started in 1983. This program will provide loans of 50 percent of the project cost up to $500,000 for cities, townships, counties, schools, and hospitals engaged in energy efficiency, energy conservation, or renewable energy projects with an expected payback period of less than 10 years. While the most common projects have been energy efficiency retrofits of public buildings, this loan program has funded the construction of a 225 kW turbine and nine wood-fired boilers (DSIRE 2004).

Renewable Fuels. Minnesota ranks third in the U.S. in the production and use of ethanol as an alternative fuel for many reasons, not the least of which is state promotional policies. One of these measures is a requirement that ethanol blended gasoline (E-10) be used on a year-round basis throughout Minnesota. This mandate was part of a state implementation plan required by the U.S. Environmental Protection Agency (EPA) under the Clean Air Act, with the end result being that all gasoline sold in Minnesota since 1997 has had at least a 10 percent ethanol content.

More direct support for ethanol fuels is visible in 1987 legislation offering a $0.20 per gallon incentive payment for producers beginning ethanol production on or before June 30, 2000. Individual producers are eligible to receive up to $3 million in incentive payments per year with a maximum total of $34 million for all producers (Minnesota Legislative Auditor 1997). Annual goals have been set and easily reached, with production capacity reaching over 400 million gallons in 2004 compared to a 300 million gallon goal (Minnesota Statute 41A.09 2004). Ethanol production capacity in Minnesota is currently 524 million gallons per year (RFA 2005).

Flexible-fueled vehicles (FFVs), including vehicles that run on a blend of 85 percent ethanol, or E-85 are also being promoted by the State. In 2004 Governor Tim Pawlenty issued Executive Order 4–10 requiring state agencies to reduce on-road gasoline use 25 percent by 2010 and 50 percent by 2015 from 2005 levels (DOE 2005b). The high production level of Minnesota ethanol plants has also led to the most extensive E-85 infrastructure in the nation, with 108 E-85 filling stations and approximately 100,000 FFVs on the road. This is not surprising since prices for E-85 fuel during 2004 averaged $0.18 less than the price of regular gasoline (MDOC 2005b).

Biodiesel is also beginning to enjoy some of the state support previously reserved for ethanol. In 2002 legislation was passed mandating that all diesel fuel sold in the state after June 2005 have a 2 percent biodiesel component, conditional upon the state reaching an annual production capacity of 8 million gallons. Although this condition has not yet been met, over 200 filling stations have begun offering biodiesel at their pumps and the law is expected to come into effect some time in the summer of 2005 with the completion of two 30 million gallon capacity plants in Albert Lea and Brewster (NBB 2005).

IOWA

Overview of Electricity Production. As is the case for many states, the last decade has brought consistent increases in electricity consumption and production capacity in Iowa. From 1993–2002, the generating capacity of the electric power industry increased at a rate of 1.1 percent per year from 8,487 MW in 1993 to 9,338 MW in 2002. Correspondingly, electricity consumption grew at a rate of 3.2 percent per year, from 32 million MWh in 1993 to 42.5 million MWh in 2002. Throughout this period, the market has been dominated by coal-fired power plants, which have consistently comprised more than 80 percent of the total electricity production.

Renewable electricity sources have experienced rapid growth in recent years in Iowa, although their market penetration is still small. Non-hydro renewable capacity grew from 5 MW in 1993 to 529 MW in 2002 with almost all of the growth occurring during the last five years of this period. Production from non-hydro renewable sources grew at 48 percent annually during this decade, from less than 30,000 MWh in 1993 to over 1 million MWh in 2002 (EIA 2004a). Almost all non-hydro renewable energy is from wind power, with smaller amounts coming from landfill gas and other biomass generation (EIA 2004b, Table C4). By the end of 2005 Iowa's wind power capacity was 832 MW (AWEA 2005). Again, this trend towards increasing use of renewables for power generation can be explained by a few important state policies.

Utility Mandates. Some of the same policies that Minnesota has used to support renewable energy have been used in Iowa, although in general policy in Iowa has been less extensive or ambitious. One of these policies, called the Alternative Energy Law, was passed in 1983 and required Iowa's two investor-owned utilities to purchase electricity from renewable facilities at rates substantially higher than their obligations under the federal

Public Utilities Regulatory Policies Act of 1978[3]. In 1991, due to legal and implementation difficulties, the Alternative Energy Law was redesigned. This resulted in a combined goal of 105 MW of renewable electricity capacity for investor-owned utilities and revised rate-setting procedures to provide incentives for renewable energy development (Iowa DNR 2002). Interestingly, a compliance schedule for achieving this goal was never set, apparently under the premise that the required renewable energy purchase rates would provide sufficient incentive for increasing production.

More recent policy has proceeded along similar lines, with subsequent energy plans stressing the need to pursue renewable energy alternatives without mandatory compliance dates. A target of 10 percent renewable electricity generation was made in the 1990 comprehensive energy plan, and current recommendations from the Governor's Energy Task Force call for a goal of 1,000 MW of renewable electricity capacity by 2010 (Iowa Utilities Board 2003). A mandatory RPS has been considered but rejected in favor of less restrictive methods for supporting renewable energy.

Even though Iowa has chosen not to set mandatory renewable electricity production goals, other recent actions obligate utilities. One of these requirements is a mandatory green-power option, which was enacted in 2001 and took effect in 2004. All Iowa electric utilities, including those whose tariff rates are not regulated by the State, are required to comply with this law although they have considerable leeway in doing so. Utilities may purchase green power from outside of Iowa if they have pre-existing contracts or a vested financial interest with out-of-state renewable energy facilities. Eligible technologies are the same as those specified under the Alternative Energy Law (Iowa Code 199–15.11 2003).

Net Metering and Interconnection Standards. Iowa has been providing support for residential renewable electricity generation through a net-metering program established in 1991 as part of the legislation mentioned earlier. Iowa's net metering program is unique in that under the original guidelines, no size limit was set on facilities eligible for net-metering treatment. Subsequent protests from Iowa utilities in the late 1990s resulted in the imposition of a 500 kW limit and gave utilities the option to roll over net excess generation from month to month rather than provide payouts on a monthly basis. Further rule clarification allows facilities larger than 500 kW the option to contract for net billing on 500 kW of their capacity with the remaining capacity addressed through utility purchase agreements (Iowa Utilities Board 2004). It is not clear how this provision applies to large single generator facilities such as large wind turbines, where the net-metered portion of energy production is not easily distinguishable from the remaining portion. All told, Iowa's net metering code grants much more freedom to personal energy generators than those in most other states, even with the recent size restrictions. Standard interconnection procedures are also in the process of development, which should further streamline the interconnection process for small generators (DSIRE 2004).

Tax Incentives. Iowa currently offers several tax incentives to renewable energy producers, most of which are available for both large and small systems. Solar and wind energy conversion systems built since 1978 are exempt from value-added property taxes, as are all anaerobic digester systems. Both residential and commercial wind energy systems are exempt from state sales taxes on actual wind energy equipment and installation materials. Renewable facilities also receive a reduced energy excise tax rate for their power generation. Finally, methane recovery facilities and wind systems are exempt from the generation taxes while large hydropower facilities pay a reduced rate (Iowa DNR 2005a).

Grant and Loan Programs. Iowa offers an wide set of grants and loans for R&D of renewable energy devices and installation of renewable energy systems. The Alternative Energy Revolving Loan Program (AERLP) is a $5.9 million fund established in 1996 with money from the State's investor-owned utilities and administered by the Iowa Energy Center. The program provides up to half the cost of renewable energy projects up to a maximum of $250,000 at 0 percent interest over a 20-year payback period. To ensure a diverse array of projects a portion of funds is set aside for specific technologies such as solar, large wind, small wind, methane gas, hydropower, or biomass. Non-specific funds available for all projects comprise 30 percent of the total funding. Past AERLP projects have included a 450 kW waste-wood facility, a 7.5 MW biomass gasifier, a 600 kW hydroelectric facility, two PV systems totaling 3 kW, and eight wind power projects totaling more than 9.5 MW. Energy production from 45 past projects, including biofuels, totaled the equivalent of nearly 1.6 million MWh from July 2003 through June 2004 (Iowa Energy Center 2005).

Additional low-interest loans for renewable energy projects are available for non-profit organizations, schools, hospitals, and government agencies through the Iowa Energy Bank established in 1986. The Energy Bank does not fund projects, but instead facilitates favorable loan agreements for project developers through private lending institutions. For the most part, these loans are aimed to finance revenue neutral building improvements with an emphasis on energy efficiency and conservation. However, projects involving wind turbines, PV arrays, and biomass utilization have been funded in the past because of their potential energy cost savings. In some cases, organizations can combine AELRP loans with Energy Bank loans to realize very significant cost savings. For example, the Spirit Lake School District saved $72,000 in interest payments on a 600 kW wind turbine by obtaining low and zero-interest loans through the Iowa Energy Bank and the AERLP (Iowa DNR 2005a).

In addition to administering the AERLP, the Iowa Energy Center provides support for new technologies through R&D and demonstration project grants. Roughly $1 million in renewable energy grants was awarded in 2004 for grant projects involving everything from crop-waste energy conversion to hydrogen production from organic wastes. Funding from the Energy Center is also used to sponsor education programs and conferences designed to promote public awareness and showcase improvements in energy technology (Iowa Energy Center 2004).

Renewable Fuels. Iowa currently has several policies that support the development of renewable fuels and has been a national leader in ethanol production since the late 1970s. Blended fuels with an ethanol content of at least 10 percent currently receive a 1.5 cents per gallon tax exemption on the state fuel excise tax, which expires in June 2007. Fuel retailers are also eligible to receive a 2.5 cents per gallon tax credit on any blended fuel sales in excess of 60 percent of total fuel sales (Iowa DNR 2005a). Biodiesel use in state-owned vehicles is supported by a revolving fund that subsidizes the extra cost ($0.15 – $0.30) of fueling vehicles with biodiesel. State government agencies have also purchased more than 500 FFVs equipped to run on E-85 blend ethanol fuel since 1993 (Iowa DNR 2005b).

Despite the weak nature of these incentives production and use of renewable fuels in Iowa is expanding rapidly thanks to the natural incentive found in producing fuels locally, the value added to corn by using it to make ethanol, and federal programs supporting renewable fuels. The Renewable Fuels Association reports a capacity of 881 million gallons per year from 15 plants in Iowa, one of the two top ethanol producers in the U.S. (RFA 2005). Four soybean oil plants make over 50 million gallons of biodiesel each year, making Iowa a leading producer of biodiesel as well (NBB 2005). E-85 fuel is sold at 16 retail service stations and eight state owned facilities serving an estimated 45,000 FFVs, while biodiesel of varying blends (B2 – B100) is available from 150 outlets. A recently proposed bill would expand the infrastructure and bring alternative fuel consumption in Iowa in line with production (Iowa DNR 2005b).

Michigan

Overview of Electricity Production. Total electricity generation capacity and production in Michigan exhibit trends similar to those in Minnesota and Iowa, though on a larger scale. Generating capacity grew at 1.7 percent per year from 1993–2002, reaching more than 29,000 MW in 2002. Actual production increased at just 1.1 percent annually, reaching almost 118 million MWh in 2002. Expansion has by no means been universal among fuel types, however, and some interesting trends have emerged, especially since 1997.

During this five-year period, gas and coal use for electric generation have exhibited opposing trends. Generating capacity and electricity production from coal-fired power plants has remained about the same, while capacity and production from gas-fired power plants has increased dramatically to keep up with demand growth. In 1997, gas-fired power plants made up 8.8 percent of the electricity generating capacity in Michigan. By 2002 they made up almost 25 percent, although their market-share of electricity production increased to a much lesser extent, from 12.5 percent in 1997 to 13.4 percent in 2002, indicating that much of the increase in capacity remains unused or is for peaking units. Renewable capacity has not changed much and remains dominated by one hydroelectric power plant, which makes up 75 percent of the total capacity (EIA 2004a). Non-hydro electricity production is composed mostly of landfill gas and wood-waste operations, with much smaller contributions from other biomass and wind energy facilities (EIA 2004b). The market share for non-hydro renewables has remained at around 2 percent in recent years. Part of the reason for this lack of development is that state support of renewable energy is quite limited compared to what we see in Minnesota and Iowa.

Utility Mandates. Nothing substantive exists in this category in Michigan. Several utilities offer green-power programs, but this is a matter of choice rather than compulsion in the State. An ambitious RPS was proposed during 2003 in the State House of Representatives but did not pass. The proposal would have required Michigan utilities to procure 7 percent of their electricity production between 2004 and 2006 from renewable sources, ratcheting up the requirement by varying degrees to a total of 15 percent in 2013 and thereafter. Additional requirements disqualified hydropower as a renewable energy source and would have required a 5 percent portion of the total renewable production come from solar energy (MREP 2003).

Net Metering and Interconnection Standards. The Michigan net metering program is still in its infancy, with a consensus agreement between the

Michigan Public Service Commission (MPSC) and 11 utilities reached at the end of March 2005. In a sense, this is still a voluntary program because it does not apply to all Michigan utilities, although it covers most of the major power providers. Under the program, eligible generators are limited to less than 30 kW and the total program size is limited to 0.1 percent of the each utility's peak demand from the previous year. The initial enrollment period is slated at five years with enrollees retaining the option to net meter their power for 10 years after enrollment (MPSC 2005). Interconnection standards were finalized in 2003 and should help prospective personal generators navigate the interconnection process (DSIRE 2004). Because of the restrictions placed on total program size, the overall market penetration of personal energy systems is destined to be small, but this would probably be the case anyway based on how programs in other states have fared.

Tax Incentives. Michigan offers a limited set of tax exemptions under the Michigan Next Energy Authority Act of 2002 (Act. No. 549) for companies engaged in R&D or production of renewable energy technologies. All such companies in Michigan are eligible to receive a personal property tax exemption on any equipment related to these activities (DSIRE 2004). In the first quarter of 2005 the Michigan Economic Development Corporation (MEDC) listed 171 Michigan businesses as "alternative energy businesses" (MEDC 2005). As Michigan is the center of the U.S. automobile industry, many of these businesses are engaged in the development of the various aspects of fuel-cell development, although some have expanded into other areas of renewable energy development. One of the most visible companies in this respect is Ovonics Corp., which has offices throughout Southeast Michigan. Ovonics currently operates the world's largest thin-film PV manufacturing facility with a yearly output of 30 MW, and is involved in R&D related to fuel cells, solid hydrogen storage, and battery technology (Ovonics 2005).

In addition to property tax exemptions, the Next Energy Authority Act has led to the creation of a technological development zone, aptly named the NextEnergy Zone in Detroit. Companies operating within this zone are eligible for additional tax incentives including exemptions from payroll taxes, the state education tax, and other taxes related to business activities (DSIRE 2004). Also within the zone is a building called the NextEnergy Center meant to function as an R&D, demonstration, and education center. This building is affiliated with Wayne State University and opened in September 2005 (NextEnergy 2005a).

Notably, these tax incentives apply only to businesses and support research activities rather than the actual use of renewable energy systems. Thus the aim of the Next Energy Authority Act seems to be to help Michigan recruit business operations rather than foster growth in renewable energy production. One could assert that this lack of support is reflected in the lack of appreciable development of renewable energy generation in Michigan.

Grant and Loan Programs. Grants and funding make up a large portion of Michigan's policy commitments to renewable energy. One of the more unique grant programs is one dedicated to funding the construction of large (>10 kW) PV arrays. Public institutions including schools and government agencies can receive grants for up to $60,000 or 90 percent of project costs, with roughly $180,000 available for grants each year. Further funding for more diverse interests is available to this sector in the form of Community Energy Project Grants, where grants of up $6,000 are available for a demonstration projects, education programs, or events (DSIRE 2004).

Michigan also offers some grants through the Michigan Biomass Energy Program (MBEP) for education programs, demonstration projects, technology development, and infrastructure investment. Grants of $5,000 to $30,000 are awarded annually to non-profit and public groups. Some renewable energy projects are may also be funded through the Michigan Low-Income and Energy Efficiency Fund, a public benefits fund created in 2000 (DSIRE 2004).

Additional funding and technical support for education programs was also offered under the Next Energy Authority Act. A portion of the state money dedicated to this program is granted to schools developing alternative energy curriculums. In 2003, the first phase of funding totaling $750,000 was granted to four Michigan colleges, resulting in the creation of 50 alternative energy courses serving 1,500 students. In 2005 the second phase of funding totaling $290,000 supported four universities and two community colleges (NextEnergy 2005b).

Renewable Fuels. The use and production of renewable fuels in Michigan is quite limited. No state incentives exist for producers or retailers of renewable fuels and the retail infrastructure is small. There are currently only two stations in Michigan offering E-85 blended fuel, although more stations offer E-10 as a result of air-quality legislation (Wozniak 2005). Ethanol production in Michigan is limited to one plant with a capacity of 40 million gallons per year, with two more in the planning phase. The Alternative Fuels Data Center (AFDC) currently lists 12 outlets that sell biodiesel and five hydrogen filling stations (AFDC 2005). NextEnergy plans to build upon this and announced a major Biodiesel Value Chain Initiative in October 2005. This Initiative will include a National Biofuels Energy Laboratory and a state-of-the-art production plant to be built by BioDiesel Industries Inc. The number of hydrogen fueling stations is also promising and should increase as progress occurs under the NextEnergy initiative, but overall Michigan lags far behind Minnesota and Iowa in promoting the use of renewable fuels.

Discussion

In the policies summarized above, three different approaches to supporting renewable energy through state programs can be identified. On one extreme is Minnesota, where a comprehensive mixture of policies covers nearly every aspect of renewable energy development from R&D and demonstration to distributed generation and large-scale commercial developments. A similar situation has arisen in Iowa, although overall policy is both less extensive and less coercive. On the other extreme is Michigan, where support for renewable energy is still in its infancy and legislation displays a visible skew towards economic development rather than actual energy production from the state's renewable energy resources. For a review of state programs supporting renewable energy see Table 2.

To some extent these differences are understandable from a political standpoint. The automobile industry in Michigan is expected to exert a prominent role in shaping state policy, and thus the emphasis on fuel cell development is not surprising. Only one U.S. state, California, has more hydrogen filling stations. The same holds true for both Minnesota and Iowa where farming is a major part of the state economy. Farming interests would predictably support the development of renewable fuels in these states because such support opens up new markets for their products and in many cases represents an added value to their crops. The case for wind power and energy crop development in Minnesota and Iowa is similar in this respect. The siting of wind turbines on agricultural lands generates income for rural residents in the form of lease payments and does little to detract from the land's productivity. The opening of CRP lands to renewable energy development acts as an added incentive, allowing farmers to reap the benefits of land preservation, CRP payments, and limited development all at the same time.

In contrast, the situation in Michigan is much different and the barriers more difficult to overcome. While Michigan has a large renewable energy potential, the costs of such development are more significant than

Table 2: Summary of State Support for Renewable Energy			
	Minnesota	Iowa	Michigan
RPS	1230 MW (Xcel) 10% voluntary objective for other utilities by 2015	105 MW mandatory (~2%) Stated goals of 1000 MW by 2010	None
Green Pricing	Mandatory	Mandatory	Voluntary
Production Incentives	Yes	Yes (high renewable purchase rates)	No
Purchase and Financing	Extensive support	Extensive support	Little support
Research, Development & Demonstration	Extensive support	Moderate support	Extensive support
Renewable Fuels	Large incentives	Small incentives	No incentives
Net Metering	All utilities	All utilities	Most utilities

in either Minnesota or Iowa. Much of Michigan's renewable potential lies in the biomass potential of its forest cover and wind potential along the shorelines and offshore in the Great Lakes. Renewable energy development in Michigan thus hinges on making significant trade-offs between preserving the natural beauty and integrity of its ecosystems while at the same time attempting to harvest energy in a sustainable way.

The nature of these obstacles makes for an interesting paradox. Political support is obviously much easier to come by where the environmental benefits of developing renewable energy resources are supplemented by significant economic benefits to the state economy and come at a small cost to natural ecosystems. However, policy support is needed most in those areas where significant barriers exist and the trade-offs are more visible. Thus the task of policy makers should be to find innovative, creative solutions to overcome these obstacles while balancing the needs and wants of state residents.

Minnesota policy provides us with an excellent example of such creativity in the Prairie Island legislation. While some might consider the obligations required of Xcel Energy onerous and unreasonable, the fact remains that Minnesota provided a service to Xcel by allowing the utility to store its excess spent nuclear fuel on site. The payment for this service allowed Minnesota to expand renewable energy production, benefited state residents, and provided funding for a more environmentally friendly energy future. The legislation also serves as a notice to other Minnesota utilities that lawmakers have the political will to impose restrictive measures to support renewable energy, making the voluntary REO program more effective.

Iowa shows us that while an RPS is generally considered the most effective policy for supporting renewable energy, it is by no means the only way. The right set of state financial incentives, coupled with existing federal incentives and laws, can be quite successful. Essential to all of this are technological development, grants, and loan programs that provide marginal or nascent technologies the funding and opportunities they need to become viable energy options. In this respect, state programs can be superior to federal programs because they spur developments in technologies specific to local or regional needs and resources. States can pick and choose renewable energy options to match their resources and needs, while at the same time addressing issues and concerns on a local level. Support in Minnesota and Iowa for anaerobic digesters and crop waste-to-energy research is a good example such a focus on local resources.

This same line of thought brings us to policy support of renewable energy in Michigan, which has thus far proven to be largely inadequate at developing state resources. In general, policy support in Michigan could be called "misplaced" because it focuses not on overcoming state barriers to renewable energy development, but instead on R&D that might be better left at the national level. To be sure, technological innovations in fuel cells stand to benefit residents of the State of Michigan to a greater extent than most other places, but such research can be done anywhere (and California's hydrogen fuel cell program will provide major competition). As such, it is probably more appropriate that it be the subject of federal programs, which are in a better position to provide the large amounts of necessary funding. This is not to say that all such research should cease in Michigan, but only that it should not be the sole basis of Michigan's contribution to a sustainable future when so many other options are available.

Future development of renewable energy in Michigan will hinge on a state commitment to addressing the barriers that currently impede resource development. Incentives for the use of waste-wood as a biomass feedstock or as a source of renewable fuels are appropriate, as are demonstration projects, education programs, and public dialogue about the future direction of renewable energy policy. To some extent, the grant programs in Michigan already serve some of these purposes, but by themselves they are inadequate. Incentives promoting the use of landfill gas could help the state more fully utilize an already viable resource. Utilities could be obligated to provide a green-power option to their customers, and public informational sessions could stress the environmental hazards of coal-fired power plants near the Great Lakes. Ideally, an RPS could be applied to state utilities, but this is not strictly necessary and the political will for such a measure appears to be absent at the moment. In any case, a variety of options are available, but it is up to lawmakers to explore them while balancing issues and concerns specific to renewable energy in Michigan and the future implications of inaction.

Conclusion

What is most apparent from this study is the importance of creative, comprehensive state policy support to renewable energy. States have the freedom to institute a variety of policy or incentive programs to support renewable energy, but the most successful policy comes from adapting a broad strategy to suit their particular needs, natural attributes, and even existing federal incentives. In light of their natural environments, it is not surprising to see wind energy developing in Iowa and Minnesota. There is little chance that such development would have occurred without state support in either case. The federal wind energy production tax credit was an essential component of development in both states, but by itself this tax credit could never have achieved the degree of success we currently see. Through formulating policies that made use of this existing federal incentive, Minnesota and Iowa were able to expand renewable energy production without entailing prohibitive costs to themselves or state residents. In addition, this had the effect of creating markets where wind energy technology could be tested and improved, hopefully to some point in the future where financial incentives are no longer necessary.

The same holds true for the ethanol industry, where federal renewable fuel incentives have been supplemented by state incentives with great success. The development of the ethanol industry in Iowa further illustrates another point. State policies need not be overly restrictive or significant to produce results, provided that the right set of natural incentives exist. Thus the goal of state energy policies should be to provide just enough support to encourage development and overcome barriers, while relying on the existing market to do the rest of the work. In this way, the natural benefits of renewable energy provide most of the impetus to development, but the initial barriers can be overcome with a little help from directed policy.

This appears to be a large part of the problem in Michigan and is responsible for the lack of recent development of renewable energy. Instead of focusing on overcoming the barriers to development of their most abundant renewable resources, wind and biomass, policymakers have instead directed their attention towards economic development with little more than token gestures to renewable energy. To be certain, the barriers to renewable energy development in Michigan are perhaps more numerous and substantial than those in Iowa and Minnesota, but this is precisely why state policy is needed. These barriers should not act as a deterrent to renewable energy development so much as they should provide a stimulus for developing policy solutions. These policies necessitate a long-term commitment on the part of the state, which Iowa and Minnesota have done, but a step that Michigan is reluctant to take.

Notes

1. The average power output takes into account wind power's intermittency and that turbines rarely operate at their nameplate capacity. These figures use a capacity factor of about one-third, meaning that for every 1 MW of average output, 3 MW of nameplate capacity must be installed.

2. The amount of production disqualified from the REO under this restriction was nearly 25,000 MWh from July 2002 through June 2003. At the end of 2003, 39 MW of installed capacity was certified for participation in this program, with 14 MW installed in 2003 alone (MDOC 2004a).

3. The Public Utilities Regulatory Policies Act of 1978 is a federal law that obligates electric utilities to purchase power from IPPs operating within their franchised service territory at the avoided cost rate, that is their cost of generating the same amount of power themselves. This rate is typically determined for individual utilities by state public utility commissions.

References

AFDC. 2005. *Alternative Fueling Stations by State and Fuel Type.* Available at *http://www. eere.energy.gov/afdc/infrastructure/station_counts.html* Accessed April 26, 2005.

AWEA (American Wind Energy Association). 2005. *Wind Energy Projects Throughout the United States of America.* Available at *http://www.awea.org/projects/index.html* Accessed May 2, 2005.

Berry, David. 2002. The Market for Tradable Renewable Energy Credits. *Ecological Economics* 42(3): 369–79.

De Fiebre, Jeremy. 2005. Minnesota Energy Information Center, Minnesota Department of Commerce, In Personal Communication, April 2005.

DOE (U.S. Department of Energy). 2004a. *Report to Congress on Analysis of Wind Resource Locations and Transmission Requirements of the Upper Midwest.* Washington, D.C.: U.S. Department of Energy, Office of Energy Efficiency and Renewable Energy.

_____. 2004b. Office of Energy Efficiency and Renewable Energy.Biomass Program: Biomass Feedstocks. Available at *http://www.eere.energy.gov/biomass/biomass_feedstocks.html* Accessed April 25, 2005.

_____. 2005a. Office of Energy Efficiency and Renewable Energy. State Energy Information. Available at *http://www.eere.energy.gov/state_energy/states.cfm?state* Accessed April 26, 2005.

_____. 2005b. Office of Energy Efficiency and Renewable Energy. *EPAct Launches Fleet Towards Minnesota's Fuel Future.* Available at *http://www.state.mn.us/mn/externalDocs/ Commerce/Minnesota_EPAct_success_story_032205011958_MNSuccess.pdf* from the Minnesota Department of Commerce. Accessed May 3, 2005.

DSIRE. 2004. Database of State Incentives for Renewable Energy. *Minnesota Incentives for Renewable Energy.* Available at *http://www.dsireusa.org/* Accessed April 26, 2005.

EIA (Energy Information Administration). 2004a. *State Electricity Profiles 2002.* DOE/EIA-0629. Washington, D.C.: U.S. Department of Energy.

_____. 2004b. *Renewable Energy Annual 2003.* DOE/EIA-0603 (2003). Washington, D.C.: U.S. Department of Energy.

Elliot, D.L., C.G. Holladay, W.R. Barchet, H.P. Foote, and W.F. Sandusky, W.F. 1987. *Wind Energy Resource Atlas of the United States.* DOE/CH 10093–4. Richland, WA: Prepared by the Pacific Northwest Laboratory for the U.S. Department of Energy.

Gupta, Shalina. 2004. *Plant Power: Biomass-to-Energy for Minnesota Communities.* St. Paul, MN: Prepared by Minnesotans for an Energy-Efficient Economy for the Minnesota Department of Commerce and Minnesota Office of Environmental Assistance.

Iowa Code 199–15.11. 2003. Database of State Incentives for Renewable Energy. Available at *http://www.dsireusa.org/library/docs/incentives/IA02R.pdf.* Accessed April 26, 2005.

Iowa DNR (Department of Natural Resources). 2002. *Renewable Energy Resource Guide 2002.* Available at *http://www.state.ia.us/dnr/energy/MAIN/PUBS/IRERG/index.html* Accessed April 26, 2005.

_____. 2005a. *Financial Assistance and Incentive Programs.* Available at *http://www.state. ia.us/dnr/energy/MAIN/renewable/incentives.html* Accessed April 26, 2005.

_____. 2005b. *Ethanol.* Available at www.state.ia.us/*dnr/energy/MAIN/PROGRAMS/ ETHANOL/index.html* Accessed May 4, 2005.

Iowa Energy Center. 2004. *2004 Annual Report.* Available at *http://www.energy.iastate. edu/news/downloads/2004Interim.pdf* Accessed April 26, 2005.

_____. 2005. *Alternative Energy Revolving Loan Program (AERLP).* Available at *http://www. energy.iastate.edu/funding/aerlp-index.html* Accessed April 26, 2005.

Iowa Utilities Board. 2003. Status of Recommendations from the 2001 Energy Task Force Report to the Governor, Memo to Governor Tom Vilsack, December 17, De Moines, Iowa.

_____. 2004. Decisions on Docket Nos. TF-03–180 & TF-03–181. Available at *http://www. state.ia.us/government/com/util/_private/Orders/2004/0120_tf03180.pdf* Accessed April 26, 2005.

Klink, Katherine, Helen D. Fisher, Geoffrey K. Force, Joanna I. Thorpe, and Jeffrey M. Young. 2003. Interannual Variability of Wind Speed and Wind Power at Five Tall-Tower Sites in Minnesota (1996–2001). *Physical Geography* 24(3): 183–95.

Launder, Kelly. 2002. *Energy Crops and Their Potential Development in Michigan.* Available at *http://www.michigan.gov/documents/CIS_EO_Energy_crop_paper_A-E-9_87916_7.pdf* from the Michigan Biomass Energy Program. Accessed May 5, 2005.

Lave, Lester B., W. Michael Griffin, and Heather L. MacLean. 2001. The Ethanol Answer to Carbon Emissions. *Issues in Science and Technology* 18(2): 73–78.

Lemus, Rocky W., Charles E. Brummer, Kenneth J. Moore, Neil E. Molstad, C. Lee Burras, and Michael F. Barker. 2002. Biomass Yield and Quality of 20 Switchgrass Populations in Southern Iowa, U.S.A. *Biomass and Bioenergy* 23 (6): 433–42.

MDA (Minnesota Department of Agriculture). 2005. *Farm Planning and Practice: Finance Programs.* Available at *http://www.mda.state.mn.us/farmplan.htm* Accessed April 25, 2005.

MDOC (Minnesota Department of Commerce). 2002. *Wind Resource Analysis Program Report.* Available at *http://www.state.mn.us/mn/externalDocs/Commerce/WRAP_Report_ 110702040352_WR AP2002.pdf* from the Minnesota Energy Info Center. Accessed April 25, 2005.

_____. 2003a. *Minnesota's Potential for Electricity Production Using Manure Biogas Resource.* Available at *http://www.state.mn.us/mn/externalDocs/MN_Biogas_Potential_Report_ 041003013143_biogasfinal2.pdf* Accessed April 25, 2005.

_____. 2003b. *Minnesota Solar Electric Rebate Program*. Available at *http://www.state. mn.us/mn/externalDocs/Commerce/Solar_Electric_Rebate_Program_110802025911_Rebate-Instructions08–04.pdf* Accessed 26, 2005.

_____. 2004a. *Quadrennial Energy Report 2004*. Available at *http://www.state.mn.us/mn/ externalDocs/Commerce/2004_Quadrennial_Report_071404101313_DraftQuadRPT11–04.pdf* Accessed April 25, 2005.

_____. 2004b. *1986–2004 Electric Utility Qualifying Facilities Report*. Available at *http://www. state.mn.us/mn/externalDocs/Commerce/1986–2003_Utility_QF_Report_091903011746_QF all.pdf* Accessed April 26, 2005.

_____. 2005a. *Renewable Energy Objective Report*. Available at *http://www.state.mn.us/ mn/externalDocs/Commerce/Renewable_Energy_Objective_Report_020305041245_-REOComplete-NoH1–13.pdf* Accessed April 26, 2005.

_____. 2005b. *Energy Information: E-85 Fuel Use Data*. Available at *http://www.state. mn.us/mn/externalDocs/Commerce/E-85_Fuel_Use_Data_041703045254_E85fueUse.pdf* Accessed April 25, 2005.

MEDC (Michigan Economic Development Corporation). 2005. *Business Directory: Alternative Energy*. Available at *http://medc.michigan.org/services/ServiceProvider/* Accessed May 9, 2005.

Minnesota Legislative Auditor. 1997. *Ethanol Programs Bring Benefits but Carry Notable Costs and Risks (Summary)*. Available at *http://www.auditor.leg.state.mn.us/ped/pedrep/9704-1pg.pdf* Accessed May 4, 2005.

Minnesota Statute 216C.41. 2003. Available from the Database of State Incentives for Renewable Energy at *http://www.dsireusa.org/library/docs/incentives/MN06F.htm* Accessed April 26, 2005.

Minnesota Statute 41A.09. 2004. Available from the Minnesota State Legislature at *http:// www.leg.state.mn.us/* Accessed April 26, 2005.

MPSC (Michigan Public Service Commission). 2005. *Electronic Case Filings No. U-14346*. Available at *http://efile.mpsc.cis.state.mi.us/efile/electric.html* Accessed April 26, 2005.

MREP. 2003. *Annual Report to the Michigan Public Service Commission*. Michigan Public Service Electronic Case Filings Case Number U-12915. Available at *http://efile.mpsc.cis.state. mi.us/efile/electric.html* Accessed April 25, 2005.

Murray, Les D., and Louis B. Best,. 2003. Short-Term Bird Response to Harvesting Switchgrass for Biomass in Iowa. *Journal of Wildlife Management* 67 (3): 611–21.

NBB (National Biodiesel Board). 2005. Current and Proposed Biodiesel Production Plants. Available at *http://www.biodiesel.org/buyingbiodiesel/producers_marketers/ProducersMap-existingandpotential.pdf* Accessed May 4, 2005.

NextEnergy Corp. 2005a. *Next Energy Center*. Available at *http://www.nextenergy.org/ nextenergycenter/* Accessed November 1, 2005.

_____. 2005b. Press Release, Next Energy Announces Education Awards. Available at *http://www.nextenergy.org/news/Press_releases.asp* Accessed April 26, 2005.

Noble, Michael T., and Steven M. Hoffman. 2002. Switching on the Future: Midwestern Models for a Clean Energy Transition. *Bulletin of Science, Technology & Society* 22(2): 132–46.

Ovonics Corp. 2005. *Research and Development Projects*. Available at *http://www.ovonics. com/res/2_0_resdev.htm* Accessed April 26, 2005.

RFA (Renewable Fuels Association). 2005. U.S. Fuel Ethanol Production Capacity. Available at *http://www.ethanolrfa.org/eth_prod_fac.html* Accessed May 3, 2005.

USDA (U.S. Department of Agriculture). 2004. Farm Service Agency. *Conservation Reserve Program: Fiscal Year 2003 Annual Summary*. Available at *http://www.fsa.usda.gov/dafp/ cepd/stats/FY2003.pdf* Accessed May 5, 2005.

Vomhof, John. 2005. Great River Energy Seeks Wind-Powered Proposals. *The Business Journal* (Minneapolis-St. Paul), October 28, 2005.

Wozniak, Shawn. 2005. Michigan Energy Office, In Personal Communication, March 2005.

Xcel Energy. 2001. *Xcel Renewable Development Fund: 2001 Project Selections.* Available at *http://www.xcelenergy.com/XLWEB/CDA/0,3080,1-1-1_11824_11838-801-5_538_969-0,00.html* Accessed April 26, 2005.

_____. 2005. Xcel Renewable Development Fund: 2003 Bidder Update. Available at *http://www.xcelenergy.com/XLWEB/CDA/0,3080,1-1-1_11824_11838_12925-11657-5_538_969-0,00.html* Accessed March 25, 2005.

6. Sustainable Energy in New Jersey

Clinton J. Andrews
Rutgers University

Introduction

New Jersey often stands out in state rankings. This rich, crowded, diverse state is number 1 in population density and median family income. It is among the top ten for housing prices, mean travel time to work, and percent of the population that is foreign born, according to the American Community Survey (2004).

What about energy? Although New Jersey is ranked 10th in population, it is only 13th in total energy consumption, and is 38th in per capita energy consumption. Looking at consumption rankings by energy type, for natural gas and petroleum it is 9th, for both gasoline and distillate fuel it is 11th, for LPG it is 14th, and for jet fuel it is 4th. For consumption of electricity it is 20th. For energy consumption by end user, New Jersey is 11th for residential use, 9th for commercial use, 22nd for industrial use, and 8th for transportation use according to Hinton (2005) and EIA (2005).

As a consumer state with few indigenous energy resources, New Jersey has often innovated in its energy policies. It currently has one of the most favorable subsidy regimes in the nation for renewable energy and energy efficiency. This chapter provides background on New Jersey, its energy economy, and its energy policies, and it critically evaluates the status of sustainable energy in New Jersey.

New Jersey Background

Located in the heart of the Northeastern megalopolis on a direct axis between New York and Philadelphia, New Jersey is a coastal state with numerous ports and extensive road, rail, and pipeline networks. These links run mostly along the Northeast Corridor, a southwest-to-northeast line connecting Philadelphia and New York, paralleling ancient trade routes and the underlying geography. Geologists divide New Jersey into four parts: in the northwestern corner of the state is the Appalachian Ridge and Valley province, southeast of that is the Highlands province, then the Piedmont Lowlands province, and finally the large Coastal Plain that encompasses a majority of the state's land area. New Jersey is bordered by the Delaware River on the south and west, by the Atlantic Ocean on the east, and by the Hudson River on the northeast. It is bisected in the middle by the Raritan River.

Three hundred and fifty years ago, colonial settlements in New Jersey spread across the coastal plain and into the Piedmont along the banks of the rivers and estuaries. Canals and railroads linked these sites by 1850. New Jersey was then an economic hinterland that provided agricultural and mined products to the large cities of New York and Philadelphia. During the latter half of the nineteenth century, New Jersey's port cities and rail terminals became natural sites for industrial activity. By 1900, Camden's Campbell's soups were feeding America, Trenton's Roebling Iron Works had provided cables for the Brooklyn Bridge, New Brunswick's Johnson brothers had sold bandages to the world, Edison's invention factory in Menlo Park had launched the electric power and sound recording industries, and Newark's tanneries had supplied hats and shoes for countless Americans. These industrial accomplishments planted seeds that sprouted into several giants of the manufacturing economy in the 20th century, including such well-known corporate names as RCA, AT&T, Johnson and Johnson, and Merck. Today, New Jersey has sectoral specializations in professional and business services; financial activities; trade, transportation and utilities; educational and health services; and petrochemical refining.

New Jersey developed one of the nation's most comprehensive commuter rail networks during the industrial years, providing regular train service into New York, Philadelphia, Newark, and other major job centers. Yet the great decanting of America's industrial cities into their rural hinterlands after World War II caused a dramatic reshaping of New Jersey's economic and social geography. Rapidly growing suburbs assimilated not only the white flight from New Jersey's own modestly sized industrial cities, but also the much larger exodus from New York and Philadelphia, two of America's largest immigrant pumps.

Decentralization was aided by the aggressive building of a highway network that not only preserved New Jersey's advantage as a port and corridor state, but also opened up new land for suburban development. The overlay of a radial-and-ring highway network on a strictly radial rail network provided a variety of transportation choices. During the past 25 years, however, as jobs have followed residents into the suburbs, the rail network has become a less viable alternative for many commuters. Today, even though New Jersey has the highest population density of any U.S. state and New Jersey Transit operates at full capacity, New Jerseyans suffer from the nation's third longest average commute (ACS 2004).

Part of the challenge is that New Jersey's population continues growing, with an increase of 8.85 percent between the 1990 and 2000 census (ACS 2004). The 2005 population is estimated to exceed 8,700,000. The rate of population growth is below the national average, but it still represents an additional 68,000 people each year to burden already crowded roads, trains, schools, and housing markets. All of these people consume energy.

New Jersey Energy Markets

The only time that New Jersey enjoyed energy self-sufficiency was during the pre-colonial and colonial eras when biomass and falling water counted as major commercial energy resources. The state has minimal fossil fuel resources.

Since the industrial revolution, New Jersey has relied heavily on energy imports. Coal imports from Pennsylvania began prior to 1830. Petroleum imports began prior to 1900. Natural gas imports began before 1920. Electricity imports began in earnest in 1927 with the creation of the Pennsylvania–Jersey–Maryland interconnection.

New Jersey's energy sector is firmly embedded in the larger energy economy, and it shares the characteristics of these larger markets.

PETROLEUM

Petroleum is traded in global markets. The United States currently imports two thirds of the petroleum it uses, and New Jersey must import all that it uses. New Jersey draws on a very diverse set of sources for petroleum products. It has no indigenous crude oil reserves, production, wells, or rigs. It has no crude oil pipelines, but it receives refined products through three pipelines: the major Colonial pipeline from the Gulf Coast, as well as the Buckeye and Sun pipelines that deliver product from ports around the Northeast. New Jersey ports that receive crude and product imports include Jersey City, Sayreville, Sewaren, Perth Amboy, Linden, Carteret, Woodbridge, Elizabeth, Bayonne, Newark, Deepwater, Crab Point, Paulsboro, Gloucester, Camden, Pennsauken, Burlington, and Duck Island. These imports come from 58 different countries, led by the United Kingdom (10 percent), Canada (9 percent), Saudi Arabia (9 percent), Venezuela (9 percent), and Nigeria (8 percent) (EIA 2005a).

New Jersey has a substantial amount of downstream refining capacity, totaling approximately 615,000 BCD (Barrels per Calendar Day, or about 26 million gallons per day) in 2005 (Hinton 2005), thus closely matching statewide demand. This distillation capacity is spread among six sites: Amerada Hess (Port Reading), Chevron (Perth Amboy), Citgo (Paulsboro), Sunoco (Westville), ConocoPhillips (Linden), and Valero (Paulsboro). As a buffer against wintertime disruptions, New Jersey has a one million barrel heating oil reserve in Woodbridge. Retail sales in New Jersey take place at 3,608 gas stations (approximately 2.1 percent of the U.S. total) as well as through home heating oil deliveries (Hinton 2005).

Over two thirds of New Jersey's use of petroleum products is for transportation, with the remainder divided among home heating, industrial, and electricity generation uses. Nineteen percent of New Jersey homes have oil heat (Hinton 2005). The demand for petroleum is dominated by transportation uses, including personal autos, commercial vehicles, and airplanes, and today there is no readily available, cost-competitive substitute fuel for these end uses.

Petroleum has been a cheap and plentiful commodity over many decades, although it has always been subject to dramatic price volatility due to a combination of lumpy supply and unresponsive demand. As result, producers and consumers have supported a series of price stabilization regimes ranging from the Standard Oil monopoly, to the Seven Sisters and OPEC cartels, to the current Saudi-American pact (Gillespie and Henry 1995). Within such constraints, oil markets have worked reasonably well. In the longer term, significant questions loom: When will this finite resource run out? When will global climate change become a significant policy driver? Will geopolitical factors limit U.S. access to foreign oil? Will energy efficiency become more palatable politically in U.S. policymaking circles?

Natural Gas

Unlike petroleum, natural gas is traded in regional rather than global markets. North America as a whole has been self-sufficient, and most of New Jersey's natural gas arrives by pipeline from the Gulf Coast. Canadian imports are growing rapidly for the Northeastern United States but little of that gas currently comes to New Jersey (Tobin 2002). Even though natural gas trade has been limited to continental markets, its price tracks that of globally traded petroleum because they can substitute for one another in many end uses.

The demand for natural gas is primarily for space and process heating, although electricity production has rapidly increased its share of gas demand since 1990. New Jersey consumed 611,780 million cubic feet of natural gas in 2004, with 38 percent going to residential end uses, 27 percent to commercial, 23 percent to electric power, and 12 percent to industrial end uses (EIA 2005b). Because the peak space heating demand occurs in the winter and the peak electric power-related demand occurs in the summer, these two uses of natural gas do not compete very much with one another for the limited pipeline capacity. However, unexpected events like Hurricanes Katrina and Rita in 2005 have periodically disrupted planned natural gas flows and thereby have caused price spikes. In spite of flat aggregate demand for natural gas in New Jersey and nationwide, there is still a strong secular trend toward higher prices because it is a clean and convenient fuel, and because of increased petroleum prices.

U.S. natural gas markets have been successfully deregulated over the past three decades, and this has encouraged exploration for new supplies, investments in new pipeline capacity, and the creation of financial instruments to manage price and availability risks. In the longer term, many view natural gas as a key bridging fuel during the transition to a cleaner hydrogen economy. This hope persists even though continental supplies of natural gas will start to diminish in the next decade or two, forcing a reliance yet again on imports, this time in the form of liquefied natural gas.

Electricity

As an energy carrier rather than a primary energy source, electricity has a distinctive role in the energy economy. It can transform a variety of primary sources into convenient, clean, and high quality energy at the point of end use. Electricity can be transmitted long distances, thus substituting for pipelines, but it cannot be stored, hence making the economic relationship to pipelines also complementary. It has regional markets that may in time grow to a continental scale. New Jersey is part of the Pennsylvania–Jersey–Maryland (PJM) regional market within which a common authority dispatches power plants, and there are strong interregional trade links to the west, north, and south. The PJM interconnection is the oldest in the United States, dating back to 1927, so the participating states and utility companies have had much practice in cooperatively managing a competitive regional market. This distinguishes PJM from certain other U.S. electrical regions where serious problems have developed.

New Jersey imports 17 percent of its electricity from other states, chiefly Pennsylvania, and in-state generation is 50 percent from nuclear, 31 percent from natural gas, 16 percent from coal, 1 percent from oil, and 2 percent from renewables (EIA 2003). These proportions have been relatively stable for the past decade. During that decade, however, power plant ownership has switched under deregulation from being predominantly in the hands of vertically integrated investor-owned utility franchises, to being in the hands of independent power producers. Traditional utilities still dominate retail sales, capturing 98 percent of customers, 97 percent of kWh sold, and 98 percent of revenues (EIA 2003). Public, cooperative, and energy service company providers share the remaining sliver of the pie.

The demand for electricity is steadily increasing in New Jersey and nationally. Residential and commercial electricity demand growth has averaged 2.5 percent annually for the past decade, although due to the loss of manufacturing in the industrial mix, aggregate demand growth has averaged only 1.4 percent annually in New Jersey (EIA 2003).

The long term outlook for the electricity sector in New Jersey is mixed. It has survived deregulation, but there are regional transmission constraints and siting problems for new power plants proposed in this crowded state. Nationally, in spite of huge potential for technological innovations, there is almost no money being invested in research and development (Margolis 2002).

New Jersey Energy Policy

As a rich and densely populated consumer state without local energy resources, New Jersey has above all sought a diverse and reliable energy supply mix. It has depended heavily on private sector leadership, but its energy policy record is not *laissez faire*. Government in New Jersey has tended to intervene in the energy marketplace according to classic rationales of improving allocative efficiency, especially to correct market failures;

plus distributional equity and macro stability (e.g., Musgrave 1959). Sometimes it has acted less defensibly, seeking to enforce widely held norms, pursue political objectives, and cater to special interests.

Business-friendly public policy has been the norm in New Jersey for most of the past century, as one would expect of a state that was home to Thomas Edison, father of General Electric, and the birthplace of Exxon Corporation, formerly Standard Oil of New Jersey. The New Jersey oil, natural gas, and electricity sectors all started mostly in private hands and remain so today. Energy policy in New Jersey thus has been primarily limited to economic and environmental regulation of private actors.

Energy taxes in New Jersey are relatively low. New Jersey's gasoline tax is only 10.5 cents/gallon compared to a weighted U.S. average state tax of 18.7 cents/gallon (note that there is an additional 18.4 cents/gallon of Federal tax) (FHA 2003). Natural gas and electricity are subject to the standard statewide sales tax of 6 percent; previous gross receipts and franchise taxes were abolished as part of deregulation (Burkhart 1997).

The oil industry gained early regulatory attention for its price volatility, and in 1938 the New Jersey legislature enacted a law defining and prohibiting price gouging at gasoline stations. This law has been dusted off periodically and used to threaten retailers and their suppliers, most recently in 2005 following the price spike due to Hurricane Katrina. Nationally, the United States learned under Presidents Nixon and Ford that gasoline price control, a stronger policy tool, was a poor public policy choice in times of disruption, and although it has periodically been discussed in New Jersey, no such controls have been used since the 1970s.

The natural gas industry grew out of the manufactured (coal) gas industry, which during the 19th century developed local gas distribution networks in many cities, originally to serve lighting needs. These networks had natural monopoly characteristics and became regulated by New Jersey and many other states during the first decade of the 20th century. The first long-distance natural gas pipeline was built in 1891, and interstate commerce accelerated during the 1920s, leading eventually to federal intervention in the form of the Natural Gas Act in 1938. This act resolved interstate conflicts and provided needed protections for consumers and investors. It was not until the 1950s and 1960s that a true national transmission network was built (NaturalGas.org 2004).

Recurring shortages and price disparities led to federal deregulation starting with the Natural Gas Policy Act of 1978, followed by administrative orders from the Federal Energy Regulatory Commission and additional legislation in 1985, 1987, 1989, and 1992. These policies led to a dramatically restructured industry. Wellhead price controls were removed, transmission pipelines were made into common carriers, and distribution systems were separated organizationally from upstream activities. New Jersey took an additional step and allowed retail customers a choice of suppliers starting in 2000; however, only 5 percent of customers have switched as of 2005 (EIA 2005c NJBPU 2005a).

Regulation of New Jersey's electricity sector followed a trajectory similar to that of natural gas. Private investors built local networks starting in the 1880s that came under municipal and then state regulation as they expanded. Interstate connections created the PJM regional market in 1927, leading to federal legislation in 1935 that reduced risks for investors and customers, and clarified rules of interstate commerce. During the 1950s and 1960s, a continental-scale transmission network was built. Deregulation commenced at the federal level with legislation in 1978, augmented by further legislation and administrative actions in 1992, 1996, and 2005. Today, federal law encourages regional power markets, competition among electricity generators, open access for transmission, and monopoly franchises for local distribution. In 1999, New Jersey required its electric utilities to divest their generation assets and to allow retail choice of suppliers, although by 2005, less than six thousand retail customers, less than 0.2 percent of the total customer base, had taken advantage of this option (NJBPU 2005a).

Environmental regulation has strongly influenced New Jersey's energy sector. Its hazardous waste site remediation policies (precursors to federal Superfund and toxics legislation) guided the cleanup of old coal gas production sites. As a downwind state, there was early support for strict sulfur dioxide emissions limits from power plants. The state's status as an ozone non-attainment area led to early fuel switching and stringent nitrogen oxides controls on power plants, and a requirement that service stations sell only reformulated gasoline. To the extent permitted by federal law, New Jersey has required consumers to buy "California cars" that meet stringent emissions limits. Thermal pollution limits on water discharges have influenced power plant siting decisions. New Jersey has acted aggressively to document and facilitate greenhouse gas emissions reductions, creating a statewide inventory of emissions in 1999, and working with neighboring states to create a regional cap-and-trade system for carbon dioxide emissions from power plants in 2005 (Heck 2005).

In sum, New Jersey's traditional energy policies have focused on security improvements (reliability of supply, self-sufficiency, non-proliferation), economic improvements (reasonable prices, less price volatility, job growth), and environmental improvements (climate change, air pollution, water pollution, land damage).

New Jersey Sustainable Energy Policies

The state is experimenting with a variety of innovative policies aimed at making the New Jersey energy economy more sustainable. Key innovations include the Clean Energy Program, a Renewables Portfolio Standard, a Smart Growth Infrastructure Investment Program, and active energy planning.

CLEAN ENERGY PROGRAM

For many years, New Jersey has directed its electric and gas utilities to provide demand-side management programs. The mechanism for funding this changed with passage of the New Jersey Electric Discount and Energy Competition Act of 1999, which put in place a Societal Benefits Charge (SBC) collected from all utility customers. The SBC provides in excess of $100 million per year for energy efficiency and renewable energy programs. These programs were run by the utilities until 2003, when the New Jersey Board of Public Utilities (NJBPU) shifted responsibility for its strategic direction, as well as partial implementation duties, to an internal Office of Clean Energy. Both before and after this transition, there was a full array of innovative and aggressive energy efficiency and renewable energy programs. Brief descriptions of current programs follow.

Energy Efficiency: Residential Gas & Electric HVAC Program. Marketed as the "Warm Advantage" and "Cool Advantage" programs, these seek to transform standard practice in the residential marketplace so that energy-efficient heating-ventilating-air-conditioning (HVAC) equipment installations become the norm. The program offers sales and technical training to HVAC installers and contractors. It also offers rebates to homeowners who install Energy Star-rated equipment in existing homes or in new homes that are located in state-designated Smart Growth areas. From 2001 through 2003, program expenditures totaled $57 million, and savings for the 79,169 participants added up to 37 MW in reduced electricity demand, 638 Gwh in lifetime electric energy savings, and 74 million therms in lifetime natural gas savings (CEEEP 2004a).

Energy Efficiency: Residential New Construction Program. Also known as the "New Jersey Energy Star Homes Program," this is a long-standing effort to make USEPA Energy Star-approved building practices the standard for new residential construction. It was designed and implemented by the seven regulated energy utilities in New Jersey as a vehicle for overcoming familiar barriers to market acceptance, including misaligned incentives for efficiency investments, inadequate information on the associated benefits, inadequate training on these technologies in the building trades, and difficulty for market actors in distinguishing between "efficient" and "standard" homes. Activities included financial incentives for builders, marketing and technical assistance for builders, development of governmental Energy Star labeling and accreditation programs, and training for municipal officials. From 2001 to 2003, program expenditures totaled $33 million, and savings for the 6,817 participants reduced total electricity demand by 15 MW, lifetime electricity consumption by 163 GWh, and lifetime natural gas use by 44 million therms (CEEEP 2004a).

Energy Efficiency: Residential Energy Star Products Program. The "ENERGY STAR Products Program" focuses on expanding the market penetration of specific energy efficient products within homes. This program, also operated by the regulated utilities, underwent significant changes in 2002, thus its performance data are not fully comparable to other programs discussed here. Three separate programs in lighting, windows, and appliances were combined into one Energy Star products program for 2003. Program activities included consumer education, creation of a retail infrastructure, marketing and training support for actors in this supply chain, standards development, and consumer rebates. A residential energy audit activity was moved to the Energy Star Products program in 2003. From 2001 to 2003, total program expenditures were $12 million, half of which took place in 2003. Impact estimates are available for only two activities, lighting and room air-conditioners. In 2003, expenditures on the lighting promotion were $4.2 million and it had 1.5 million participants, achieving lifetime electric energy savings of 359 GWh. Expenditures on the room air-conditioner promotion were $872,000 and it had 25,387 participants, achieving lifetime energy savings of 14 GWh (CEEEP 2004a).

Energy Efficiency: Residential Low Income Program. The "New Jersey Comfort Partners" program seeks to improve energy affordability for low-income households by subsidizing installation of energy efficiency measures, providing information and counseling, and working collaboratively with the weatherization assistance program of the New Jersey Department of Community Affairs. This program is operated by the state's regulated natural gas and electric utilities. From 2001 to 2003, program expenditures totaled $39 million, reached 18,356 participants, and reduced demand by 2.5 MW, electricity usage by 337 GWh, and natural gas usage by 46 million therms (CEEEP 2004a).

Energy Efficiency: C&I Energy Efficient Construction Program. The "New Jersey SmartStart Buildings®" program was created in 2003 from the merger of existing energy efficiency programs in commercial and institutional construction, building operations and maintenance, and compressed air systems. These activities were reorganized into three groups, including commercial new construction, retrofits, and schools new construction. The program was designed to encourage a general market transformation, provide incremental funding to capture otherwise "lost opportunities" for energy efficiency, stimulate small commercial customer investments in energy efficiency, and increase compliance with New Jersey's updated, efficiency oriented building code. The state's regulated utilities carried out this program, under which they provided tailored technical assistance and financial support on an as-requested basis for individual C&I customers. Total expenditures from 2001 to 2003 were $82 million on 15,818 participants, reaping total savings of 71 MW in reduced demand, 5.6 GWh in lifetime electricity use, and 26 million therms in lifetime natural gas use (CEEEP 2004a). Although it was the intent of the NJBPU to shift the reorganized program's emphasis toward new school construction (in parallel with a massive statewide school-building effort), very little of the actual expenditures went in that direction due to lack of requests from school districts.

Energy Efficiency: Appliance Cycling Program. This decade-old program has been operated by individual electric utilities for load management purposes, providing remote control of central air-conditioning equipments for peak-shaving on hot days. It is currently in maintenance mode, meaning that existing customers continue to participate, but there is no effort to enroll new customers. Aggregate expenditures totaled $21 million from 2001 to 2003, achieving electricity demand reductions but no energy savings. In 2003, some 223,689 customers participated, at a cost of $5.9 million and a savings of 195 MW (CEEEP 2004a).

Energy Efficiency: Cool Cities Program. This innovative program is funded by the NJBPU and administered by the NJDEP. It subsidizes the planting of trees in urban areas to reduce heat island effect and thereby reduce air-conditioning loads. The program started in 2003, and allied with volunteer labor, expended $1 million to plant several thousand trees in Trenton, Paterson, and a few other downtowns. Energy and demand savings have not yet been estimated. This program is being targeted towards municipalities seeking a "Sustainable Community" or "Energy Smart Community" designation from state government (CEEEP 2004a).

A cost-benefit analysis of the state's energy efficiency programs suggests that in total the benefits exceed the costs of $81 million by at least two to one, with the ratio exceeding three to one when the economic value of environmental impact reductions ("externalities") is included (CEEEP 2005).

Table 1: New Jersey Statewide Energy Efficiency Program Economic Impacts

Program	Total Resource Costs, Present Worth in 2003 Dollars	2003 Program B/C Ratio without Externalities	2003 Program B/C Ratio with Externalities
Residential Programs			
Energy Star Room AC	$872,000	1.92	2.29
Energy Star Lighting	$4,219,000	9.72	13.68
Residential New Construction Electric	$7,733,500	1.09	1.23
Residential New Construction Gas	$7,631,500	1.18	1.38
Residential New Construction Total	$15,365,000	1.13	1.30
Residential HVAC Electric	$10,152,500	1.51	1.83
Residential HVAC Gas	$4,291,500	1.96	2.28
Residential HVAC Total	$14,444,000	1.64	1.96
Low Income Comfort Partners Electric	$8,797,000	0.36	0.50
Low Income Comfort Partners Gas	$5,959,000	0.77	0.90
Low Income Municipal Partner	$679,000	0.35	0.47
Low Income Comfort Partners Total	$15,435,000	0.52	0.65
Subtotal Residential	$50,335,000	1.82	2.35
Non-Residential Programs			
C&I New Construction Electric	$1,900,000	3.80	5.20
C&I New Construction Gas	$1,932,000	0.28	0.33
C&I Retrofit Electric	$24,315,500	4.65	6.32
C&I Retrofit Gas	$779,500	5.90	6.95
C&I Schools Electric	$1,445,000	2.73	3.65
C&I Schools Gas	$183,000	3.39	3.99
Subtotal Non-Residential	$30,555,000	4.25	5.75
Total	$80,890,000	2.74	3.63

Source: CEEEP 2005

Specific programs perform better than others, so there is room for improving this portfolio.

RENEWABLES

Energy efficiency programs of various types have existed in New Jersey for many years. Renewable energy programs are relative newcomers, starting in 2001 as an initiative of Governor James McGreevey, a Democrat, and continuing under Acting Governor Codey, also a Democrat. The goals of the renewable energy programs are, first, renewable energy technology market transformation and cost-reductions by means of demand stimulus, and second, economic development achieved by capturing experience and growth in this industry within New Jersey firms. In its April 2001 order, the NJBPU directed that its renewable energy budget be evenly divided between utility-side and customer-side initiatives.

Renewable Energy: Customer On-Site Renewable Energy Program (CORE). This program, designed in 2001 and launched in 2002, encourages renewable energy investments on the customer side of the electric meter. It targets residential and commercial customers, and provides substantial rebates (up to 70 percent of installation cost) for small solar photovoltaic (PV), wind, biomass, and fuel cell systems. Total expenditures from 2001 to 2003 were $15 million, with annual budgets going forward of about $7 million. Through 2003 there were 110 participants, of which over 90 percent were solar PV projects, and the remainder was evenly divided among biomass, wind, and fuel cells. Seventy-nine percent of PV projects are under 10 kW in size (Aspen 2004). Estimated lifetime energy savings are 9 MW of demand, 166 GWh of electricity, and 210,240 therms of natural gas (CEEEP 2004a).

Renewable Energy: BPU Grid Program. Aimed at spurring investment in large scale renewable energy projects in New Jersey to supply electricity to the PJM regional market, this program has regular solicitations in the $10 million range. Actual expenditures have lagged considerably behind this rate, as implementation difficulties have slowed some installations. In response to two RFPs, five projects had been awarded $11.6 million in funding as of 2004. Projects included three wind farms (7.5 MW, 21 MW, 90 MW), one solar PV project (1 MW), and a landfill gas reclamation project (4 MW). However, actual expenditures totaled only $642,000 by the end of 2003 (CEEEP 2004a).

Renewable Energy: Renewable Energy Advanced Power Program (REAP). For this new program, launched in 2003, the NJBPU is providing approximately $20 million in funding to the New Jersey Economic Development Authority (NJEDA). Some $30 million in matching private funds will be raised by NJEDA for distributed renewable energy projects. No results are yet available for evaluating the program's efficacy.

Renewable Energy: Renewable Energy Economic Development Program (REED). Another new initiative was launched by the NJBPU in early 2003, this one to support the development of renewable energy businesses, technologies, and market infrastructure in New Jersey. By means of a competitive solicitation, $2.7 million was awarded to ten projects ranging from PV demonstration projects to new technology development for thin film PV, power-conditioning electronics, hydrogen production, and ocean wave power. No results are yet available for evaluating this program.

The NJBPU commissioned a third party process evaluation to learn whether the renewable energy elements of the Clean Energy Program were well managed. The evaluators found that participants well generally satisfied with the program, but there were numerous administrative improvements needed, ranging from reducing application backlogs, to improving training of staff, to documenting expenditures more thoroughly (Aspen 2004). The generous subsidy regime for renewable energy in New Jersey is very clearly a work in progress.

IMPACTS OF THE CLEAN ENERGY PROGRAM

In aggregate, the New Jersey Board of Public Utilities' various Clean Energy Program energy efficiency and renewable energy elements cost $177 million in 2003. Estimated associated lifetime savings of items installed in 2003 included 351 MW of demand reduction, 7,997 GWh of electricity, and 203 million therms of natural gas (CEEEP 2004a). Without even making a precise allocation of costs to electricity and gas projects, this works out to less than $500/kW, 2 cents/kWh, and 87 cents/therm avoided — a very attractive investment relative to supply-side alternatives. Two elements have been recognized nationally: the American Council for an Energy Efficient Economy designated the Residential HVAC program as "one of the best energy efficiency programs in the nation" and the US Environmental Protection Agency named the ENERGY STAR Homes Program its "2002 Partner of the Year" (CEEEP 2004a).

OTHER NEW JERSEY SUSTAINABLE ENERGY POLICIES

Renewables Portfolio Standard (RPS). This order by the NJBPU requires that a certain percentage of the electricity sold in New Jersey in a given year be generated from renewable sources. In 2003, the required percentage was set at 4 percent by 2008, and the NJBPU is currently considering a proposed new rule setting the RPS at 20 percent by 2020 (NJBPU 2005b). This mandate encourages utilities and independent power providers to bring additional renewable resources online. Energy providers must demonstrate compliance by acquiring tradable Renewable Energy Certificates (RECs), issued by the NJBPU. To help it decide whether to pursue a more aggressive target, the NJBPU has commissioned a variety of consultant studies of its technical and economic feasibility (CEEEP 2004b; KEMA 2004; Navigant Consulting 2004) and sought advice from its Clean Energy Council.

An economic evaluation of New Jersey's proposed 20 percent RPS suggests that it would raise electricity prices by a little less than 4 percent in the year 2020 but have a negligible impact on economic growth (CEEEP 2004b). Among the policy's expected effects is an uptick in local employment, a slight decrease in natural gas prices, and modest reductions in air pollution, all subject to uncertainty associated with the rate of technological improvement achieved through this renewable energy pump-priming effort.

Net metering. This allows customer-side renewables to earn revenue by running the electric meter backwards. New Jersey's 1999 electricity restructuring law and subsequent NJBPU rulemakings have enshrined net metering as a standard operating procedure for small customers. The 1999 law limited the net-metered customers to 100 kW each (PV and wind only) and total impact to 0.1 percent of system peak capacity, but a 2004 rulemaking lifted this cap and allowed up to 2 MW each for a wider array of technologies, subject to local distribution system capabilities (AWEA 2005). Generators earn money at wholesale energy rates plus tradable RECs.

Smart Growth Infrastructure Investment Program (SGIIP). In 2005, the NJBPU took the significant step of aligning public utility expansion incentives with the New Jersey State Development and Redevelopment Plan, to preferentially encourage infrastructure development in the state's officially designated growth areas. Utilities can recover the costs of distribution infrastructure at twice the normal rate in the preferred locations and, following a phase-in period, they are prohibited from recovering these costs in non-preferred locations (NJBPU 2005c). Preferential cost recovery is further enhanced if utilities invest in infrastructure in special areas under the Targeted Revitalization Incentive Program. When applied to electric, gas, telecommunications, and water utilities, this initiative provides a substantial economic incentive for developers to avoid greenfield locations and instead invest in revitalizing the state's urban areas.

Energy Planning and Targets. New Jersey undertakes a State Energy Master Plan process every few years in order to adjust its strategic policy vision for the energy sector. This process has been *ad hoc* in the past, undertaken sometimes by the NJBPU and other times by other agencies. As part of the current planning effort begun in 2005, NJBPU has commissioned the New Jersey Sustainable State Institute to orchestrate a process of analytic deliberation to set explicit long-range energy sector targets (NJSSI 2005). This very public effort will make the policy choices affecting energy supply and demand much more visible than they have been traditionally. It will also highlight the environmental tradeoffs associated with different energy choices.

Much sustainable energy innovation is playing out at the municipal or organizational level in New Jersey. For example, the Borough of Highland Park, NJ, has put a solar PV array on the roof of its borough hall while also investing in energy efficiency improvements ranging from HVAC and lighting to hybrid vehicles. Its schools are being rehabilitated for energy efficiency including such technologies as geothermal heat pumps, and it has launched a public education program with greening tips for residents (HPGCWG 2005). Other communities also have active sustainability initiatives (BSCT 2005).

The state's universities have created the New Jersey Higher Education Partnership for Sustainability, under which the presidents of all 56 member colleges and universities in 2001 signed a Greenhouse Gas Action Plan, pledging to reduce their institution's greenhouse gas emissions to 3.5 percent below 1990 levels by 2005. An audit shows that over 80 percent of the colleges have reduced their energy intensity, and in spite of dramatic growth in student enrollments and square feet of buildings, some 46 percent have also met their emissions targets (NJHEPS 2005).

New Jersey's public schools should be on track to become much greener, because an $8 billion school-building initiative encouraged compliance with the U.S. Green Building Council's LEED standards. However, that building program has suffered from severe implementation problems, mostly related to financial and quality concerns. The green building aspect has been overshadowed by — and hindered by — the initiative's financial scandals (McNichol 2005).

Conclusion

New Jersey is relatively rich, diverse state with few indigenous energy resources and a mature energy infrastructure. Its energy economy is mostly in private hands, and government has tended to intervene only judiciously in the marketplace. The result is a reasonably professional and aggressive sustainable energy program.

New Jersey's sustainable energy programs are substantial and mostly well thought out. With costs averaging about 1 percent of the $20 billion in annual statewide public and private energy expenditures, these mandated programs are significant enough to help transform New Jersey's energy economy, subject to some significant caveats. First, they must be better managed, even becoming hard-headed, and second, they must persist, even as governors come and go.

It is common in some states for regulatory agencies to be captured by the industries that regulate them (Stigler 1971), but in New Jersey the NJBPU has instead been in the hands of progressives and environmentalists for the past few years. This could be viewed as another form of capture, but perhaps a better model for explaining the New Jersey case is competitive, reputation-enhancing innovation among professionalized state regulators (Barkovich 1989). It is also clear that much of this innovation is driven by a desire to fill a sustainable energy policy vacuum at the federal level.

Critics note that demand-side stimuli for energy technology innovations do not help New Jersey firms very much because the benefits tend to leak out to producers elsewhere. However, this misses the substantial localized market-priming benefit of getting regulators, contractors, and citizens familiar with these new technologies. Many of the barriers to expansion of conservation and renewables markets lie at this downstream end of the supply chain.

A signal achievement of the current New Jersey policy regime is that it has begun to coordinate energy policies with land use policies. Given the strong links between land use and transportation, and the central role of automobile transportation in petroleum consumption, it is an obvious step toward energy independence. New Jersey's SGIIP program provides a powerful incentive to channel development into existing centers and away from greenfields. But it should be matched on the transportation side with an appropriate increase in the gasoline tax, which is currently inordinately low.

This brief tour of sustainable energy activities in New Jersey shows that much is happening and many actors are involved. New Jersey regulators have a history of risk-taking that sometimes pays off and sometimes fails spectacularly. The failures have not been on the scale of California's botched electricity sector deregulation, but the New Jersey landscape contains some persistent reminders such as its troubled school construction program, and a municipal refuse-derived fuel plant costing $80 million that operated for one day before being declared uneconomic. The point here is not to condemn reasonable risk-taking, but to ensure that this "laboratory of democracy" documents and shares appropriate lessons learned. Sensible policy innovation is a prerequisite for achieving a sustainable state.

References

American Community Survey (ACS). 2004. U.S. Census Bureau. *American Fact Finder Data Sheet for New Jersey.* Available at *http://factfinder.census.gov/* Accessed December 4, 2005.

American Wind Energy Association (AWEA). 2005. *Small Wind in New Jersey.* Available at *http://www.awea.org/smallwind/newjersey.html* Accessed December 4, 2005.

Aspen Systems Corp (Aspen). 2004. Report and appendices. *Process Evaluation of the Renewable Energy Programs Administered and Managed by the New Jersey Board of Public Utilities Office of Clean Energy.* Available at *http://policy.rutgers.edu/ceeep* Accessed December 4, 2005.

Barkovich, Barbara. 1989. *Regulatory Interventionism in the Utility Industry: Fairness, Efficiency, and the Pursuit of Energy Conservation.* New York: Quorum.

Bureau of Sustainable Communities and Innovative Technologies (BSCT). 2005. New Jersey Department of Environmental Protection. *Environmentally Sustainable Communities Initiative.* Available at *http://www.state.nj.us/dep/dsr/bscit.htm* Accessed December 4, 2005.

Burkhart, Lori. 1997. New Jersey Kills Gross Receipts Taxes. *Public Utilities Fortnightly*, September 1, 17. Available at *http://www.pur.com/pubs/2638.cfm* Accessed December 4, 2005.

Center for Energy, Economic, and Environmental Policy (CEEEP). 2004a. Rutgers University. *2003 Program Evaluation: New Jersey Clean Energy Program Energy Efficiency and Renewable Energy Programs.* Available at *http://policy.rutgers.edu/ceeep* Accessed December 4, 2005.

_____. 2004b. Rutgers University. *Economic Impact Analysis of New Jersey's Proposed 20% Renewable Portfolio Standard.* Available at *http://policy.rutgers.edu/ceeep* Accessed December 4, 2005.

_____. 2005. Rutgers University. *Program Cost-Benefit Analysis of New Jersey Clean Energy Council Energy Efficiency Programs.* Available at *http://policy.rutgers.edu/ceeep* Accessed December 4, 2005.

EIA (Energy Information Administration). 2003. U.S. Dept. of Energy. *State Electricity Profiles 2002.* Available at *http://www.eia.doe.gov/cneaf/electricity/st_profiles/new_jersey.pdf* Accessed December 4, 2005.

_____. 2005. U.S. Dept. of Energy. *State Energy Data 2001: Consumption.* Available at *http://www.eia.doe.gov/emeu/states/sep_sum/html/pdf/rank_use_all.pdf* Accessed December 4, 2005.

_____. 2005a. U.S. Dept. of Energy. *Company Level Imports.* Available at *http://www.eia.doe.gov/oil_gas/petroleum/data_publications/company_level_imports/cli.html* Accessed December 4, 2005.

_____. 2005b. U.S. Dept. of Energy. *New Jersey Natural Gas Consumption by End Use.* Available at *http://tonto.eia.doe.gov/dnav/ng/ng_cons_sum_dcu_SNJ_a.htm* Accessed December 4, 2005.

_____. 2005c. U.S. Dept. of Energy. *Retail Unbundling — New Jersey.* Available at *http://www.eia.doe.gov/oil_gas/natural_gas/restructure/state/nj.html* Accessed December 4, 2005.

FHA (Federal Highway Administration). 2003. U.S. Dept of Transportation. *Tax Rates on Motor Fuel.* Available at *http://www.fhwa.dot.gov/ohim/mmfr/dec03/mf121tpg1.htm* Accessed December 4, 2005.

Gillespie, K., and C.M. Henry. 1995. Introduction. In *Oil in the New World Order* edited by K. Gillespie and C.M. Henry, 1–17. Gainesville, FL: University Press of Florida.

Heck, Kelly. 2005. Press release. *Codey Takes Crucial Step to Combat Global Warming.* Available at *http://www.state.nj.us/cgi-bin/governor/njnewsline/view_article.pl?id=2779* Accessed December 4, 2005.

Highland Park Green Community Working Group (HPGCWG). 2005. *Green Community Outreach Project.* Available at *http://greenhp.org/* Accessed December 4, 2005.

Hinton, D. (2005). *Petroleum Profile: New Jersey.* Available at *http://tonto.eia.doe.gov/oog/info/state/nj.html* Accessed December 4, 2005.

KEMA Inc. 2004. *New Jersey Energy Efficiency and Distributed Generation Market Assessment.* Available at *http://policy.rutgers.edu/ceeep* Accessed December 4, 2005.

Margolis, Robert M. 2002. PhD dissertation. *Photovoltaic R&D Policy.* Woodrow Wilson School, Princeton University.

McNichol, Dustan. 2005. Residents demand action on construction of new schools. *Star Ledger.* May 25.

Musgrave, Richard A. 1959. *The Theory of Public Finance.* New York: McGraw Hill.

NaturalGas.org. 2004. *History of Natural Gas.* Available at *http://www.naturalgas.org/overview/history.asp* Accessed December 4, 2005.

Navigant Consulting. 2004. *New Jersey Renewable Energy Market Assessment.* Available at *http://policy.rutgers.edu/ceeep* Accessed December 4, 2005.

New Jersey Board of Public Utilities (NJBPU). 2005a. *New Jersey Electric and Gas Switching Statistics September 2005.* Available at *http://www.bpu.state.nj.us/home/energy.shtml* Accessed December 4, 2005.

_____. 2005b. *Current Rulemaking NJAC Title 14:4 Energy.* Available at *http://www.state.nj.us/bpu/home/secDiv.shtml* Accessed December 4, 2005.

_____. 2005c. *Rules Currently in Effect NJAC Title 14:3 All Utilities.* Available at *http://www.state.nj.us/bpu/home/secDiv.shtml* Accessed December 4, 2005.

New Jersey Higher Education Partnership for Sustainability (NJHEPS). 2005. *Greenhouse Gas Action Plan Update.* Available at *http://www.njheps.org/projects/energy+emissions.htm* Accessed December 4, 2005.

New Jersey Sustainable State Institute (NJSSI). 2005. *Sustainable Energy Targets for New Jersey.* Available at *http://www.njssi.org* Accessed December 4, 2005.

Stigler, George J. 1971. The Theory of Economic Regulation. *Bell Journal of Economics and Management Science* 2: 3–21.

Tobin, James. 2002. *Expansion and Change on the U.S. Natural Gas Pipeline Supply Network.* Available at *http://www.eia.doe.gov/pub/oil_gas/natural_gas/feature_articles/2003/Pipenet03/pipenet03.html* Accessed December 4, 2005.

7. Wind Power in Colorado: Small Steps Towards Sustainability

Paul Komor
University of Colorado at Boulder

Introduction

Sustainability can take many forms, but regardless of how one defines it, it's clear that a sustainable energy system will need to make significant use of renewable energy sources. Fossil fuels are finite, and there will have to be a transition to renewable fuels at some point in our future.

Colorado has in the past 10 years taken some significant, if lurching, steps toward a sustainable energy system. As of 2005, Colorado had 220 megawatts (MW) of wind power and plans to build 500 MW more. Although those numbers are not exactly overwhelming relative to Colorado's total installed capacity of 9,400 MW, they represent a significant first step. And it's even more significant when one considers that fossil fuel development — coal mining and oil and gas extraction — is economically and politically powerful in Colorado and, furthermore, that the state as a whole tends to be fiscally conservative. How then did such a state end up building all that wind power capacity? The answer is through seemingly endless rounds of political negotiation, using a variety of strategies and venues.

This chapter tells that story. It starts with an overview of Colorado, describing the state's physical, economic, and political context. It then describes five rounds of negotiations — which serve as case studies — each illustrating another battle in the effort to move Colorado's electricity system toward greater use of renewables. It ends with a discussion of the lessons learned in Colorado about the process of moving toward a sustainable energy system.

Colorado— Physical and Political Context

THE TWO COLORADOS

There are two Colorados: the Front Range and the rest. "The Front Range" refers to the narrow north-south band of cities and suburbs located between the plains and the mountains. In the middle is Denver—large, growing, and with extensive suburbs in all directions. To the north are the college towns of Boulder and Fort Collins; to the south are Colorado Springs and Pueblo. Much of the Front Range is growing at a rapid pace, and residential developments continue to spread north, east, and south. (The mountainous terrain limits growth to the west.)

The rest of the state is geographically diverse but similarly rural, agricultural, and sparsely populated. The physical settings of both Colorados are impressive: From the Front Range toward the east is the astoundingly flat, and quite dry, central plains, extending into Kansas and points east. Eastern Colorado is sparsely populated, agricultural, and far from wealthy. To the immediate west of the Front Range are the Rocky Mountains, peppered with high peaks (some over 14,000 feet). Much of this land is federally owned and uninhabited. There are pockets of population (and wealth) centered around the skiing of Aspen, Vail, and Breckenridge. Formerly wealthy, now-struggling mining towns such as Leadville and Ouray are scattered about as well. Farther west, the topography settles down a bit, and what's called the Western Slope supports farming and ranching. A number of smaller towns—including Grand Junction, Montrose, and Durango—are supported largely by agriculture and tourism.

COLORADO'S ENERGY RESOURCES AND ENERGY PRODUCTION

Colorado is blessed—or cursed, depending on your political views—with energy resources of all types. First on the list, in both energy output and economic impact, is natural gas. From 1995 to 2004, Colorado's annual natural gas production doubled, exceeding 1 trillion cubic feet in 2004. That was about 5 percent of total U.S. production (EIA 2005b). Corresponding gross revenue for that natural gas production was about $5.2 billion.

Oil production, although less impressive than that of natural gas, is significant as well: about 22 million barrels in 2004 (about 1 percent of U.S. production), worth about $880 million (at $40/barrel) (EIA 2005c).

Colorado is one of the U.S.'s top 10 coal-producing states and produces about 30 million tons of low-sulfur coal annually (EIA 2005a, EIA 2005d). About half of that coal is exported to other states, the remainder is used within the state for electricity production. Gross revenues from Colorado coal sales are about $600 million annually (assuming $20/ton).

Although Colorado gets most of its electricity from fossil fuels (Table 1), Colorado's renewable energy resources are considerable. Wind leads the list. Much of Colorado's eastern plains have class 3 or 4 wind resources, which are often suitable for utility-scale electricity production. This area is suitable for wind turbines for additional reasons: It is sparsely populated and thus there are fewer siting conflicts, and wind development is compatible with the current land uses of ranching and farming.

Colorado has other renewable resources as well, although none is as promising as wind for large-scale electricity production. Much of Colorado receives, on average, about 5.5 kilowatt-hours (kWh) per square meter per day of solar insolation. That's more than most other states (with the exception of those in the desert Southwest) (DOE 2005a), making solar photovoltaic and solar thermal generation technically feasible (but rarely cost-effective) for much of the state. There are low-temperature geothermal resources in scattered parts of the state (there is a geothermal-heated alligator farm in the southern Colorado mountains), but none is hot enough to support electricity production. There is technical potential for electricity from biomass due to Colorado's heavy agricultural and forestland uses; however, this potential is somewhat speculative with today's technologies and costs. Finally, there are 1.2 gigawatts (GW) of installed hydropower (EIA 2002) but little potential for more. Competing claims for limited water and environmental concerns mean that new hydro capacity will mostly be small, run-of-river installations.

Table 1: Colorado's electricity generation by source, 2002		
Type	Megawatt-hours (millions)	Percentage
Coal	35.4	77
Natural gas	9.0	20
Hydro	1.0	2
Other	0.2	<1
Source: EIA 2002		

THE STAKEHOLDERS

The story of Colorado's electricity system, and the lurching steps it has taken toward sustainability, is a classic one of political compromise. This story is best understood by first taking a look at the stakeholders who play the key roles: the electricity industry, notably the large investor-owned utility Xcel Energy; the advocates, notably the environmental groups; and the state government.

Electricity industry. The electricity system in Colorado is an eclectic mix of public and private entities. Unlike many other states, Colorado has not restructured its electricity system and thus is still served by monopoly retailers. The investor-owned utility Xcel serves much of the Front Range and accounts for over half of Colorado electricity sales; a mix of municipal utilities, rural electric associations (REAs), smaller investor-owned utilities, and cooperatives provide the rest.

In 1913, a handful of small hydropower-based utilities combined to create the Colorado Power Company, which was renamed in 1924 as Public Service Company of Colorado (PSCo). PSCo evolved into the state's dominant electricity provider, serving Denver and much of the more densely populated Front Range. In 1997, PSCo became an operating company under the New Century Energies, Inc. holding company. In 2000, New Century Energies and Northern States Power merged, creating the current company, Xcel Energy. Xcel operates in 10 states, has annual revenues of $8.3 billion (2004), and operates over 15 GW of electricity generating capacity (Xcel Energy 2005). Within Colorado, Xcel has 10 fossil-fueled power plants along with a handful of small hydro and wind facilities.

Many of the renewable energy struggles in Colorado have been between Xcel and various advocacy groups; however, the other electricity providers in the state have occasionally been involved. Colorado has 22 rural electric associations that distribute and sell electricity in rural areas. The service area of these REAs covers much of the state, but not the more heavily populated areas. The larger REAs—notably, Intermountain REA, which serves more than 120,000 customers—do get involved in state-level politics.

Advocacy groups. A wide range of advocacy groups, from unions to chambers of commerce to public health groups, have gotten involved in Colorado's electricity decisions. A smaller number have made significant impacts.

The most influential advocacy group has been a Boulder-based environmental nonprofit, Western Resource Advocates (WRA). Founded in 1989 as the Land and Water Fund of the Rockies, WRA has just 22 employees and an annual budget of about $2 million, but it has played a major role in Colorado electricity politics. It has been a lead environmental group, both before the Public Utilities Commission (PUC) and in negotiations with Xcel, and has achieved several notable environmentally friendly policies and decisions.

Several other environmental groups have been active as well. The Interwest Energy Alliance, a trade association of energy technology firms and other groups supporting renewables, has been active in Colorado renewable politics. The Colorado Renewable Energy Society, the state chapter of the American Solar Energy Society, focuses mostly on education and training; however, it has at times been involved in political work as well. Environment Colorado is a small, grassroots environmental group that focuses on political advocacy.

Government. The third leg of the major stakeholders tripod is the state government — particularly the PUC, the legislature, and the governor's administration. Relationships among these three groups are complex and change as elected and appointed members come and go. The best way to understand Colorado's energy decisions is to first understand each group individually.

The Colorado PUC has direct jurisdiction over the two investor-owned utilities that operate in Colorado: Xcel and Aquila. (Aquila provides less than 4 percent of Colorado's electricity and thus is not discussed here.) Although Colorado considered electric utility restructuring in the late 1990s, it rejected it and, therefore, Colorado retains the traditional structure of a vertically integrated, investor-owned utility providing monopoly service and regulated by a PUC.

What's notable, however, is that in Colorado, Xcel and Aquila combined provide just 60 percent of Colorado's electricity; the remaining 40 percent is provided by municipal utilities and REAs that are not under the jurisdiction of the PUC. The municipal utilities answer to their city governments, while the REAs are cooperatives that must answer to their members; in both cases the PUC has no direct say or control. So the Colorado PUC is certainly influential, but it directly regulates only the 60 percent of Colorado electricity provided by the two regulated utilities.

The PUC is headed by three commissioners, who are appointed by the governor for four-year terms, and a professional staff, numbering about 100, which is responsible for the detailed analysis and regulatory activities of the commission.

Colorado's legislature is active, engaged, and independent-minded.

On energy issues in particular, just about all the interesting and progressive energy legislation has originated with elected members of the legislature rather than with the governor. The legislature, officially known as the General Assembly, consists of the House and the Senate. The legislature typically meets January through May of each year. The 65 House members are elected for two-year terms and are term-limited to four consecutive terms. The 35 Senate members serve four-year terms and are term-limited to two consecutive terms. Term limits, combined with a roughly equal number of Democrats and Republicans in each body, have enabled frequent majority status changes in recent years, particularly in the Senate. The Senate switched from a Republican to a Democratic majority in 2000, switched back in 2002, and then switched to Democratic again in 2004. The House switched to a Democratic majority as well in 2004, for the first time since the early 1960s.

The administration in Colorado reflects the governor's interests and positions. Governor Roy Romer, who held office from 1987 to 1999, was a moderate on energy issues and did not make energy a main issue of his administration. Similarly, Governor Bill Owens (1999 to present) has been a moderate supporter of energy efficiency and renewable energy, but it has not been a leading issue for him. He has been a strong supporter of market-based energy efficiency and has supported efforts to increase building energy efficiency through performance contracting. In considering energy bills sent to him by the legislature and in appointing PUC commissioners, he has shown a preference for market forces over regulation. For example, in a letter to the legislature explaining his veto of a bill setting energy-efficiency standards for certain appliances, he noted: "Market forces provide powerful, and often unpredictable, incentives for consumer goods to become more efficient, and less expensive. They do so, in most cases, without the heavy hand of government mandates and central planning ... if this bill were to become law: the costs on businesses and consumers will rise. And when government mandates increased costs on businesses, these mandates can cost jobs" (Owens 2005). As discussed below, this philosophy is common in Colorado, particularly in rural areas.

The First Step: Windsource

Colorado's first, tentative step toward wind power came about in the mid–1990s due to a strange (and short-lived) movement in the electricity industry: the restructuring and partial deregulation of the utility industry. The then-looming threat of restructuring provided incentives for both the utility and the environmental community to work together, in a rather uneasy partnership, to promote a green energy pricing program.

Through the mid–1990s, Xcel (then PSCo) and the environmental community were in a continual battle over renewables—and Xcel was winning. Environmental advocates, led largely by WRA (then the Land and Water Fund), spent their advocacy and lobbying resources trying to force Xcel to put significant funds into wind power and other renewable technologies. Although the environmentalists did get some language on renewables into Xcel's 1996 Integrated Resource Plan (IRP), Xcel later withdrew from a planned wind project, and the end result of several years of adversarial jostling was essentially nothing. Xcel had little interest in renewables, because it was rewarded by the PUC for producing low-cost reliable power, and it saw little reward in investing in higher-priced, less technically proven technologies like wind turbines.

In 1996, however, a number of factors combined to encourage Xcel and WRA to work together on an innovative renewables project that led the way to significant new wind power development in Colorado.

At that time, "restructuring" was all the rage in the U.S. California was the first state to jump in with its groundbreaking AB 1890 bill that opened up that state's electricity system to wholesale competition and retail choice. (That program would lead to blackouts, massive price increases, and bankrupt utilities in 2000/2001; but, of course, no one knew that in the late 1990s.) Other states soon followed, and although Colorado was not a leader on restructuring, some in the state saw it as inevitable. Restructuring was quite threatening to regulated utilities, because they had no experience in marketing to consumers and had historically paid little attention to fundamental marketing concepts such as branding, new product development, and advertising.

Xcel saw in green energy pricing an opportunity to stick a toe in the scary ocean of competitive markets. Green pricing programs offer electricity buyers the option, at a higher price, to purchase some or all of their electricity in the form of renewables. Strictly speaking, buyers don't "get" actual renewable electricity at their electrical outlets; instead, the utility or other green provider typically ensures that an amount of electricity produced from renewable resources goes into the grid equivalent to what is purchased. As of 2005 there were hundreds of green pricing programs across the U.S.; but in 1996 they were largely unknown.

Xcel also saw green pricing as a way to introduce renewables in a manner consistent with a then-popular ideology at both the utility and the state government: Green energy pricing was "market-driven." If consumers wanted renewables, they would be willing to pay for them, and the amount of new renewables would be determined by consumer demand, not by regulation or market intervention.

So that explains Xcel's interest in green pricing. But why was Xcel willing to work with environmental groups—which it had been battling for years—to implement a green pricing program? Largely because Colorado's IRP process gives "intervenors" (such as environmental groups) the opportunity to argue before the PUC that Xcel's resource plans are not appropriate or optimal for the state. The PUC may or may not agree, of course, but the IRP process makes it possible for intervenors to delay or even disrupt Xcel's plans. And, as seen in this and the other case studies, the IRP process (which was in 2002 renamed the least-cost planning, or LCP, process) has been fundamental to giving the environmental community some say in Colorado's electricity future.

A second motivation for Xcel to partner with environmental groups was that it would give the company's green pricing program some sorely needed credibility with potential buyers—those concerned with the natural environment.

Why, however, did the environmental community support the idea of green pricing programs? Well, not all in that community did. Some were opposed to the idea of a few altruistic electricity users paying for renewables that all would benefit from in the form of reduced environmental impacts from overall electricity generation. And one PUC commissioner expressed doubts as well, noting that "the subscribers [to Xcel's green pricing program] are subsidizing brand equity, new product development, environmental benefits, portfolio diversity and future resource planning" (Colorado PUC 1997).

Most members of the environmental community, however, decided to work with Xcel on the green pricing program. They had achieved little success from their adversarial tactics, they had been unable to get regulations in place requiring Xcel to obtain new renewables, and they saw the then-looming restructuring of the electric utility industry as an opportunity to promote new renewables.

So, due to curious and largely unexpected motivations and strategic choices, the former adversaries decided to work together in making Xcel's green pricing program a success.

Not surprisingly, there were significant disagreements between the utility and environmental groups. First was the issue of how to price the green product. Xcel wanted to set the price based on willingness to pay—that is, to let the market set the price. Environmental groups, in contrast, favored a cost-of-service pricing strategy, in which the price would reflect actual costs of production. The two did not come to terms on methodology, but they did on outcome. They agreed that the price of the new wind product, dubbed Windsource, would be set at a premium of 2.5 cents per kWh above the standard rate (that premium would later be reduced). Noted one analysis, "Essentially, the parties agreed on a specific number and remained silent on the methodology used to reach the number" (Mayer et al. 1999, 4). Pragmatism outweighed methodological purity, as it usually does outside of academia.

A second issue was how Xcel's coal-fired generation would be portrayed in the marketing of Windsource. Xcel obtains more than half of its electricity from coal, and it did not want Windsource marketing to emphasize the detrimental environmental effects of coal. The two parties agreed that the marketing would focus on the advantages of renewables rather than on the problems of coal-fired generation.

There were, of course, other issues as well, but after the pricing skirmish settled down, the two parties worked on assembling a grassroots marketing campaign. Partnerships were established with municipalities and businesses, the governor's energy office kicked in some funds for marketing, chambers of commerce helped out, and the result was an impressive level of sign-ups. Marketing began in March 1997, and wind farm construction began in August 1997. At that time, Xcel planned to install 10 MW of new wind capacity; however, Windsource sign-ups continued to exceed expectations, and over the next few years Xcel continued to build more wind to meet Windsource demand. By October 2001, 60 MW of new wind generation capacity had been built in Colorado, driven entirely by Windsource demand. By the end of 2004, Windsource was the largest green pricing program in the country (as measured by the number of participants), with more than 40,000 participants in Colorado and Minnesota (DOE 2005b).

Just as important as the wind capacity that Windsource built was the experience Xcel gained with this new and largely unproven technology. As noted above, as a regulated utility, Xcel is consistently rewarded for providing low-cost, reliable electric service. Windsource was outside the rate base, so shareholders rather than ratepayers were at risk for technical failures or other problems. However, there were few major technical issues, which gave Xcel confidence that utility-scale wind power could contribute to the electric grid.

There's irony in this story: The threat of restructuring provided the main incentive for the oddball partnership that built Windsource, yet that threat faded away soon after Windsource started up. That threat, however, provided an important first step toward integrating wind power into Colorado's electricity system.

The Lamar Wind Farm: 162 MW

Colorado's second big step toward greater use of renewable generation sources came about via the big stick, when the PUC directed Xcel to
buy the output from a wind farm. There was nothing cooperative, subtle,
or particularly innovative about the process; it was purely regulatory. What
was significant was why the PUC made this decision. In the PUC's view,
the purchase would save ratepayers money. And subsequent events have
proven the commissioners right.

As in the Windsource case study, the requirement that Xcel do its
resource planning in a public process before the PUC was pivotal. Xcel's
1999 resource plan included a process by which Xcel would publish a
request for proposals (RFP) for new electricity supply. Xcel put out that
RFP in 1999/2000 and received 300 separate bid proposals for over 9,000
megawatts of power (Colorado PUC 2001, 10)—much more than it needed.
Among those bids was one submitted by Enron Wind for a 162-MW wind
farm to be located near Lamar, Colorado. Xcel assessed these bids via a
computer model to identify the set of bids that would, in the company's
view, satisfy the least-cost requirements of the IRP process. It concluded
that an "all-gas" portfolio—that is, a set of bids consisting entirely of natural gas–fired generation, and excluding the Lamar wind farm, would be
the least-cost solution.

The PUC scheduled hearings in January 2001 to review and, if appropriate, approve the Xcel bid review. Many different parties submitted testimony on a range of topics. Of particular interest to the environmental
community was the wind bid. In short, the environmental groups argued
that the Lamar wind bid should be accepted because it was a least-cost
option. This led to a detailed and technical discussion on just what it means
to be least-cost and how wind's cost and performance characteristics could
be fairly and accurately compared with those of traditional fossil-fired technologies—topics that are still under discussion today.

The costs of any generation technology can be divided into three
components: first (also called capital) costs, operating (sometimes called
operating and maintenance or O&M) costs, and fuel costs. For both wind
and natural gas–fired technologies, the capital and operating costs are
fairly well documented. The fuel costs for natural gas, however, are not.
(Fuel costs for wind are, of course, zero.) Natural gas prices are very volatile and have bounced around from $3 to $9 per 1,000 cubic feet (ft^3) in
the past three years. (These are wellhead prices; prices seen by residential
users are higher.) Committing to natural gas–fired generation, however,
means committing to buying natural gas in the future, whatever its price.

(It is possible to hedge this risk via futures contracts, but doing so adds costs and is increasingly difficult as natural gas price volatility has increased.) So the question for the PUC was what should be assumed for future natural gas prices. A low price assumption meant that wind power would be more expensive than natural gas, whereas a high natural gas price assumption meant the reverse. Not surprisingly, Xcel testified that future natural gas prices would be low — $3 or less; while an environmental advocate predicted prices of $4 or higher.

Disagreements over wind's capacity value and ancillary service costs were complex, and just as polarized. Wind power, unlike power from coal or natural gas, is subject to the natural variability of the wind and cannot be switched on and off at will. In technical terms, wind is not "dispatchable," meaning that it cannot be turned on (dispatched) to meet electricity needs. So the question is, in essence, how much less is wind power worth because of its intermittent nature? There are several ways to measure this relative worth. One is with ancillary service costs, which is a measure of costs that wind power imposes on the rest of the electricity system. An example of an ancillary service cost is "spinning reserve," which refers to the need to have other power plants ready to generate in case the wind doesn't blow. Xcel estimated the ancillary service costs of the proposed wind farm at $61 million, whereas the PUC staff and the environmental community estimated them at $3 million to $6 million (Lehr et al. 2001).

In both cases, the PUC — surprisingly, as that PUC was not seen as particularly renewable-friendly — sided with the pro-wind group. In its decision, the PUC noted that "it is prudent to lean toward the higher range of the gas [price] forecast" and that Xcel's ancillary cost estimates were "excessive." More importantly, the PUC concluded that the wind farm was in fact cost-effective: "We find that adding Enron's Lamar wind energy bid to PSCo's preferred resource plan is in the public interest and comports with the IRP rules. This determination is based solely on our finding that the acquisition of the Lamar facility will likely lower the cost of electricity for Colorado's ratepayers. After a careful analysis of the economics of the wind bid, we find that it is justified on purely economic grounds, without weighing other benefits of wind generation that could be considered under the IRP rules" (Colorado PUC 2001, 34).

One could imagine other scenarios in which a political agency, motivated by reasons such as environmental protection, economic development, or employment, directs a utility to build renewable energy capacity. In this case, however, the PUC was very clear: It did not consider any environmental externalities or other factors; it looked only at electricity costs, and it found that wind would "likely lower the cost of electricity."

Subsequent events proved the PUC right. Since the Lamar decision, natural gas prices have typically been $3 to $9 per 1,000 ft^3 and are expected to remain high. Ancillary service costs are still a topic of debate but are thought to be in the range of 0.1 to 0.5 cents per kWh (Milligan 2004), which comes out to $4 million to $18 million dollars for the Lamar wind farm (assuming a 30 percent capacity factor and a discount rate of eight percent). This is much closer to the PUC staff and wind advocates' estimates than to Xcel's estimates.

More telling, however, was Xcel's 2003 testimony before the Federal Energy Regulatory Commission that the Lamar wind farm would "displace higher-cost generation" and reduce costs by $4.6 million (Darnell 2003, 18).

Overall, the Lamar story's significance is not in the process, which was clear and unremarkable — the PUC told the utility what to do. What is notable is the evidence it uncovered: Wind can save money and reduce electricity costs.

RPS in the Legislature: Three Strikes

The third case study of Colorado renewable energy turns to the legislature and is a much more political story, driven by personalities, legislative process, and ideology. Although the result of this three-year battle was a stack of failed legislation, it did set the stage for a significant and groundbreaking citizen initiative on renewables.

Starting in the late 1990s, a number of states passed renewables portfolio standards (RPSs)—requirements that utilities (or other electricity retailers) obtain an increasing percentage of the electricity they sell from renewables sources. Texas, for example, passed a law in 1999 that required companies selling electricity in that state to purchase 2,000 MW of new renewables by 2009 (later legislation increased that number). As of 2005, about 20 states had RPS requirements in place.

Then-state-Senator Terry Phillips (D) introduced an RPS bill in the Colorado Senate in 2002. That bill set an RPS standard of 10 percent for 2010 — meaning that Colorado utilities, notably Xcel, would have to obtain 10 percent of their electricity from renewable sources by 2010. Groups testifying in favor of the bill included Western Resource Advocates (due largely to the environmental benefits of renewables), representatives of wind project developers, and the Rocky Mountain Farmers Union (a grassroots organization of family farmers and ranchers whose interests include environmental stewardship). Xcel initially testified against the bill, arguing that it would increase consumer's electricity bills and require significant new transmission capacity. (However, Xcel later agreed to not oppose the bill.) The bill passed the Senate and moved on to the House, where it passed by a comfortable majority, due largely to the support of then–House majority leader Lola Spradley (R). However, the bill failed at the last minute because the Senate did not consider the House changes to the bill before the legislative session ended.

RPS proponents were pleasantly surprised that the bill had gotten as far as it had. A common legislative experience is that it takes three sessions to get a new idea through the process. The first session introduces the concept and puts it on the agenda. The second session defines supporters and opponents. The third session is needed to actually get the bill through, using coalitions built ahead of time.

So proponents tried again in the 2003 legislative session, expecting success. This time, however, the opposition was better organized and killed the legislation in the Senate. A first RPS bill passed the House but was defeated by a 4–3 vote in a Senate committee. A second, less-aggressive RPS bill passed the Senate committee that had defeated the first bill, but it lost in another Senate committee by a 6–4 vote.

Several groups raised concerns about the 2003 RPS bills, including the Colorado Mining Association and a consortium of large industrial energy users. However, the most significant opposition came from the rural electric associations. These groups opposed the bills for two reasons: their possible effects on electricity costs and the fact that they were a "mandate." Even though the second proposed RPS bill exempted REAs from the RPS, the REAs argued that, because some of them purchased wholesale power from Xcel, they would still see the effects of any electricity price increases that might result from the RPS. And REAs have a strong philosophical bent against government mandates of any sort. "Our biggest objection is that [the proposed RPS bill] is mandatory," said Stan Lewandowski, general manager of the Intermountain Rural Electric Association. "We're not opposed to renewables as such" (as quoted in Raabe 2003).

After the surprising 2003 defeat, Colorado RPS proponents worked hard to ensure that they would succeed in 2004. The 2004 bill included shrewd "sweeteners" intended to build support in rural areas. For example, the bill gave a 50 percent bonus credit to renewable energy installations in rural areas. The bill also exempted REAs from the RPS requirements. Notably, Xcel did not oppose the 2004 bill and even offered mild support for it. "We support the bill," said Xcel spokeswoman Margarita Alarcon. "It provides for a level of diversity in our supply portfolio and offers planning certainty for the company. The mandate is achievable" (as quoted in Fletcher and Proctor 2004).

However, the REAs continued to oppose the bill, mainly on philosophical grounds. Noted Ray Clifton, executive director of the Colorado Rural Electric Association, "We are not opposed to renewables. Our concern is in the public policy area. Is it the best public policy to put into Colorado statutes a mandate for a particular fuel mix? If you make a decision today based on a set of circumstances, is that going to be the same set of circumstances years down the road? We would also have this position if they legislated requirements on the use of coal, nuclear or gas" (as quoted in Valenti 2004). The 2004 RPS bill passed the House and a Senate committee but was narrowly defeated 18–17 by the full Senate due largely to opposition from some REAs.

Overall, both sides spent considerable amounts of political capital in this three-year fight. And the result of the final loss was that the RPS supporters switched tactics, as discussed below, and ended up with a much stronger RPS than the bill that was narrowly defeated in 2004.

Amendment 37: The First RPS Passed by Ballot Initiative

Even before the 2004 RPS bill died in the Colorado legislature, several Colorado environmental groups were raising the possibility of passing an RPS requirement by ballot initiative — that is, by a direct vote of Colorado residents. The ballot initiative process is daunting. It requires obtaining more than 60,000 signatures to just get it on the ballot, and then, of course, there's an expensive public campaign to convince voters to approve it. However, the RPS bill seemed a good candidate for such a strategy. Polls had consistently shown significant popular support for renewables in Colorado, and RPS proponents were increasingly frustrated with the compromises they needed to make in the legislature.

The ballot initiative wording went through many drafts, but in the end the proponents decided on an aggressive strategy. Rather than work with potential opponents (notably Xcel) to come up with wording that all could agree on, they decided instead to ask for just what they wanted, and forego cooperation with opponents. The ballot initiative, known as Amendment 37, required the following: That Xcel and Aquila obtain 3 percent of their electricity from renewables by 2007 and 10 percent by 2015. That 4 percent of the required renewable generation come from solar technologies, and that those utilities offer customers a rebate of $2/watt for solar electric generation.

The fight over Amendment 37 was a very public one, as both sides took their arguments to the voters in preparation for the November ballot. The most involved proponents were environmental groups, but a wide range of other organizations joined in as well, including various cities in Colorado, economic development councils, unions, the American Lung Association, and a ski industry organization. Proponents settled on the phrase "Cleaner air. Cheaper energy." They argued, in numerous public meetings, seminars, newspaper articles, and elsewhere that Amendment 37 would help the environment, provide jobs in rural areas, and save money — giving the Lamar decision as evidence that wind power can be less expensive than that from natural gas. An independent consultant found that the impact of Amendment 37 on electricity costs would be that "state-wide electric rates will be virtually unchanged" (Binz 2004a, 2); his report was widely quoted by Amendment 37 supporters. And the *Denver Post* supported Amendment 37 in an editorial.

Opponents— of which there were many — decided on the key phrases of "Right idea, Wrong solution" and "Say no to unfunded mandates." Xcel and the Colorado Rural Electric Association, along with several other groups, created a lobbying group called Citizens for Sensible Energy Choices. Its stated goal was to "educate the public about the impacts of adopting a poorly drafted ballot initiative on renewable energy" (Citizens for Sensible Energy Choices 2004). It argued that the costs for Amendment 37 could approach $2 billion, that Colorado utilities were already using renewable energy, that consumers already had the option of more renewables through Windsource, and that it would be unfair for all consumers to subsidize solar systems installed by a small number of people. The city council of Colorado Springs, Colorado, passed a resolution opposing Amendment 37.

In the end, Amendment 37 passed by 54–46 percent. Support was strongest in Front Range counties such as Boulder, Jefferson, and Denver Counties, while the amendment lost in most rural counties. It appeared that the feel-good appeal of renewable energy, coupled with the vague dislike many consumers have of their utility, overcame concerns about costs.

As of 2005, actual implementation of Amendment 37 was mired at the PUC, and it's unclear what impact it will have on Colorado's electricity future. If the settlement (discussed below) is fully implemented, then it's possible that much of Amendment 37 may turn out to be irrelevant, because its goals will have been met even without the amendment. Even if that turns out to be the case, however, Amendment 37 was significant because it was a ballot initiative, an aggressive step toward a sustainable energy system taken directly by the voters.

The Settlement: Bypassing the PUC

In 2004 there were visible and public fights over an RPS for Colorado, first in the legislature and then over Amendment 37. While that was going on, however, a rather private fight was ongoing over Colorado's energy future that was more important, from the perspective of fossil fuel dependence and carbon emissions, than the RPS. This fight was over a proposed new 750-MW coal-burning power plant.

As mentioned above, Xcel is required to conduct a least-cost planning process every four years. To grossly simplify a very complex process, Xcel must forecast future electricity needs and then show how it will meet them with a least-cost set of resources (such as fossil-fueled plants, renewable energy sources, and energy efficiency). Xcel submits this proposed plan to the PUC, which reviews it and allows intervenors (such as environmental groups) to comment. The PUC then either approves the plan or requires some changes.

In its 2003 least-cost planning submittal to the PUC, Xcel forecasted the need for an additional 2,000 MW of electricity by 2013. It proposed meeting that demand with a mix of resources—some wind, some efficiency, some natural gas—but, most significantly, with a new coal-burning power plant. Most of the new electricity generation in the U.S. in recent years had been natural gas–fired. For many reasons—notably, air quality concerns, high construction costs, and long lead times—few utilities had proposed new coal-burning power plants. The last new coal plant in Colorado went on-line in 1981. Xcel, however, argued in its 2003 LCP submittal that Colorado's electricity demand was expected to grow, due to increased electrification and a growing population, and that a new, large coal-burning power plant was a key element for meeting that growing demand at least cost.

Xcel, in its 2003 LCP plan, argued that this 750-MW, $1.3 billion coal plant should be exempt from bidding requirements, but that instead Xcel should be permitted to build the plant itself and, should be prepaid, in effect, by adding a surcharge on ratepayers' bills to partially fund construction of the plant.

The environmental community did not greet this proposed new coal plant warmly. John Nielsen of Western Resource Advocates testified for the PUC that "the resource screening analysis used by Public Service to provide a cost-benefit justification for Comanche 3 is flawed because the Company failed to consider energy efficiency and demand side options in the analysis, understated the capacity contribution of wind towards planning reserves, failed to evaluate a smaller coal plant among its resource choices, and understated the risks to ratepayers of coal plant capital cost overruns and future CO_2 compliance costs" (Nielsen 2004, 3). ("Public Service" is Xcel, and "Comanche 3" is the proposed new coal plant.)

Others were also unhappy with Xcel's proposal. A consortium of large industrial energy users testified that the bidding exemption and prepayment proposals could raise energy costs (Binz 2004b). The Office of Consumer Council testified that "The major flaw in PSCo's determination of its least-cost plan is that it did not include all cost-effective demand-side management (DSM) programs in its plan" (Rosen 2004, 6).

The debate covered many issues, but one particularly relevant to sustainability was "CO_2 regulatory risk." The 750-MW coal plant, if built, would emit about 5.8 million tons CO_2 per year (assuming 2.2 pounds CO_2 per kWh and 80 percent capacity factor). If, at some point in the future, regulations were passed that limited or reduced CO_2 emissions, then those CO_2 emissions would be a liability to Xcel — and to Colorado ratepayers. For example, Western Europe has a carbon trading system, and in 2005 the market price for CO_2 was about \$24/ton. If Xcel had to pay that amount for carbon emissions from the proposed coal plant, then that cost would be \$140 million annually.

Such regulations don't appear to be likely in the short term, as in 2005 neither the U.S. Congress nor the Bush administration seems particularly interested in the issue of climate change. But the proposed coal plant would likely operate for at least 20 years, and perhaps for 50 years or more, and significant CO_2 regulation over that time period is certainly possible. Hence, the term "regulatory risk."

Some argued that a carbon tax or other CO_2-related regulation was likely over the life of the coal plant and that Xcel should therefore consider such a tax in its economic analysis of least-cost options. Xcel countered that, even if it assumed a reasonable CO_2 tax, the coal plant was still a cost-effective option.

This debate — mainly over the coal plant but also over what's appropriate to assume for future carbon regulation, how much wind and energy efficiency to support, and other issues — seemed headed for an eventual decision, one way or the other, by the PUC. This, however, is where things got interesting. For a variety of reasons — notably, that Xcel wanted to move ahead quickly, and the environmental community did not view the PUC as friendly to its cause — the parties privately agreed to work toward a settlement. This is analogous to an out-of-court settlement in civil litigation. The parties agree among themselves and present their agreement as a fait accompli to the PUC. The PUC is not required to accept their agreement, but it likely will if opposing sides agree to it.

So while all parties continued to grind through the official PUC LCP process, they were also meeting privately, trying to work out an agreement. They were successful and presented their agreement to the PUC in late 2004. In summary, in that settlement the environmental community agreed not to fight the coal plant. In return, Xcel offered a number of actions the environmental community wanted, notably: Acquisition of up to 320 MW of demand-side power savings. Retrofitting of two existing coal plants (Comanche 1 and Comanche 2) with advanced pollution-control equipment, including controls for mercury emissions. Use of a $9/ton implied CO_2 cost in evaluating future potential power contracts. Xcel also agreed to continue its pursuit of up to 500 MW of wind power, as it had proposed in its original 2003 LCP proposal.

The PUC approved the settlement in total — although one of the three PUC commissioners dissented. In his dissent, the chair of the PUC noted: "The carbon tax imputation especially stands out as extra-jurisdictional, speculative, and utterly without foundation. Based on the grim-faced testimony of experts who have no expertise in divining what Congress may or may not do in the coming decades, the Commission has apparently been persuaded that such a tax is 'likely.' The only competent evidence on the issue — that Congress has never passed such a measure, all going down to substantial defeat for fear of harming the economy — has been given little weight" (Colorado PUC 2004, 47). His view, however, was in the minority, and the settlement — included the implied CO_2 cost — was approved.

Ten Lessons Learned

These five case studies illustrate a range of tactics and strategies for getting new renewable energy in place. Each one has both direct and indirect outcomes (see Table 2) and, in some cases, these hinged on small, almost random occurrences. One switched vote, for example, would likely have caused the 2004 RPS bill to pass the Colorado legislature, which would have meant the ballot initiative would not have occurred, and the language in the 2004 RPS bill was much weaker than language in the ballot initiative. Details aside, however, there are some valuable overall lessons to be learned from these case studies, which I distill into 10 points below.

Name/title	Description	Direct outcomes	Indirect outcomes
Table 2: Outcomes of the five case studies			
Windsource	Voluntary green pricing program	62 MW of installed wind power	Utility experience with wind power eased the way for more wind in the future
Lamar	PUC directed utility to buy wind	162 MW of installed wind power	Provided strong evidence that wind power can reduce electric rates
RPS* in the legislature	Colorado legislature narrowly defeated RPS bill three times	None	Frustration with legislature led to ballot initiative
Amendment 37	Ballot initiative to implement an RPS	10 percent renewables by 2015	First state RPS via ballot initiative in the U.S.
Settlement	Agreement regarding proposed new coal plant	Increased spending by utilities on efficiency and pollution controls	Precedent for bypassing the PUC

*RPS = renewables portfolio standard, a requirement that utilities get an increasing percentage of their electricity from renewables.

Sustainability and environmental protection are a tough sell. Although environmental protection was the underlying motivating factor for the environmental advocates in Colorado, that argument did not prove particularly effective in the gritty reality of political negotiations. Environmental protection does not translate well into money, jobs, or other tangible short-term benefits.

Costs, economic development, and jobs are politically powerful motivators. Arguments that renewable energy meant jobs in rural areas, contributed to economic development, and could cut energy costs were behind renewables' political successes in Colorado.

Wind power can be cost-effective. As the Lamar case study shows, even if one ignores environmental externalities, installing new wind-powered electricity generation can save money and reduce electricity costs.

This is of course dependent on prevailing natural gas prices, transmission access, and other site-specific factors; but the stunning technical advances and price drops in utility-scale wind turbines mean that wind can compete financially with fossil-fueled generation.

Institutions respond to the incentives they face. Colorado utilities are under continual pressure from the PUC and from their customers to deliver dependable, low-cost electricity and to not take risks. It's no surprise, therefore, that they are not particularly enthusiastic about new technologies, such as wind, that they have little experience with, that do not have a well-documented cost and performance record, and that do not help them meet their goals. One way to change their minds is to change the incentives. Instead of pressuring an institution to do what's not in its perceived self-interest, work instead from the outside to redefine its self-interests.

Take small steps before big ones. In the early days of Colorado's wind story, Xcel was willing to install small amounts of wind power as long as ratepayers were insulated from the technical and financial risks. The company found that wind power worked well, which paved the way for larger wind installations. Grand steps toward sustainability can be threatening, but small, safe, low-risk steps can get you to the same goal — sometimes more easily.

Policy can best be understood in terms of winners and losers. Any policy change — whether at the state or national level, whether about energy or defense or anything else — means that some parties will gain and some will lose. Another way to say this is that energy policies are often neither "good" nor "bad" in general — only in the particular. An RPS, for example, is good for the wind industry but potentially bad for the coal industry.

There are two implications of this truism. First, if people say a policy is good or bad, they usually mean that it's good or bad for them. So when you hear spokespersons evaluating a policy, keep in mind who they are and what they want from the policy.

Second, policy positions are a function of the amount of perceived gain or loss. Policies to promote sustainability, if presented as such, don't directly translate into significant gain or loss for anyone and therefore are unlikely to garner much interest. In contrast, policies to promote economic development (which can be true of policies to promote sustainability, such as an RPS) are much more likely to see significant support.

Both content and process are necessary. There are two sides of any proposed policy change: content and process. Both are critical. Content is what the legislation or regulation actually says—the proposed policy itself. Process is the tortuous path that legislation must follow to become law. Unfortunately, good content isn't enough. Getting legislation or regulations passed requires expending a lot of effort on the process as well.

In the example of the RPS in the legislature, it had little opposition in the first (2002) attempt but failed at the very end of the process because the legislature adjourned before a final vote on the bill could take place. Process, not content, killed the bill. By next year, it was too late, because the opposition had gotten organized.

It's all in the details. It's tempting to make broad generalizations about energy policy—such as "subsidies are bad" or "RPSs get results"—but the reality is more complicated. For example, the Texas RPS was a driving force behind that state's 1.4 GW of wind installed as of November 2005. But Maine's 1999 RPS has driven no new renewables installations. Why? Because Maine set the RPS goal below its actual renewable capacity and thus did not provide incentives for new renewables. The lesson here is that just about any policy can be influential, but it can also be irrelevant.

Policy goals vary widely. This is a fundamental difference between the public sector (policy) and the private sector (business). Most businesses have a clear goal: to make money. There will, of course, be differences of opinion on how to best do this (offer new products or services? raise prices? change marketing strategies?), but the overall goal is simple and shared across the organization.

Policy goals, unfortunately, lack this clarity. In the case of energy, there are many possible goals, including (Komor and Bazilian 2005): Maintaining a dependable supply, building a sustainable energy system, decreasing environmental impacts, keeping energy prices low, and increasing employment and economic vitality.

And each goal has a constituency. Large energy users, for example, will often be most concerned with price and dependability, while the environmental community will often focus on CO_2 and other pollutants. Politicians are left with the difficult job of trying to satisfy diverse constituencies with different goals.

Disagreements over policy are often fundamentally disagreements over goals. Arguments in favor of opening up new areas for oil and gas drilling, for example, are driven in part by supply security and price goals, whereas arguments against such action stem from environmental goals.

It's often helpful to recognize that others don't share your goals. The renewables advocacy community, for example, often views policy as a tool to implement its goal of getting the most renewables in place in the shortest period of time. A utility, in contrast, views policy as a tool to help it meet their goals of low-cost, reliable electric service.

It's sometimes possible, therefore, to save time and effort by shifting the discussion from specific policy options to policy goals, because that's the root of the disagreement. Doing so can prompt discussion of solutions that can meet diverse goals.

Everyone's an advocate. Too many policy discussions start with the view that there's a right and a wrong. It's useful instead to keep in mind that everyone is an advocate. Everyone wants something from policy: support for their favorite technology, pursuit of their favored goal, or business for their company. There's nothing wrong with being an advocate — it's all part of the democratic process—but it is helpful to recognize that all interests are "special."

Acknowledgments

Insightful comments and suggestions were provided by Adam Capage, Craig Cox, Frank Laird, Gail Reitenbach, and Suzanne Tegen.

References

Binz, R. 2004a. The Impact of the Renewable Energy Standard in Amendment 37 on Electric Rates in Colorado. Public Policy Consulting. September. Available at *www.rbinz.com/ RES.htm*. Accessed October 15, 2005.

_____. 2004b. Testimony of Ronald J. Binz on behalf of Colorado Consumers Group, before the Public Utilities Commission of the State of Colorado. September 13. Available at *www. dora.state.co.us/puc/docket_activity/HighprofileDockets/04A-214E_-215E_-216E.htm*. Accessed October 15, 2005.

Citizens for Sensible Energy Choices. 2004. *2004 Colorado Renewable Energy Ballot Initiative*. Available at *www.coloradomining.org/Issues/Initiative145ppt/CMACSEC_pres_final_ files/frame.htm*. Accessed November 7, 2005.

Colorado PUC (Public Utilities Commission). 1997. Decision No. C97–203, February 19. Available at *www.dora.state.co.us////puc/decisions/1997/C97–0203_96A-401E.doc*. Accessed November 7, 2005.

_____. 2001. Decision No. C01–295. February 23. Available at *http://www.dora.state.co.us/ puc/decisions/2001/C01–0295_99A-549E_PHASE%20II.pdf*. Accessed November 7, 2005.

_____. 2004. Decision No. C05–0049. December 17. Available at *www.dora.state.co.us/puc/ docket_activity/HighprofileDockets/04A-214E_-215E_-216E.htm*. Accessed October 15, 2005.

Darnell, R. 2003. Testimony before the Federal Energy Regulatory Commission (FERC), June 16, 2003. Exhibit PSC-1.

DOE (U.S. Department of Energy). 2005a. *Colorado Solar Resources*. Available at *www.eere. energy.gov/state_energy/tech_solar.cfm?state=CO*. Accessed November 14, 2005.

_____. 2005b. *Green Power Network — Green Pricing Markets*. Available at *www.eere.energy. gov/greenpower/markets*. Accessed November 14, 2005.

EIA (Energy Information Administration). 2002. *State Electricity Profiles — 2002*. Available at *www.eia.doe.gov/cneaf/electricity/st_profiles/colorado.pdf*. Accessed November 14, 2005.

_____. 2005a. *Colorado Coal Profile*. Available at *www.eia.doe.gov/cneaf/coal/statepro/ imagemap/co.htm*. Accessed November 14, 2005.

_____. 2005b. *Natural Gas Navigator.* Available at *http://tonto.eia.doe.gov/dnav/ng/ng_prod_sum_dcu_NUS_a.htm.* Accessed November 14, 2005.

_____. 2005c. *Petroleum Supply Annual 2004.* Vol. 1. June 2005. DOE/EIA-0340(04)/1. Available at *www.eia.doe.gov/oil_gas/petroleum/data_publications/petroleum_supply_annual/psa_volume1/psa_volume1.html.* Accessed November 14, 2005.

_____. 2005d. *State Coal Profile Image Map.* Available at *www.eia.doe.gov/cneaf/coal/statepro/imagemap/usaimagemap.htm.* Accessed November 14, 2005.

Fletcher, A., and C. Proctor. 2004. Renewable Energy Bill Moves Forward. *Denver Business Journal,* February 6.

Komor, P. and M. Bazilian. 2005. Renewable energy policy goals, programs, and technologies. *Energy Policy* 33(14): 1873–1881.

Lehr, R., J. Nielsen, S. Andrews, and M. Milligan. 2001. *Colorado Public Utility Commission's Xcel Wind Decision.* National Renewable Energy Laboratory (NREL) report. NREL/CP-500-30551. September.

Mayer, E., E. Blank, and B. Swezey. 1999. *The Grassroots Are Greener.* Renewable Energy Policy Project, Research Report No. 8. June. Available at *www.repp.org.* Accessed November 14, 2005.

Milligan, M. 2004. "Wind Integration Impacts: What Have We Learned?" Presentation to ENVS 5100 class, University of Colorado at Boulder, October.

Nielsen, J. 2004. Prefiled direct testimony of John Nielsen on behalf of Western Resource Advocates, before the Public Utilities Commission of the State of Colorado, September 13. Available at *www.dora.state.co.us/puc/docket_activity/HighprofileDockets/04A-214E_-215E_-216E.htm.* Accessed October 15, 2005.

Owens, B. 2005. Letter to the Colorado Senate dated 28 April 2005. Available at *www.colorado.gov/governor/press/april05/hb1162.html.* Accessed November 14, 2005.

Raabe, S. 2003. Wind-power bill to get 3rd airing. *The Denver Post,* April 9, C-01.

Rosen, R. 2004. Answer testimony and exhibits of Dr. Richard A. Rosen on behalf of the Colorado Office of Consumer Counsel, September 13. Available at *www.dora.state.co.us/puc/docket_activity/HighprofileDockets/04A-214E_-215E_-216E.htm.* Accessed October 15, 2005.

Valenti, R. 2004. Renewable energy bill passes Colorado House. *The Colorado Daily,* February 9.

Xcel Energy 2005. *www.xcelenergy.com.* Accessed November 14, 2005.

8. Massachusetts's Policy in Context: Utility Deregulation, Regional Initiatives, and Constrained Renewable Resources

Nicholas A. Hiza
Greenlight Energy

Introduction

Over the past decade, Massachusetts has enacted policies promoting sustainability that are among the most aggressive and advanced in the nation. These policies can be roughly grouped into two categories, distinguished by their primary objectives: those that deal with the regulation and curtailment of greenhouse gas emissions, and those that promote the greater use of renewable energy.

The first category has become a focus of state regulation relatively recently. Perhaps formally beginning with the state's acceptance of the New England Governors/Eastern Canadian Premiers Climate Change Action Plan in 2001, Massachusetts has taken a number of steps to regulate greenhouse gas production: ranging from the passage of targeted regulations capping CO_2 emissions from existing power plants, to the state's self-imposed commitments in its Climate Protection Plan to cap and reduce its total greenhouse production by as much as eighty percent. Though potentially of greater influence over the long term, the formal adoption of the greenhouse gas reduction as a state goal is a relatively recent occurrence.

150

Consequently, it has not yet become deeply entrenched in existing regulation, and it is uncertain to what extent state commitments will translate into enforceable laws. However, the commitments themselves place Massachusetts among the leaders of national sustainable policy.

But more influential — and enjoying more regulatory force — are those policies in the second category: promoting the development and use of renewable energy. These began with the suite of laws passed as part of the deregulation and restructuring of the state's electrical industry in the 1990s. The central objective of these policies was to establish a competitive marketplace for renewable energy within the broader electrical markets being developed at that time. To support the initial formation of this market, Massachusetts passed a number of measures both promoting a greater demand for renewable energy and investing in the development of its supply. To date, the most important source of state support for sustainable energy is the demand created by its Renewables Portfolio Standard (RPS), which requires that 4 percent of its electricity come from "renewable sources" by 2009. But the state has also created the opportunity for conscientious consumers to purchase amounts of renewable energy in excess of these minimum requirements by promulgating standardized labeling and disclosure requirements to empower a voluntary market for sustainable energy. The state charged its economic development agency, the Massachusetts Technological Collaborative (MTC), to address remaining barriers to the development of supply. To fund this mission, the state enacted an ongoing ratepayer surcharge to create the Renewable Energy Trust. Combined with tracking systems that allow for the verifiable purchase or sale of renewable energy, Massachusetts has successfully created a stable yet vibrant market demand for renewable energy.

Yet despite the state's two-pronged strategy — enacting programs encouraging both demand for and supply of renewable energy — the development of a renewable industry has been slower than expected. While the state has set a goal to support the development of 1,000 Megawatts (MW) of renewable generation by 2009, by late in 2005 — eight years after the RPS was announced and two years after it came into effect — only 5 projects were waiting to interconnect to the Massachusetts electrical grid. With only two of these projects larger than 30 megawatts in size, these facilities would add less than 540 megawatts of new renewable capacity to the state's system. Furthermore, 80 percent of this capacity comes from the highly contentious Cape Wind Project proposed off the shores of Cape Cod. Were this hotly debated project to fail, only 115 megawatts of new capacity would remain. This contrasts sharply with the experience of states like New York, which has seen many more projects proposed than will be required to satisfy its RPS. Granted, demand in New York is greater than in Massachusetts: by 2009, the New York RPS is expected to generate three times the demand of the Massachusetts RPS. But as of 2006, only three years since the announcement of its RPS, New York has fully ten times more renewable projects waiting to connect to the grid than Massachusetts (and nearly fifty times the capacity if Cape Wind were withdrawn). What has hampered Massachusetts has not been a lack of state support or demand for renewables, but the lack of easily accessible wind resources. Throughout the United States, what has driven the expansion of renewable energy supply in recent years has been the construction of large, utility-scale wind power facilities. In New York, wind has made up 98 percent of the first round of procurements for the state RPS. Though the situation may change as other technologies mature, it is largely the fragmented and constrained nature of the land-based wind resource in Massachusetts that explains why the state, even equipped with aggressive and well-formulated policies to promote renewable energy, is not meeting its goals as quickly as some of its neighbors.

To address this potential issue, Massachusetts is exploring two large-scale initiatives to expand the supply of renewable energy available under the RPS: one to allow limited development of wind resources on state land, and the other to allow currently ineligible biomass facilities to qualify as new source of renewable energy under the Massachusetts RPS.

Both of these proposals could substantially alter the face of the state's renewable energy industry, in addition to their immediate goal of easing supply constraints. The first proposal — the inclusion of state lands for consideration and development — could more than double the potential wind resources available, and result in a substantial expansion of renewable generation in the state. The second — relaxing the RPS definition of new renewable sources to include existing biomass — would undercut the growth of truly new renewable capacity, and would be viewed by many as an effective reduction in the amount of renewable energy required by the state. By demonstrating a willingness to relax its qualification criteria, the state risks rendering the remaining requirements in its RPS meaningless, since market participants will have little assurance they will not be further decreased. Signaling such a lack of stability could be very detrimental for the state's burgeoning renewables industry, chilling new development and exploration.

Massachusetts is entering into a critical time when its policy requirements are being tested against market realities and resource challenges. If the state maintains its requirements and works to address the particular challenges posed by the state's resource constraints, its system of strong and stable incentives will help a robust market to develop. However, if the state begins to ease these requirements, in effect diluting the demand for renewable energy, the instability this will signal to the market will undercut the interest of the development community — who, without the assurance that state mandates are reliable, will be reluctant to invest the necessary time and capital to pursue projects in the state. Counter-intuitively, then, an easing of requirements now will in fact inhibit the development of the Massachusetts market in the long term.

Regional GHG Initiatives and the Massachusetts Climate Protection Plan

The history of greenhouse gas reduction as a codified state goal in Massachusetts probably begins formally with its adoption of the New England Governors/Eastern Canadian Premiers Climate Change Action Plan in 2001. The state has made a number of commitments to regulate greenhouse gas emissions, both through its participation in broader regional initiatives like the 2001 Climate Action Plan and the Regional Greenhouse Gas Initiative (RGGI) CO_2 cap-and-trade program, and in its own resolutions. These commitments were formally outlined in 2004 with the publication of the Massachusetts Climate Protection Plan. The Climate Protection Plan includes a number of measures aimed at achieving the state's broader pledge to reduce greenhouse gas emissions to 1990 levels by 2010, and to continue these reductions until a sustainable emissions rate 75–85 percent below current levels is reached. While it is not concrete regulation, the Plan put forward a number of clearly stated and actionable steps to reduce greenhouse gas (GHG) emissions. These steps vary widely in focus and in scope, ranging from structural improvement like better accounting of GHG emissions, to incorporating smarter growth principals in town planning, to achieving specific targets such as reducing CO_2 from state facilities by 25 percent by 2012 (Office for Commonwealth Development 2004).

While it is still too early to understand the extent to which these commitments will resolve into enforceable regulations, Massachusetts had already begun to control CO_2 production even before the Climate Protection Plan was released. The state Department of Environmental Protection implemented CMR 310 7.29 in May of 2001, establishing "output-based emission rates" (Department of Environmental Protection 2001, 1). for existing power plants. These efficiency rates limit the amounts of NO_x, SO_2

and (interestingly) CO_2 allowable measured in terms of pounds of pollutant produced per megawatthour of electricity generated, and even established a cap on CO_2 and Hg emissions from operating facilities.

These caps prohibit affected facilities from rising above their 2004 or 2006 levels of CO_2 production (the benchmark year depending upon whether generators choose simply to install pollution controls to meet their efficiency requirements, or repower their facility to do so), and within two years of their cap date facilities must meet an overall emission rate of less than 1,800 pounds of CO_2 generated per megawatthour produced (Department of Environmental Protection 2001). For plants that cannot meet these emission requirements, credits for off-site reductions of CO_2 emissions can be obtained through carbon sequestration or renewable energy projects (Department of Environmental Protection 2001). No plants had yet engaged in such measures by the summer of 2005, but the Massachusetts Department of Environmental Protection was developing regulations that would determine what projects could qualify as reductions, along with how to approach greenhouse gas banking and trading (Energy Information Administration 2005a). As it stands, Massachusetts is the first state in the country to regulate the emission of greenhouse gasses from existing power plants (Conference of New England Governors and Eastern Canadian Premiers 2002). Though only a first step, the state's willingness to pass such pioneering measures offers promise the broader regulation of CO_2 production called for in the Climate Protection Plan may translate into specific regulatory action.

Electrical Utility Restructuring Act and the Market for Renewable Energy

Though in time the goal of regulating greenhouses gasses may come to be a prime mover of state policy, today it is market mechanisms formulated during the deregulation and subsequent restructuring of electrical markets in the 1990's that are the most important supports of sustainable development in Massachusetts.

Accordingly, to understand sustainable policy in the Commonwealth it is first necessary to examine the historical changes in the electrical industry that set the context for its formation. Traditionally, the United States has employed a highly regulated electricity market, where everything from the area a utility might service to the price it could charge was set by regulators. Though reforms to this system were introduced in 1978 with the passage of the Public Utility Regulatory Policies Act (PURPA), it was not until 1996 when the Federal Energy Regulatory Commission (FERC) implemented regulations requiring open and equal access to jurisdictional utilities' transmission lines for all electricity producers that this system truly began to change. The passage of these regulations drove the formation of open markets and prompted many states to restructure their electric industries to allow customers direct access to retail power generation (Energy Information Administration 2005b). At the same time, FERC encouraged the states to require utilities to sell off their power plants and to gradually eliminate regulator-set rates in favor of prices determined by the markets (New England Independent Systems Operator 2005a). It was believed that competition would encourage innovation, incentives for investment, and increased efficiency, much as it had done in the fields of transportation, telecommunications, and financial services. Although the optimism associated with this initial period of deregulation was soon tempered by experiences like the California brownouts, the die had been cast and many states continued along the road of deregulation and restructuring throughout the latter part of the 1990s.

FERC also created a number of regional Independent System Operators (ISOs) to manage the transition to competitive electricity markets, and to ensure system reliability and oversight of the wholesale markets thereafter (New England Independent Systems Operator 2005a). In this way, a desirable hybrid was created: market forces would increase system efficiency and lower costs to consumers, but each ISO would act as a single, regulated body accountable for system reliability, much as the utilities had done in the past. ISO New England was created in 1997 to manage the transition in the six-state region comprised of Massachusetts, Maine, New Hampshire, Vermont, Connecticut, and Rhode Island. This was a natural subdivision of the National Grid, as the area had operated as a regional grid since the formation of the New England Power Pool (NEPOOL) in 1971.[1] By 2005, five of the six NEPOOL states had required their utilities to divest their generation, and nearly 90 percent of the region's power plants were unregulated — making New England the most deregulated market in the country (New England Independent Systems Operator 2005a).

The transition to deregulated energy markets began for Massachusetts when the Massachusetts Department of Telecommunications and Energy (DTE) issued its "Order in Electric Industry Restructuring" on August 16, 1995. In it, DTE proposed principles for the transition to — and operation of — a restructured electrical industry (Massachusetts Department of Public Utilities 1995). Over the next sixteen months, it developed the necessary rules and regulations to implement the principles established in this order, which it issued in draft form in May of 1996[1] and finally as actionable "Model Rules" in December of that same year (Massachusetts Department of Public Utilities 1996). The model rules were meant to provide the regulatory framework for an efficient market structure that would "minimize long-term costs to consumers while maintaining the safety and reliability of electric services with minimum impact on the environment" (Massachusetts Department of Telecommunications and Energy 1998, 6).

As part of minimizing environmental impacts, several supports for renewable energy were proposed. These included the establishment of a fund to invest in industry development, the formation of fair interconnect standards, and the requirement that information on these technologies should be distributed to electrical customers. These proposals would have substantially advanced sustainable energy policy in the state. But their implementation, along with that of the Model Rules at large, was forestalled when the Massachusetts Legislature undertook a comprehensive review of electric restructuring in 1997 (Massachusetts Department of Telecommunications and Energy 1998).

The Legislature's review resulted in the passage of the Electrical Utility Restructuring Act on November 25, 1997. The purpose of the Act closely paralleled that of the Model Rules formulated earlier by the DTE: it sought to create a comprehensive framework for restructuring the utility industry (Massachusetts Legislature 1997).

The primary goal of this new structure was to allow competitive electrical markets to function effectively in Massachusetts. To achieve this, the Act broke apart the vertically integrated structure of the existing electric utilities, unbundling prices and functionally separating generation services from transmission and distribution services (Massachusetts Legislature 1997). It encouraged competitive markets to develop at both wholesale and retail levels in all sectors: from generation to brokering services to the final marketing and supplying of electricity to consumers. While all market participants must be licensed by the DTE to operate in Massachusetts, it is the market — not the state — that determines the rates participants charge for their services (Massachusetts Legislature 1997).

It was hoped that, by dispensing with all but the regulations necessary to protect the environment and maintain system stability the Act would foster competition among generators and retail suppliers that would, in turn, drive down costs to consumers and increase the general efficiency of the system (Massachusetts Legislature 1997). The maintenance of the transmission and distribution systems would be left to the traditional utility companies, who would continue to provide metering, billing, and information services at rates regulated by the DTE (Massachusetts Legislature 1997). DTE was also charged with setting standards to ensure the reliability of the transmission and distribution system (Massachusetts Legislature 1997). Reliability of the larger competitive markets would remain the responsibility of ISO New England.

But the Act was as concerned with the profile of the generation supplying the market as with its price, and it included supports for sustainable forms of energy which noticeably exceeded its antecedents. The purpose of these measures was to harness the advantages created by the broader context of deregulated electrical markets to encourage the formation of a competitive market for renewable energy. Measures were designed to accomplish this goal in one of two ways: either by enhancing demand for renewable resources, or by investing in their supply.

The Renewables Portfolio Standard and the Voluntary Market

Legislating Demand

The most critical addition to earlier proposed supports was the enactment of a Renewables Portfolio Standard (RPS) mandating that a steadily increasing percentage of electricity sold in the Commonwealth would come from new sources of renewable generation. Today, the stable demand this measure creates is by far the strongest incentive for renewable energy development in the state.

The structure of the RPS takes full advantage of the deregulated market it was formed in. It is based on a model of individual procurement; all retail suppliers of electricity in the Commonwealth (with the exception of Municipal Light Districts) are required to include a minimum threshold of electricity from new renewable sources in the energy they sell (Massachusetts Register 2002). This minimum increases annually, beginning at 1 percent in 2003 and increasing by 0.5 percent each year thereafter until 2009. After this time, the increases will accelerate to 1 percent per year until the Department of Energy Resources (DOER) elects to suspend them (Massachusetts Register 2002). As is necessary for the RPS to foster long-term investment, there is no mechanism for decreasing these renewable energy requirements, either in the original Act set forth by the Legislature, or in the regulations DOER promulgated pursuant to it, which go so far at to state explicitly that the percentage required must never decrease (Massachusetts Register 2002). At most, the DOER may suspend further increases.

Meeting this demand will require substantial growth in available renewable capacity in the coming years. Roughly 51,000,000 megawatt-hours of electricity was sold in Massachusetts in 2005, 1,000,000 megawatt-hours of which were required to come from new sources of renewable generation. As the RPS increases .5 percent each year, roughly enough new renewable capacity must be added to supply an additional 280,000 mega-watt-hours of electricity. To put this in perspective, if these requirements were to be satisfied with wind energy alone, the RPS would require over 100 megawatts of new capacity to begin operation annually, from 2005 until 2009. By 2009, there would need to be more than 800 megawatts of wind supplying power to the state.[2] Installed today, this would likely take an investment in excess of $1 billion. The surety of a long-term demand for the renewable energy produced is critical in incentivizing the commitment of the capital necessary for these facilities, which often would be uncompetitive based on their electrical sales alone. The time necessary to permit, construct, and repay the loans on a renewable energy project may span decades. Because the RPS guarantees that the demand for renewable energy will only rise from year to year, suppliers can feel secure they are competing for a market that will still be present when their facilities become operational.

TRACKING THE MARKET

Though a mandate, the RPS is still fundamentally a market mechanism. Only the percentage of energy required from new renewable sources is set by the state; thereafter each market participant determines the most cost-effective way to achieve that percentage. For this concept to be put into practice, however, a method had to be devised to track the attributes of energy bought and sold in Massachusetts. It was decided this would be best accomplished by contractually separating the renewable attributes of the generation from the electricity produced. These attributes could then be bought and sold as a tradable commodity, called a Renewable Energy Certificate (REC), to meet the RPS requirements. Considered technically, this would require developing a system to track these attributes and effectively tag each unit of electricity sold into the market as either renewable or conventional. To accomplish this, NEPOOL contracted with the private firm APX Inc. to assist New England's ISO in developing this mechanism. When launched on July 15, 2002, the scope and level of detail this system would track made it the first of its kind in the nation.

This system, termed the New England Generation Information System (or NE GIS), tracks the attributes of every MWh of electricity sold onto the New England grid. It is of fundamental importance for renewable generators, since it certifies the renewable energy attributes associated with the electricity they produce — allowing for the verifiable sale of these attributes to retail electrical suppliers. But the GIS tracks over fifty different attributes of each MWh of electricity produced by every generator on the NEPOOL system, including the technology used, the age of the facility, the fuel source, and the emissions released during production. Each MWh generated is assigned a certificate, issued quarterly,[3] which records all of these attributes (New England Power Pool Generation Information System Operating Rules 2005). The certificates that the GIS assigns are therefore useful to a number of different market participants. Generators use these certificates to demonstrate compliance with state emissions regulations. Qualifying renewable facilities sell their certificates to retail suppliers of electricity, also called Load Serving Entities (LSE). LSE's, in turn, base their fuel source labels on these certificates to meet state disclosure requirements, and use renewable energy certificates to demonstrate compliance with the state's RPS.

Eligibility

To qualify as a source of REC's on the NE GIS, a facility must meet specific eligibility requirements, including some consideration of its fuel source and generation technology, how long it has been in operation, how its generation is metered, and its location. For the purposes of the RPS, a renewable generation unit must use one of the following fuels: solar photovoltaic or solar thermal electric energy, wind energy, ocean thermal, wave or tidal energy, fuel cells using an eligible "New Renewable Fuel," landfill methane gas and anaerobic digester gas used onsite, or low-emission, advanced biomass power conversion technologies using an eligible biomass fuel (Massachusetts Division of Energy Resources 2005a). However, there is no differentiation between eligible sources; all qualifying generators will receive one REC for each megawatt hour produced. Because the RPS seeks to drive demand for new sources of renewable energy, no facility in operation before December 31, 1997, can qualify under the RPS. If upgrades or other factors result in an otherwise qualified existing facility producing more than its "Historical Generation Rate," it may apply for a vintage waiver to receive RECs for only the amount of generation in excess of what the site historically produced. In this way, the RPS incentives target generation that has been newly added to the system. Finally, in examining location Massachusetts does permit out-of-state supply to qualify under its RPS. However, production must be verified by the

NE-ISO, which creates some practical limitations to purchasing RECs from outside the NEPOOL region. The exception to this is off-grid and behind-the-meter generation, both of which must be located in Massachusetts to qualify. If a unit meets all these criteria, DOER will provide the facility with a Statement of Qualifications, at which time it may sell RECs for compliance with the state's RPS.

The careful formulation and enforcement of these criteria is obviously critical to the RPS achieving its goals. More inclusive criteria or lenient enforcement will increase the likelihood that the RPS will be satisfied at a lower cost, but with greater levels of emissions. This might be true for a number of reasons, such as the inclusion of existing renewable generation in the RPS, which would reduce the amount of conventional generation displaced, or the qualifying of facilities which utilize "dirtier" technologies, such as the co-firing of biomass with non-renewable fuels like coal.

COST

If an LSE does not purchase enough RECs to satisfy its requirements under the RPS, it must make Alternative Compliance Payments (ACPs) to the state. In 2003, a retail supplier of electricity had to pay $50 per MWh in ACPs for each MWh it did not manage to procure RECs for (payments for 181 MWh were actually made) (Massachusetts Division of Energy Resources 2005a). ACPs effectively set a cap on the cost of RECs in Massachusetts—since, if the price that renewable energy suppliers charged for their RECs ever rose too high, LSEs would simply buy ACPs instead. To prevent ACPs from eroding the price of RECs over time, this rate is adjusted up or down annually in relation to the previous year's consumer price index. So in 2005, the published rate per MWh for ACPs was $53.19 (Massachusetts Division of Energy Resources 2005b). As such, this price is and remains very competitive: $53 per MWh might be as much or more than a generator would receive for their electricity. To put this in perspective, the value of a MWh on Massachusetts's spot market has averaged around $55 since March of 2003 (New England Independent Systems Operator 2005). In theory then, the extra revenue a renewable generator could receive through the sale of the attributes of its power could double its revenue. Importantly, the option of making ACPs instead of buying RECs from certified energy suppliers has been structured so as not to undercut the growth of the renewables market. Not only does the cost of ACPs adjust over time, but the payments are directly used to fund the Massachusetts Technology Collaborative, the organization charged with facilitating the development of renewable energy in the Commonwealth.

Thus, even when LSEs opt out of buying RECs from renewable energy suppliers, their ACP payments seed the development of new renewable technologies and facilities.

COMPLIANCE MARKET

The demand generated by the RPS (usually referred to as the compliance market) is expected by many to be the main engine of renewable energy purchases for the foreseeable future. However, it is possible the demand for sustainable energy in the voluntary market could be greater than the minimum level required by the RPS.

The advent of competition meant, of course, that energy retailers could differentiate their product from a rival's by price. But the Electrical Utility Restructuring Act introduced a new basis for competition: the characteristics of the power's production. This was achieved through the implementation of uniform labeling requirements, enabling consumers to compare a number of aspects of competing electrical products, such as whether or not the source of the generation was renewable (Massachusetts Legislature 1997).

After September 1998, all companies selling power in Massachusetts are required to provide a disclosure label to their customers, once before delivering service and on a quarterly basis thereafter. Disclosure labels include five categories of information on the power's attributes: price as compared to that of other suppliers, terms of contract, power sources, pollution emitted from these sources (as compared to both regional averages and the averages for new power plants), and labor data about the conditions of workers in these facilities (Massachusetts Legislature 1997). Thus, conscientious consumers looking to support anything from lower emissions to unionized labor can now act on these convictions in the selection of their electrical provider.

Whether or not consumer preference will result in a demand for renewable energy greater than that mandated by the RPS remains to be seen. In part this will depend on how large the competitive market becomes.

Though by the summer of 2005 there were 15 retail suppliers of electricity and 25 licensed power brokers active in at least one of the four Massachusetts distribution company service areas,[4] the amount of customers who had migrated from default services to a competitive supplier of any form, green or otherwise, had been small (5 percent in July of 2004) (Massachusetts Division of Energy Resources 2005a).

But though the number of customers shifting to competitive supply has not been large, the total volume of electricity purchased from competitive suppliers in Massachusetts has increased considerably since competition began in April of 1999. This growth has been largely driven by increasing purchases in the commercial and industrial sectors. This stands to reason; there are far fewer actors in these sectors than the residential markets, consuming much more electricity per capita, with a proportionally increased sensitivity to the cost of energy and any potential for savings.[5] Indeed, of the 2.5 million electrical customers on the 2004 rolls of the Investor Owned Utilities (IOUs) in Massachusetts, the 7,000 customers classified by the Massachusetts DOER as large industrial and commercial users purchased 40 percent of the total electricity sold. As such (and because such large customers need not necessary be price-takers), it is logical that they would more quickly move to the competitive market to try and capture greater savings. Commercial and industrial users purchased eleven million megawatt hours of electricity from some form of competitive supply in 2004, which made up 24 percent of total electric sales in the state, 38 percent of sales to industrial users, and 96 percent of purchases from competitive supply (Massachusetts Consumer Affairs and Business Regulation 2005).

For proponents of the voluntary RECs market, this is a promising shift. Nationally, the non-residential market has emerged as the primary driver of voluntary demand for renewable energy. For example, the U.S. Environmental Protection Agency (EPA) Green Power Partnership has grown from 21 Founding Partners in 2001 to over 600 non-residential associations collectively purchasing over 3.1 billion kilowatt hours of green power in 2005. This figure has doubled since mid 2004, and increased ten fold since the Partnership began in 2001 (Environmental News Network 2005).

By comparison, residential migration to competitive sources has lagged behind. In 2004, residential users purchased only 420,000 megawatt hours of electricity from some form of competitive supply, which made up a little less than 1 percent of total electric sales in the state, 3 percent of all sales to residential users, and 4 percent of purchases from competitive supply (Massachusetts Consumer Affairs and Business Regulation 2005). However, customers have had little financial incentive to switch from default services whose prices had been kept artificially low during the transition to deregulated markets. With the termination of the old default services in March of 2005, it is likely more residences may begin to select competitive supply. Initially, this expectation that has been borne out; by July of 2005 the number of residential customers obtaining their electricity from some form of competitive supplier had grown 150 percent, to over 180,000 (Massachusetts Consumer Affairs and Business Regulation 2005).

By the summer of 2005, a third of all electricity sold through IOUs in Massachusetts had come from competitive suppliers. At these levels, only 7 percent of the competitive marketplace would have to elect to buy pure renewable energy products for the demand to be greater than of the RPS mandate. This would be in excess of what has been in observed in competitive markets to date, but voluntary purchases of renewable energy are on the rise, and some top performing utility green pricing programs have achieved participation rates of 15 percent. (Massachusetts Environmental Policy Act Office Regulations 1998a). Thus, it is possible that even at current levels, consumer preference — especially of industrial customers — could create demand for renewable energy in excess of percentages mandated by the state's RPS.

Building Supply

Massachusetts has enacted a number of policies that both successfully formed a market and encouraged robust demand for renewable energy. However, though this helped to address the comparatively high expense of renewable generation, many systemic barriers remained to renewable facilities entering the marketplace. At the core of these difficulties was the general lack of familiarity with such technologies found in the utilities, regulators, financiers and the public (Massachusetts Department of Telecommunications and Energy 1998). This inexperience engendered a number of problems for proposed projects, from the inability to secure long-term finance to effectively being unable to link to the electrical grid under current interconnection standards.

Massachusetts Technological Collaborative

Rather than attempting to solve all such problems at the passage of the Act, the Legislature charged the Massachusetts Technological Collaborative (MTC) with the broader task of fostering renewable energy supply in the state: under this larger objective it could address these impediments and others that would likely arise in time. MTC is the state's development agency for renewable energy and what it calls "the innovation economy." The MTC was originally formed in 1982 to address a lack of engineers familiar with semiconductor design, but by the end of the eighties a severe recession and major advances in semiconductors decreased the demand for such individuals. Its training center and program were slated for termination in 1993, but the MTC's charter was broadened to encompass a wider directive of promoting economic growth in the Commonwealth, with a focus on more advanced sectors of the economy. Over the next few years it completed a number of successful development initiatives, and by the passage of the Electrical Utilities Restructuring Act in 1997 the Massachusetts Legislature had determined it was the organization best suited to provide ongoing support to the emergent renewable energy sector.

RENEWABLE ENERGY TRUST

To give this organization the resources necessary to achieve its goals, the Legislature established the Massachusetts Renewable Energy Trust Fund (MRET) as part of the passage of the Act (Massachusetts Legislature 1997). MRET was implemented with the stated goal to "generate the maximum economic and environmental benefits over time from renewable energy to the ratepayers of the Commonwealth" both by promoting the use of renewable energy and the development of the renewable energy manufacturing industry in the state (Massachusetts Legislature 1997). It is the MTC's task to determine how best to allocate MRET resources to accomplish these economic goals and others assigned by the Legislature, such as the protection of the environment and the diversification of the Commonwealth's fuel supply (Massachusetts Legislature 1997). The funding MRET supplies is significant, replenished by an ongoing surcharge of .05 ¢/kWh on electrical bills in Massachusetts[6] — which generates an annual revenue stream of approximately $23 million per year for the MTC to invest in encouraging supply(United States Department of Energy 2005).

The formation of MRET was not uncontested, and no monies were dispensed for the first two years after the surcharge began in 1998. In what would later be referred to as the Shea Lawsuit, eight customers of investor-owned utilities disputed the fund's legitimacy through legal action against the eight companies that provided their electricity, and against the DTE, the DOER, and the MTC (Shea 2000). The plaintiffs asserted that the surcharges set forth in the electrical restructuring act in 1997 violated the Massachusetts Constitution by imposing unreasonable excise taxes and also that they violated the equal protection clause of the Fourteenth Amendment, since they did not apply to customers in Municipal Light Districts (Shea 2000). It was not until April of 2000, with the court's unanimously ruling that the surcharges were constitutional, that MTC was free to begin accessing the fund.

In pursuing its goals, the MTC has minimized direct investment in large-scale energy facilities. Instead, MTC has funded initiatives that address barriers to all project proposed in the state. For example, the MTC has funded efforts to develop consistent interconnection standards for renewable energy technologies tying into the Massachusetts grid, addressing a substantial stumbling block to the industry. They have given extensive grants to organizations focused on public outreach and education, which is a critical support to the smaller projects likely to be permitted in the state. Even programs through which MTC provides direct support for individual projects often seem as directed at education as development.

Consider the Community Wind Initiative: in this program the MTC will partner with townships interested in installing a few turbines to run a local load, such as a desalination plant. This decentralized model of developing numerous small wind farms has higher risks and smaller rewards than utility scale facilities, and is not likely occur in the market with any regularity at this time. Therefore, what small capacity each success in this program adds is a positive expenditure of MTC funds, in that it is likely without this intervention the facility would not have been built. But what is likely to have a much greater impact is that even a few successes in this program — distributed throughout the state — will drastically decrease the distance to the nearest operational renewable energy facility for the average Massachusetts residence. Increasing the public's exposure to renewable energy (in this case, wind energy) is hugely important in dispelling myths about that technology, such as quelling fears about noise or unsightliness. Inarguably, MTC's Community Wind Program may be helping to increase the number of renewable energy facilities in the state. But more importantly, and perhaps more to its purpose, MTC is working to erode a substantial barrier to other proposed developments by addressing a general lack of familiarity with the technology. Especially in a state that is so densely populated, public acceptance will be a key determinant of the success of the renewable energy industry — and of the RPS.

Development of the Renewable Industry in Massachusetts

Despite robust demand and well formulated state support for bringing supply to the market, the development of a renewable industry has been slower than expected. The MTC has set a goal to support the development of 750 to 1,000 operational Megawatts (MW) in renewable generation by 2009 (Database of State Incentives for Renewable Energy 2005). But by November 2005 — a full eight years after Massachusetts announced its RPS and two years after it had come into effect — a total of 5 projects were waiting to interconnect to the Massachusetts electrical grid. Only two of these projects had capacities greater than or equal to 30 megawatts, and taken together these facilities would add less than 540 megawatts of new renewable capacity to the state's system. Furthermore, 80 percent of this capacity is contributed by the highly contentious Cape Wind Project proposed off the shores of Cape Cod. Were opposition to this project to prevail, only 115 megawatts of capacity would remain.

This contrasts sharply with the experience of states such as New York. By 2009, the New York RPS is only expected to generate three times the demand of the Massachusetts RPS, but the state has a full ten times the renewable projects waiting to connect to the grid (and nearly fifty times the capacity if Cape Wind were withdrawn).

New Policies

As of the summer of 2005, Massachusetts was considering two substantial changes in state policy that would seek to accelerate the fulfillment of the RPS by expanding the supply of renewable energy available from wind and biomass respectively. However, these two policies would take dramatically different approaches to achieve this goal. In the case of wind, the state has recognized that the amount and distribution of the land it owns has substantially impeded the development of wind resources in the state. As such, a shift in policy that made some portion of this land available for development could have a dramatic impact on the profile of renewable resources in the Commonwealth.

Just how dramatic an impact such a policy could have becomes clear on a thorough examination of the states wind resources. Wind resources in Massachusetts are concentrated in two regions: in the mountains in the west and along the eastern coast. A survey of wind resources rated Class 4 and greater reveals a concentration of 97 percent of the state's land-based commercial wind resource in only four counties: Berkshire County, the westernmost county in state, and the counties of Barnstable, Dukes, and Nantucket, which make up Cape Cod and the Islands—one of the northeast's major tourist destinations. Arguably, the greatest renewable resources in the state are to be found blowing over the waters off the shores of these coastal counties. However, though offshore wind technology is advancing, it has not yet reached a point where the majority of New England's ample offshore wind resources are viable for development. Regions where the water is shallow enough and the wind resources great enough to support sites are often close to heavily developed shorelines. Residents in such regions often paid a premium for a view of the uninterrupted horizon, which raises concerns about strong public resistance to proposed development (such as the fierce and well funded opposition to the Cape Wind Project proposed in Nantucket Sound).

LAND-BASED RESOURCES

To date, the distribution and characteristics of land-based wind resources in the state have been the most important influence on the industry's development. Land-based wind resources along the Cape Cod coast are abundant, but sites are tightly constrained by existing development, environmentally sensitive areas, and high property values. A developer will typically site turbines one and a half times the turbine's height from structures and roads, and over a thousand feet from an occupied dwellings. Outside of protected areas such as the National Seashore, the Cape is thickly settled, and though distributed sites of low capacity may be available for development, it is unlikely that sites exist which could support large scale wind farms. In the near future at least, development along the coast will likely be limited to small, distributed on-shore or near-shore sites, such as the single 660 kW wind turbine installed in the town of Hull.

The remaining commercially viable wind resources in Massachusetts are concentrated on ridge tops in the western part of the state. There are 80 to 90 miles of ridgeline in Western Massachusetts with an expected Wind Class of 4 or greater. To understand the potential of this resource, some rough estimates may be informative. Though such estimates have a high margin of error, they can give us a very general idea of the contribution possible.

A rule of thumb often employed in estimating site capacities is that turbines will be spaced 3 to 5 rotor diameters apart perpendicular to the prevailing wind. As most of the ridgeline in Massachusetts runs north to south, and the prevailing winds come out of the west, it is reasonable to estimate one modern GE 1.5 MW wind turbine might be placed every three rotor diameters (or 760 feet for a model with a 77 meter rotor diameter) along a ridgeline. With one more assumption, that wind power facilities in a Class 4 wind resource will have average annual capacity factors of at least 30 percent, we can calculate some approximate figures for the generation potential of the state's wind resources. Based on these assumptions, every mile of ridgeline represents 10 MW of potential capacity, and 27,500 MWh of annual generation. Therefore, ridgelines in western Massachusetts could support 800 to 900 MW of capacity, generating 2.2 to 2.5 million MWh of renewable energy each year (roughly 4–5 percent of expected demand in 2005).

DEVELOPMENT ISSUES

However, not all of this land is suitable for development. Some resides in sites that are too small to be financially viable, some is unavailable due to its ownership and associated conservation easements. Indeed, in Massachusetts the two are closely related. The partial ownership of many sites by public entities such as the state in effect fragments the remaining private and developable lands into sites too small to viable, a concept that will be discussed at length below. Whether a site's size is constrained by wind resources or conservation restrictions on a portion of the property composing it, the small size of sites in Massachusetts severely hampers wind power development in the state.

Traditionally, developers look for large continuous stretches of ridgeline, preferably contained within a single permitting jurisdiction (a single town in the case of Massachusetts), so as not to incur extra permitting and interconnecting expenses. The impact of reducing project size is at least twofold. First, many facility costs will not scale linearly with the size of the project. The smaller the site, the more cost each megawatt must bear to cover the fixed costs of construction, such as building a transmission line and substation to interconnect a project to the transmission grid. Furthermore, larger plants can often negotiate better prices for their wind turbines. Since the turbines themselves may make up 80 percent of the total facilities cost, reducing this expense can have substantial impacts on the overall economic return a project may see. Indeed, under current market conditions— where the demand for turbines far exceeds their supply — a smaller project may not be able to secure turbines at all, unless the developer is also negotiating contracts for larger turbine procurement at the same time. Finally, with few exceptions (such as the possibility that a smaller project will not have to file an Environmental Impact Statement), the amount of capital expended in permitting and the associated public outreach and education is similar for large and small projects. As the economic picture grows more precarious, risk increases steadily since even minor unexpected costs can scuttle a project. As importantly, the compensation for developing a small project is proportionally reduced, whether this is the direct fee a group will receive when passing the project to an owner-operator or simply the value a small number of megawatts will bring to the overall portfolio of the company.

The minimum project size a developer may be willing to undertake will be contingent upon a number of factors; the expected value of the project, financial resources, tolerance for risk, etc. To get an idea what developers feel may be a viable project size in the Massachusetts's market, consider the projects currently proposed by private development groups: the average capacity of the three land-based wind projects who have filed requests to connect to the state's electric grid is 18 megawatts. However, one of these three projects actually utilizes two ridges for its 30 MW proposal, at 13.5 MW and 16.5 MW respectively. Therefore, the average continuous site size is 14 MW. It is worth mentioning that many developers would consider this a very low average; the average capacity for land-based proposals requesting interconnect in New York 119 MW, though most of these are not ridgeline sites. However, these are real proposals that experienced development groups have demonstrably deemed worth the investment of considerable funds and years of time, and therefore valid guides for our purposes. Based on this average, we might take an initial look at how much ridgeline with class 4 wind resources exists in continuous stretches with potential capacities of 10 MW or greater, or (based on our rules of thumb discussed earlier) sections greater than 1 mile long. Without considering ownership of the land, there are around 30 sites in the state with Class 4 wind for a mile or more — a total of roughly 70 miles. As much 10–20 percent of the resource resides in sites with capacities too low to support development.

Though this does reduce the states wind resources, the impact is not extreme. Of far greater importance is the effective reduction in average site size which results from much of the state's ridgelines being contained in recreation and conservation lands, hereafter referred to as "open space," and therefore being subject to many potential permitting restrictions. Of the initially mentioned 80 to 90 miles of ridgeline with Class 4 wind resources, only 34 percent is privately owned.[7] The bulk of the resource is public-owned and held under conservation restrictions that prevent development of any kind. Even where development is not restricted outright — for example, on lands with limited or temporary protection — the extra level of complexity required for permitting on such land is a strong disincentive to a developer.

Of the remaining two-thirds of Class 4 wind resources held publicly, roughly 80 percent is owned by agencies of the state, and is therefore preserved under Article 97 of the state's constitution. Article 97, adopted in 1972, requires that no land or easement taken or acquired for natural resource purposes shall be used for other purposes unless the Massachusetts Legislature approves the change by a two-thirds vote. Article 97 was intended to be a legislative check to ensure that lands acquired for conservation purposes were not exploited for uses inconsistent with those intentions, and any proposed conversion requires the completion of an Environmental Notification Form and review under the Massachusetts

Environmental Policy Act (MEPA) (Massachusetts Environmental Policy Act Regulations 1998a). That said, it is possible to lease state land preserved under Article 97. For example, there are a number of marinas in Massachusetts which lease land from the state. But such leases are revocable at any time, and cannot be granted for longer than a five year term, at the end of which they may be renegotiated. It is extremely unlikely that any group would construct a wind power facility with such an insecure and short term lease, and leasing land under an irrevocable contract for the length of time necessary to secure financing for a wind power facility would almost certainly be seen as a disposition under Article 97, whether or not any land transfer actually occurred.

Although the Executive Office of Environmental Affairs (EOEA) can transfer Article 97 land in some circumstances, dispositions usually happen through the legislative action mentioned above (Massachusetts Environmental Policy Act Regulations 1998b). Though the two-thirds threshold was intended as a formidable hurdle to development, such legislative actions have in fact become very common in recent years, constituting over 20 percent of all roll calls over the course of any given legislative session (Resor 2004). Bids in the Legislature for such land dispositions are almost always successful, and about one third of the transfers make public open space available to private development. That said, most developers would be extremely hesitant to begin work on a project whose viability depended upon a two-thirds legislative vote. This is especially true when considered in light that development in these areas— often used for recreation — may encounter substantial public resistance.

IMPACT

As already stated, the impact of roughly two thirds of the land-based class 4 wind resources in the state being potentially unavailable for development reaches beyond the land excluded from consideration. These restrictions impede the development of private sites which are fragmented by public land, effectively reducing the size of many potential projects to a point where they are no longer viable. When publicly-owned sites are excluded, though only a little over 60 percent of the resource has been removed from consideration, the total number of developable sites is reduced from 30 to as few as 7, totaling some 12 miles of privately owned ridge — over an 80 percent reduction in total resource.

Given this situation, it is clear than any measure which allows for some development on state land may dramatically increase the number of potential sites available. Especially where state land borders substantial stretches of elevated ridgeline, the selective release of some property may increase the available wind resources in the state many times.

In response to these facts and broader pressure for state involvement, Massachusetts has begun developing a policy on the siting of wind generation facilities in the Commonwealth. This policy is likely to be the first of its kind in the nation, and though as of the summer of 2005 the details of this policy were not yet known, it will almost certainly address the availability of renewable resources on publicly held land. Whether the state will use its new policy as an opportunity to remove or relax restrictions on the use of public land, or on the contrary to reaffirm them, remains to be seen. However, there are a number of indications that state lands may be opened to some limited form of development in the coming years. One such indication can be found in a recent positive ruling by the EOEA which may allow the use of state land for access to a proposed wind farm in the town of Princeton, MA.

THE PRINCETON PROJECT

The Princeton project consists of the redevelopment of an existing wind farm on a 16-acre inholding parcel owned by the Princeton Municipal Light Department and surrounded by the Mountain State Reservation (WMSR), which is owned and managed by the Massachusetts Department of Conservation and Recreation (DCR) and protected under Article 97 of the State Constitution. Current access to the site traverses parkland, and the project has sought a formal easement from the DCR to render this a permanent part of the facility. As expected, the EOEA found that the granting of such an easement would result in the conversion of Article 97 land. However, pursuant to approval from the Massachusetts General Court, the EOEA did not take issue with this. Indeed, the Secretary went on to write:

> the project as designed has positive impacts both to the state reservation surrounding the project site and to air quality... I find that development of the Princeton wind farm is compatible with the surrounding WMSR. The Princeton wind farm project demonstrates that renewable energy development and successful stewardship of state parkland can be complementary goals ... it would be appropriate (indeed necessary) for the Commonwealth to develop general standards and policies regarding development of wind energy infrastructure on protected open space prior to undertaking a systematic program of development of WTG arrays on state-owned protected open space. Toward that end, I have directed my policy staff to work with EOEA's land holding agencies and stakeholders to develop a general guidance document that advances the Commonwealth's Renewable Portfolio

Standard goals while upholding the underlying purpose and integrity of constitutionally protected open space. (Princeton Wind Farm Infrastructure Improvements 2004, 11–12).

A call for the consideration of wind power development on state lands was repeated in the 2004 Massachusetts Climate Protection Plan, mentioned above. By the summer of 2005, David W. Cash, Director of Air Policy at the EOEA, had held a series of stake-holder meetings to gather comments about the development of such guidelines. It seems at least possible that some development will be allowable, though whether the terms and processes associated with such development will make more projects in Massachusetts possible remains to be seen. However, if well formulated such policies could have a dramatic impact on the amount of resource available.

Addressing Growth of the Industry

Proposed changes in the state's policy on wind power facilities would seek to address slow growth in renewable capacity by encouraging the installation of new facilities. In contrast, the Commonwealth has considered expanding supply by increasing the amount of existing biomass capacity that can qualify to sell renewable energy in the state. If fully enacted, this proposal could have the effect of satisfying the RPS without the addition of any new facilities. Many fear that such an eventuality would undermine the mandate's ultimate goal; indeed, some critics argue that even the consideration of such revisions has already had a noticeable effect of slowing investment in new renewable generation in the state.

By mid–2005, proposed revisions to eligibility requirements for generators utilizing biomass fuels became the focus of much debate. Qualifying criteria for such facilities are fairly strict. Plants using pile burn, stoker combustion, or similar technologies (which make up the bulk of existing biomass generation in the northeast) cannot qualify under the RPS. Operations must instead utilize an "advanced technology," demonstrate that their emissions are consistent with comparable biomass units in the state, and use an eligible biomass fuel (a provision which bars the use of municipal and construction waste).

On July 1, 2005, DOER and the DEP jointly issued a Notice of Inquiry (NOI) proposing changes in the definition of "low-emission biomass power conversion technology" and other matters relating to qualification under the RPS. The proposed revision to the RPS alters at least three of these constraints: it expands the list of allowable fuels to include at least some construction and demolition material. It eases current restrictions on what technologies are eligible, lifting the outright exclusion of pile-burn and stoker combustion technologies and instead evaluating whether a technology is considered "advanced" by an examination of its "Net Heat Rate." And it allows existing biomass facilities which install pollution controls to qualify as "new" sources under the RPS (Massachusetts Division of Energy Resources 2005a). As such, the entire output of such a facility — not just the amount of generation above its historical average — would be considered eligible under the RPS, a fact that has generated substantial concern in market participants and the financial community. Existing regulations had only allowed generation in excess of historical levels to be considered new, and then only with a vintage waiver (though in truth, prior to issuing this NOI DOER had already allowed a plant's full generation to be eligible after a retrofit in several Advisory Rulings).

Of primary concern to many is the impact these combined alterations will have on the REC market in Massachusetts. Biomass is already expected to contribute substantial amounts of renewable energy in the coming years. Literature-based estimates place the woody biomass production potential of the Commonwealth at 4.41 million tons per year from residues and sustainably harvested forest resources. This supply stream could provide significant feed stock for new or upgraded existing biomass facilities. The Union of Concerned Scientists (UCS) estimates that existing biomass plants that have already received their Statements of Qualifications in accordance with the RPS vintage waiver requirement are likely to account for as much as 500,000 megawatt hours of new renewable generation, satisfying about half the amount mandated by the state for 2005. If all the plants in the region who can upgrade their technology to be eligible do so, over one million megawatt hours of renewable energy will be available for RPS compliance. This by itself would satisfy roughly half the RPS demand through 2009, even before the addition of new advanced biomass facilities (Fallon and Breger 2002).

Furthermore, even before the NOI, the DOER waived the vintage requirements for several biomass facilities. UCS estimates just these facilities alone will supply another 1 million megawatt hours of renewable generation to the market (Donovan 2005). It is therefore possible that through just a few exceptions to the vintage waiver requirements, the Massachusetts RPS could be satisfied until 2009. However, only half of the electricity generated will be in addition the initial baseline of renewable generation already taking place in New England before the RPS, with a proportional reduction in the amount of new generation the state RPS will support.

If this is coupled with an easing in requirements so that current technologies like stoker and pile-burn generators with updated pollution controls may qualify for the RPS, enough capacity is already present in the region to completely satisfy the RPS into the next decade. Daniel V. Gulino of Ridgewood Renewable Power posits that, including stoker retrofits, enough biomass generation already exists in New England to satisfy 120 percent of the demand created by the Massachusetts, Rhode Island and Connecticut RPSs combined through 2010. He goes further to point out that biomass generators in Canada and New York would also be eligible. All told, enough generation already exists in the region to supply 160 percent of the 2010 demand of all three RPSs, without the addition of any new capacity (Gulino 2005).

In short, if codified, the NOI and complimentary Advisory Rulings may render the Massachusetts RPS moot. Whether or not the proposals in the NOI are enacted, the short-term impact of their consideration will certainly be a dramatic slowing in investment in the region's renewables market. It is quite reasonable to expect that buyers will want shorter-term REC contracts at lower prices, lenders will hesitate to invest in projects whose revenue streams may evaporate as existing biomass capacity is retooled, and developers, expecting both results, will look elsewhere to invest their time and capital.

Conclusion

Even if the current proposed amendments to the qualification criteria for biomass are not enacted, such proposals will continue to be put forward as long as the growth in renewable capacity remains slow. Policymakers must be prepared to resist such pressures if they are to preserve the efficacy of the RPS. Indeed, the slow rate of growth observed to date is not a symptom of an intractable problem with the RPS. Rather, it presents a challenge that requires creative solutions— solutions crafted with a clear understanding of the state's renewable resources.

Renewable resources in Massachusetts, and importantly wind resources, are not as plentiful or accessible as they are in many states. In the short term, these constraints on the accessibility of the resource can be mitigated in at least two ways. In developing its siting policy, the state could choose to open some of its own land to development. As we have seen, intermittent parcels of state land present a critical constraint on the accessibility of the current resource, and so allowing some utilization of this land offers one of the clearest ways the state could support greater renewable energy production. This will surely be a complicated process, as the state continues to hold stakeholder meetings to solicit input and to weigh the various trade-offs that would be involved in allowing access to its land for such development. But if a compromise is reached, a policy allowing limited development on state land could make many projects viable that are currently too small to be feasible.

Ongoing education efforts will also be critical in fostering the public understanding necessary to allow for the utilization of what resource is available. The permits required for siting and developing projects in Massachusetts are extensive, and because Massachusetts is so densely populated, the number of stakeholders necessarily involved in the permitting process (directly or indirectly) will be greater than in many other places. The ongoing efforts by the MTC to increase public awareness— not only about the environmental benefits of renewable energy, but also about the economic benefits that accrue to communities hosting renewable energy facilities— are therefore a critical form of support. The better informed all the involved parties are, the more likely it is that the permitting process can reach a workable resolution in an efficient and truly participatory way, facilitating project development and therefore fulfillment of the RPS mandate. Concurrently, public education efforts effectively decrease permitting costs for renewables, making these facilities more competitive with conventional forms of energy production. A concerted public-education effort on the part of the state is thus very important, as many renewable projects in Massachusetts will likely be relatively small, and unable to shoulder the substantial additional cost of an extensive permitting process or multi-million dollar public outreach effort, like that undertaken by the Cape Wind Project.

In the longer term, the state must also focus its energies on supporting technological advancement, in the search for new ways to make more efficient use of the renewable resources available. Advancement in offshore wind technology would allow Massachusetts to utilize tremendous wind resources currently blowing over waters too deep to site turbines in. Similarly, advances in low-speed or distributed wind technology may significantly expand capacity in smaller, land-based sites in the years ahead. Already, biomass is likely to be a major contributor to the fulfillment of the Massachusetts RPS. But continued research into advanced biomass technologies such as gasification may yield both a more cost-effective source of electricity, and a competitive source of carbon neutral fuels for the region's transportation fleet. If the RPS is maintained, perhaps even more innovative solutions will develop to satisfy the market created.

Finally, for those most interested climate change, it must be borne in mind that the facilitation of a renewable energy market is a means to an end: the end being a reduction in the emission of greenhouse gasses. Movements in state policy towards directly limiting CO_2 production are critical complements to, and the eventual successor of, the renewable development incentives we have reviewed here. Focusing on the reduction of CO_2 emissions increases the number of paths by which the state may achieve this end. Eventually, the expansion of renewable energy generation in the state may be coupled with conservation and even sequestration to produce a truly sustainable pattern of energy production and consumption.

In the meanwhile, Massachusetts has enacted many forward-looking measures that have formed an effective network of market supports, increasing both the demand for renewable energy and the investment in developing its supply. By better understanding and addressing the resource constraints currently stalling the market, Massachusetts will be well positioned to meet its goals following its current path. However, if the state chooses to address the current slow growth of renewable resources by diluting its standards or easing the demand for renewable energy, it will lose what is essential to the RPS's success: the element of stability. Currently, the RPS ensures steady demand for renewables, encouraging investment in what remains a risky and emerging sector. If the state sends the signal that this demand is unreliable, investors and entrepreneurs will shift to more certain markets—inevitably further stalling or even halting development in the state. The policies Massachusetts chooses to enact now, in the first years its requirements come under pressure, will set the tone for the future by setting the expectations of the market. It now remains to be seen whether state policy makers will secure and expand upon the gains of the past decade, or reverse course just as their work finally begins to bear fruit. As the evidence of our impact on the global environment continues to mount, it is clear that their decision, and the decisions of many other policy makers throughout the country and indeed the world, will be of the greatest importance to us all.

Notes

1. NEPOOL was one of three such "power pools" formed to increase system reliability following the Great Northeast Blackout of 1965.

2. Massachusetts Department of Public Utilities. Investigation by the Department of Public Utilities upon its own motion commencing a Notice of Inquiry/Rulemaking, pursuant to 220 C.M.R. §§ 2.00 et seq., establishing the procedures to be followed in electric industry restructuring by electric companies subject to G.L. c. 164, D.P.U. 96–100.

3. An average capacity factor of 30% is assumed.

4. Certificates will be created quarterly on the 15th day of the calendar quarter (the "Creation Date") that is the second calendar quarter following the calendar quarter in which the Energy associated with a Certificate was generated. Therefore, for example, the Certifi-

cates associated with Energy generated in January, February and March of a year will be created on July 15 of that same year.

5. Company websites: Fitchburg Gas and Electric Light Company, Massachusetts Electric Company, NSTAR Electric, Western Massachusetts Electric Company.

6. For an average large industrial user in Massachusetts. A 1 cent decrease in the cost per kWh would save $30,000 a year, based on 2004 MDOER Migration data.

7. ...Said charge shall be the following amounts: three-quarters of one mill ($0.00075) per kilowatt-hour in calendar year 1998; one mill ($0.001) per kilowatt-hour in calendar year 1999; one and one-quarter mill ($0.00125) per kilowatt-hour in calendar year 2000; one mill ($0.001) per kilowatt-hour in calendar year 2001; three-quearers of one mill ($0.00075) per kilowatt-hour in calendar year 2002; and one-half of one mill ($0.0005) per kilowatt-hour in each calendar thereafter.

8. This does not include privately owned 'open space' such as privately owned summer camps. These are considered open space because of their function, but are actually unprotected. However, they compose such a small part of the open space commercial wind resource, they were left in the 'restricted' category.

References

Conference of New England Governors and Eastern Canadian Premiers. 2002. Report Update: Technology Options and Recommendations for Reducing Mercury and Acid Rain Precursor Emissions from Boilers.

Database of State Incentives for Renewable Energy. 2005. Public Benefits Funds: Massachusetts Renewable Energy Trust Fund. Available at *http://www.dsireusa.org/dsire/library/includes/seeallincentivetype.cfm?type=PBF&currentpageid=7&back=regtab* Accessed January 28, 2006.

Department of Energy. 2005. *Electric Industry Restructuring in Massachusetts; Updated April 2005.* Available at *www.eere.energy.gov/regions/northeast/docs/massachusetts_4_05_update.doc* Accessed October 6, 2005.

Department of Environmental Protection. (2001). *Emissions Standards for Power Plants 310 CMR 7.29.* Available at *www.mass.gov/dep/bwp/daqc/files/regs/729final.doc*

Donovan, Deborah. 2005. Reply Comments to Notice of Inquiry/Proposed Revisions to Biomass Regulations.

Energy Information Administration. 2005a. *Annual Energy Outlook 2005.* Available at *www.eia.doe.gov/oiaf/aeo/* Accessed June 12, 2005.

_____. 2005b. *Electric Power Industry Restructuring Fact Sheet.* Available at *http://www.eia.doe.gov/cneaf/electricity/page/fact_sheets/restructuring.html* Accessed June 12, 2005.

Environmental News Network. 2005. *Voluntary Green Power Purchasing up 1000 Percent in Five Years; Large Corporations Purchasers Driving Growth.* Available at *http://enn.com/biz.html?id=1193* Accessed October 27, 2005.

Fallon, Mike and Dwayne Breger. 2002. *The Woody Biomass Supply in Massachusetts: A Literature Based Estimate.* Available at *http://www.mass.gov/doer/programs/renew.htm* Accessed January 1, 2006.

Gulino, Daniel V. 2005. Notice of Inquiry/Stakeholder Follow Up.

Massachusetts Consumer Affairs and Business Regulation. 2005. *Electric Customer Migration Data.* Available at *http://www.mass.gov/portal/site/massgovportal/menuitem.8caa6 fb493e931c14db4a11030468a0c/?pageID=ocaterminal&L=5&L0=Home&L1=Consumer&L2 =Energy%2c+Fuel+%26+Utilities&L3=Electricity&L4=The+Power+Is+Yours%3a+Electricity+Industry+Restructuring&sid=Eoca&b=terminalcontent&f=_doer_pub_info_migrate &csid=Eoca* Accessed September 25, 2005.

Massachusetts Department of Public Utilities. 1995. *Investigation by the Department of Public Utilities.* Available at *http://www.magnet.state.ma.us/dpu/electric/95–30.pdf* Accessed April 24, 2005.

_____. 1996. *Model Rules and Legislative Proposal.* Available at *http://www.magnet.state.ma. us/dpu/restruct/96–100.pdf* Accessed April 24, 2005.

Massachusetts Department of Telecommunications and Energy. 1998. *Investigation by the Department of Telecommunications and Energy,* 6. Available at *http://www.mass.gov/ dte/restruct/96–100/master.pdf#DPU/DTE%2096–100%20Order%20issued%202/20/98* Accessed April 24, 2005.

Massachusetts Division of Energy Resources (MDOER). 2005a. CMR 225. Available at *www.mass.gov.doer/rps/225cmr.pdf* Accessed July 16, 2005.

_____. 2005b. Alternative Compliance Payment. *Available at www.mass.gov/doer/rps/acp.htm* Accessed January 27, 2006.

Massachusetts Environmental Policy Act Office Regulations. 1998a. Available at *http://www. mass.gov/envir/mepa/thirdlevelpages/meparegulations/301cmr1103.htm.* Accessed October 21, 2005.

_____. 1998b. EOEA Article 97 Land Disposition Policy. Available at *http://www.mass.gov/ envir/mepa/fourthlevelpages/article97policy.htm* Accessed October 28, 2005.

Massachusetts Legislature. 1997. *Electrical Utilities Restructuring Act.* Available at *http://www. mass.gov/legis/laws/seslaw97/s1970164.htm* Accessed May 2, 2005.

Massachusetts Register. 2002. Renewable Energy Portfolio Standard, 225 CMR 14.00. Available at *http://www.mass.gov/doer/rps/regs.htm* Accessed July 16, 2005.

New England Independent System Operator. 2005a. *Establishing the Grid.* Available at *http://www.eia.doe.gov/cneaf/electricity/page/fact_sheets/restructuring.html* Accessed June 12, 2005.

_____. 2005b. *Monthly Summary of Hourly Data.* Available at *http://www.iso-ne.com/markets/ hstdata/znl_info/monthly/index.html* Accessed October 29, 2005.

New England Power Pool Generation Information System Operating Rules (NEPOOL). 2005. NEPOOL GIS Rules, January 2006 version. Available at *http://www.neopolgis.com/* Accessed January 27, 2006.

Office for Commonwealth Development, Massachusetts Climate Protection Plan. 2004. Available at *http://www.mass.gov/portal/site/massgovportal/menuitem.1163aed4641a31c14db 4a11030468a0c/?pageID=ocdmodulechunk&L=1&L0=Home&sid=Eocd&b=terminalcon- tent&f=_ocdfrontpage_climateplanchuck&csid=Eocd* Accessed January 12, 2006.

Princeton Wind Farm Infrastructure Improvements. 2004. Certificate of the Secretary of Environmental Affairs on the Environmental Notification Form.

Resor, Pam. 2004. *An Act to Protect the Natural and Historic Resources of the Commonwealth.* MassAudbon. Available at *http://www.massaudbon.org/PDF/advocacy/leg0506/Article 97–2005–2006.pdf* Accessed November 10, 2005.

Shea, William E. and Others v. Boston Edison Company and Others. 2000. Docket number SJC-08160.

United States Department of Energy. 2005. *Electric Industry Restructuring in Massachusetts, Updated 2005.* Available at *www.eere.energy.gov/regions/northeast/docs/massachusetts_4 _05_update.doc* Accessed October 6, 2005.

9. Sustainable Energy in the Oceans: Offshore Wind in the U.S.

Christine Santora
Pew Institute for Ocean Science

Introduction

Offshore wind is a relatively new form of wind energy generation that combines the well-developed technology of onshore wind farms with desirable offshore conditions. In fact, it is considered by some to be the most promising and economically feasible of all renewable ocean energy prospects (Pelc and Fujita 2002; Hartnell and Milborrow 2000). A number of offshore wind farms are already operational in Europe, and several have been proposed in U.S. waters. There are, however, challenges in implementing such facilities in the United States. Legal, social, economic and environmental concerns have emerged, and technical issues with installation and transmission are still being addressed. Governance for this new ocean use was initially uncertain and is now being determined at the federal and state levels. This chapter will review offshore wind as an energy source, discuss various governance issues, and examine the role of states— particularly those with active offshore wind proposals— in the regulation and implementation of this new offshore use.

Why Offshore Wind?

Wind energy is one of the cleanest forms of energy generation, and has become cost-competitive with traditional fossil fuels (Pelc and Fujita

2002) in recent years with the development of technology and improvement of market conditions. Offshore locations are advantageous for wind energy generation, generally because winds are stronger and more consistent than over land. One study off the coast of Denmark showed that wind speeds located 2 km and 11 km offshore were approximately 30 percent and 50 percent higher than a site located 10m off the coast (Pryor and Barthelmie 2002).[1] Since wind power increases exponentially with speed, higher wind velocities over the ocean means increased potential for energy generation — up to 70 percent higher than on land (Pelc and Fujita 2002, DTI 2002). Persistence, or the duration of surface wind speeds within specified classes, is also higher offshore (Pryor and Barthelmie 2002). Turbulence, on the other hand, is lower because wind is unobstructed by landforms or infrastructure, and because the difference in temperature between the sea surface and air is smaller than the temperature difference over land (Krohn 2002; Pelc and Fujita 2002). Less turbulence translates into less wear and tear on wind turbines, lower maintenance costs (Krohn 2002; Hartland 2003) and more electricity generated per square meter of swept rotor area (Musial and Butterfield 2004). Other reasons for going offshore include short supplies of land-based sites and vast quantities of the resource (Krohn 2002).

Spatial elements also give offshore wind an advantage, such as the ability to transport and erect large structures (Musial and Butterfield 2004). While land-based infrastructure and equipment can limit the size and capacity of turbines handled, such issues are less problematic offshore where installation requirements can be met more easily. Additionally, space limitations for the overall footprint of a wind farm that exist on land are less of an obstacle to siting wind farms offshore.

Offshore wind design is similar to its land-based counterpart (Pelc and Fujita 2002), and its technological feasibility has been demonstrated (Hartnell and Milborrow 2000). Current offshore wind turbine manufacturers have taken conventional land-based turbines, upgraded their electrical and corrosion control systems to "marinize" them, and placed them on concrete bases or steel monopiles to anchor them to the seabed (Musial and Butterfield 2004). An offshore substation then "boosts the collection system voltage" (Musial and Butterfield 2004), and high voltage cables are installed under the seabed to transport electricity from the wind farm to the land-based grid. Other modifications have recently appeared, such as a design change that increases rotor speed by 10 percent, the addition of platforms to allow helicopter access, and the use of camouflage paint that make the turbines less visible (Krohn 2002).

Challenges exist, however, in perfecting this technology in the marine environment without rendering it cost-prohibitive. Construction is more complicated, and structures must be considerably strengthened to withstand corrosion from saltwater and added loads from waves and ice (Musial and Butterfield 2004). In addition, the fixed costs of undersea cables, steel foundations, installation, maintenance, and grid connections are higher (Krohn 2002; Russell 2004). These increased complexities and costs mean that offshore wind developments must be larger in terms of both turbine size and project scale (Krohn 2002; Musial and Butterfield 2004). Economies of scale favor large wind farms; optimal size of an offshore wind project is likely to be 100 MW or greater, with large turbines of 2 MW and above (Krohn 2002).

Siting Issues

Most offshore wind farms to date have been constructed in shallow depths where waters are relatively protected. While several European countries such as Denmark, the Netherlands, Germany, and the U.K. have abundant shallow sites, the U.S. is more limited in shallow water areas. The U.S. has abundant offshore wind resources; however estimates indicate that only about 10 percent are in shallow water, while the rest are in waters 30 meters (m) and deeper (Musial and Butterfield 2004).

Deeper offshore waters have stronger winds but higher investment costs due to installation, transmission and monitoring (Gaudiosi 1999). At depths less than 30 m, established foundation technologies can be deployed without significant research and development effort. Offshore wind developments planned for deeper waters will require significant technological advances (Musial and Butterfield 2004).

In order to fully take advantage of offshore wind resources, especially in the U.S., new technologies such as floating platforms will likely be needed to deploy wind turbines in deeper waters. These structures would replace conventional steel monopiles or concrete bases, and must be able to provide enough buoyancy to support the weight of the turbine and to restrain motions caused by wind and wave forces (Musial and Butterfield 2004). A major challenge for deep water wind turbines will be to merge the developed but expensive technologies borne of the oil and gas industry with the experience and low-cost economic factors driving the shallow water offshore wind energy industry (Musial and Butterfield 2004). Since offshore wind farms rely on underwater cables to transmit power to a land-based grid, the further out a wind farm is located, the more expensive and difficult transmission issues will be.

Despite challenges for wind power generation in the marine environment, the physical characteristics of offshore locations and vast quantities of the resource make offshore wind development attractive. For the U.S. in particular, offshore wind presents an opportunity to site new energy facilities in closer proximity to major load centers— particularly the energy-constrained northeast (Offshore Wind Energy Collaborative 2005). Geography can play a major role in renewable energy feasibility. The Great Plains, for instance, may offer large quantities of potential wind energy, but storage capacities and transmission capabilities are limited. The U.S. Department of Energy estimates that there are more than 900,000 MW of potential wind energy off the coasts of the United States, a number that approaches the total current installed U.S. electrical capacity (Offshore Wind Energy Collaborative 2005). Another estimate suggests that wind farms off the coast of the U.S. could provide up to 54 GW of capacity, or 102 TW h/yr of energy, with most production coming from the northwest, northeast, and Gulf of Mexico (Pelc and Fujita 2002). Because the U.S. population is concentrated at the coasts, plentiful offshore wind resources are located fortuitously close to densely populated areas with high energy demands (Hartland 2003; Musial and Butterfield 2004). Offshore wind may therefore be able to provide large coastal cities and population centers with renewable energy access that was previously limited or nonexistent.

Governance

Until the first offshore wind proposals emerged, neither the federal government nor the states had experience in permitting or regulating offshore wind farms. When faced with the first offshore wind farm proposal in federal waters, the government used a "default" regulatory process using applicable laws and jurisdictions to respond in the absence of a specific and comprehensive legal framework. Governance for this new ocean energy use, including permitting, regulation and agency jurisdiction is still being developed, and is just starting to be addressed by the federal government and coastal states.

Offshore wind presents a unique combination of legal and management issues. Unlike most land parcels, oceans and submerged lands are not subject to traditional private property rights. Rather, they are held in the public trust. The Public Trust Doctrine was adopted in the U.S. as part of English common law, and for centuries it has preserved the rights of the public to use tidal waters for commerce, navigation, and fisheries

(Christie and Hildreth 1999). In the 1950's the doctrine was further codified through the Submerged Lands Act, which gave coastal states title to submerged lands and resources from the shoreline out to three miles, including the "right and power to manage, lease, develop, and use" them (43 USC 1301). The Outer Continental Shelf Lands Act (OCSLA) established federal control of the outer continental shelf (OCS) beyond three miles (43 USC 1301).

Historically, leasing has been used to validate the use of public lands by private entities. For instance, OCSLA authorizes the Secretary of Interior to lease OCS lands to the highest bidder for mineral production, and stipulates a detailed regulatory framework for leasing and production. When a publicly-owned resource is made available to the private sector, public compensation, or resource rent, is usually collected. For offshore oil and gas uses, lessees make three categories of payments: bonus bids when a lease is issued; rental payments before a lease produces, and royalties on any production from the lease. From 1953 to 2002, these payments have contributed approximately $145 billion in federal revenues (USCOP 2004). This principle has also clearly been established on public lands, where the government collects rent from ranchers through grazing fees, royalties from timber and mining companies, and both rent and royalties from land-based wind development (USCOP 2004; Firestone et al. 2004).

Until recently, there was no similar framework for renewable energy activities on the OCS; previous law specified that leasing apply to "extractable" resources only. The nature of offshore wind as a renewable resource in the marine environment exempted it from existing lease programs. The Energy Policy Act of 2005 recently amended OCSLA to include alternative energy sources. The Act also granted the Department of Interior, through the Mineral Management Service (MMS), new responsibilities over offshore renewable energy projects. Section 388 of the Act specifically authorizes MMS to: act as the lead agency for renewable energy uses on OCS lands; ensure consultation with states and other stakeholders; grant easements, leases, or right-of ways for renewable energy uses of the federal OCS; issue regulations on such leasing programs; enforce violations; require financial surety so that facilities are properly removed; and regulate, monitor, and determine fair return to the nation. The Act also establishes leasing on a competitive basis and revenue sharing between the federal government and affected states (those with coastlines located within 15 miles of a project's center). As of this writing, MMS has not yet published regulations for a renewable energy leasing program on the OCS, and is just beginning to transition into the lead regulatory agency for offshore wind projects. The MMS has stated that it will assume oversight of existing projects (e.g. those that have already been proposed — the Cape Wind project off the coast of Massachusetts and the Long Island Power Authority project off the coast of Long Island, NY) while developing a longer-term strategy for offshore wind.

Aside from the recent changes brought about by the Energy Policy Act in 2005, other laws that govern the use of the OCS for offshore wind energy projects are the Rivers and Harbors Act (RHA) and the National Environmental Policy Act (NEPA). The former regulates obstructions to navigable waters. Section 10 of the RHA establishes permit requirements to prevent unauthorized obstruction or alteration of navigable waters, and gives authority to grant such a permit to the U.S Army Corps of Engineers (USACE) via Secretary of the Army. Section 4(f) of OCSLA extends this authority to OCS lands, including "artificial islands, installations, and other devices." Offshore wind developers must apply to the USACE for a Section 10 permit in order to gain authorization for their projects.

NEPA governs the environmental review process for proposed offshore wind projects. NEPA requires federal agencies to prepare an Environmental Impact Statement (EIS) for major federal actions that significantly affect the environment. An EIS identifies and evaluates the impacts of a proposed action, and describes a range of alternatives. In the case of offshore wind, the USACE has acted as the lead agency conducting the EIS; however the MMS is now transitioning to take over the role. Many other federal, state and local agencies with jurisdiction over affected resources are consulted in the review process as well. A more comprehensive review of those agencies and other federal laws that apply to offshore wind (e.g. Migratory Bird Treaty Act, Magnuson-Stevens Fishery Management and Conservation Act, etc.) can be found elsewhere (Santora et al. 2004; USACE 2004).

Role of States

States will have a significant role in offshore wind development, whether a project is proposed in federal or state waters. Where the entire turbine array, or wind farm, is located in federal waters, states still have permitting and regulatory authority over parts of the project occurring in state waters, such as the undersea cables connecting the wind farm to the land-based grid. States also have authority to review the project to ensure that it is consistent with its coastal policies. To date, the active proposals for offshore wind located in federal waters exist off the coasts of Massachusetts and New York. At the time of this writing, Texas announced that it granted a lease to a Louisiana-based company for a 150 MW wind farm in its state waters. In future cases such as Texas's where an entire offshore wind farm is proposed within three miles of a shoreline, states will have an increased role.

States have regulatory authority over projects in federal waters under the Clean Water Act and the Coastal Zone Management Act. Section 401 of the Clean Water Act requires that an applicant for a federal license or permit provide a state water quality certification, showing that the facility or project will comply with the Act and water quality standards. Section 404 of the CWA regulates the discharge of dredged and fill material into navigable waters of the U.S.; the USACE and the Environmental Protection Agency jointly administer this program. A dredge and fill permit may or may not be needed for offshore wind farm projects, depending on the type of activity proposed to install the turbines and cables. For instance, the jet-plowing technique to be used in the proposed wind farms off of Massachusetts and New York will not require a dredge and fill permit (Santora et al. 2004; New York State/USACE 2005).

States also play a role in authorizing offshore wind projects in federal waters under the Coastal Zone Management Act (16 USC 1456). Under Section 307 of the Act, if a state has a federally approved Coastal Zone Management Plan (CZMP), it has authority to determine whether federal activities in the coastal zone are consistent with their CZMP. The precedent for this is clear; after a Supreme Court ruling in *Secretary of Interior v. California* (464 U.S. 312 (1984)) that excluded OCS activities in federal waters from state consistency review, Congress amended the law to include federal activities outside a state's coastal zone. Thus, states have some assurance that projects in federal waters will not result in a violation of state CZMPs (Flynn 2005). Through the CZMA, states have statutory authority to reject a proposal if it conflicts with state coastal policies and values. On the other hand, the opposite does not hold true; if a state seeks to *encourage* an activity, such as offshore wind development, consistency cannot be used to force the federal government to license a project (Russell 2004).

If a state determines the proposed activity to be consistent with their CZMP, permits are issued by the state CZM authorities accordingly. If the activity is found inconsistent, the state may negotiate conditions for issuing a permit. One benefit of the consistency provision is that states may leverage their consistency review power to revise and improve projects (Russell 2004). The 2000 amendments to the CZMA emphasize the role of negotiation; applicants are directed to cooperate with state agencies to develop conditions that are suitable to the consistency review. If negotiations fail, a state must describe the unsatisfied conditions in the consistency objection it makes to federal authorities (Russell 2004). If a state ultimately finds a project inconsistent with its coastal policies, an applicant can appeal the decision to the Secretary of Commerce. The Secretary may overturn a state's finding only if the proposal is found to be consistent with objectives of the CZMA or is essential for national security purposes. The most recent regulatory changes to the CZMA in 2000 identify energy facility siting as an activity that "significantly" advances the national interest (Russell 2004)—this may have substantial implications for a state's ability to use consistency as a way to veto an offshore wind project in federal waters.

State regulation of offshore wind through consistency certification will not be uniform. Under the CZMA, there are three acceptable frameworks for how a state program can be structured: (1) direct management of land and water uses by a centralized CZM state agency; (2) state establishment of criteria and standards for local implementation, subject to administrative review and enforcement; and (3) local establishment and implementation of regulations, with state level review of program decisions (Flynn 2005). While a few states, such as California and Rhode Island, have created centralized coastal zone management agencies, most state CZM programs are "networked," consisting of various pre-existing laws and management programs with agency roles defined through policies or Memoranda of Understanding (Beatley et al. 2002; Flynn 2005). For instance, in Massachusetts, a variety of different agencies have a role in coastal zone management, including the Departments of Environmental Protection, Environmental Management, Fisheries and Wildlife, and Food and Agriculture. Other agencies such as the Metropolitan District Commission, the Energy Facilities Siting Board, and the Executive Office of Transportation and Construction are also involved (Flynn 2005). Depending on the affected state, offshore wind projects can be subject to permitting authority located within multiple state and local level agencies (Flynn 2005).

Consistency provisions could possibly lead to *interstate* conflicts when a state's activity that requires a federal permit or approval is not consistent with the coastal program policies of another state. Referring to a conflict between North Carolina and Virginia over water being drawn from a lake between its borders, the Secretary of Commerce found that while the CZMA does not give one state direct authority to control activities in another, it does grant states the right to seek conditions on or prohibit the issuance of federal permits that would "affect" their state or further degrade their coasts. As a precaution against states' unrestrained use of this authority, an applicant can appeal for override by the Secretary of Commerce (Christie and Hildreth 1999). While this has yet not been directly challenged by offshore wind, it is feasible that offshore wind projects proposed along state borders could pose a conflict, especially in areas with dense borders such as the Mid-Atlantic and New England.

Some argue that the CZMA is ill equipped to handle offshore wind, and is actually structured to disfavor offshore wind development. Russell (2004) argues that since the benefits of wind energy are realized well beyond coastal borders (e.g. addressing climate change and energy security), the perceived costs to local communities (e.g. aesthetics, effects on other coastal users) might outweigh the benefits, causing offshore wind to be "inconsistent" or undesirable with CZM policies. Another shortfall is that CZMPs themselves do not yet offer specific guidelines on offshore wind (for instance, where development is appropriate) within state jurisdictions.

Examples of State Laws
That Apply to Offshore Wind

Individual state laws and regulations will also apply to offshore wind, but will vary among states, since each has different coastal, environmental, and energy policies. Offshore wind developers will have to comply with state and local requirements such as wetland permits, building permits, zoning ordinances, subaqueous permits, and state National Pollutant Discharge Elimination System permits (Firestone et al. 2004). Although laws and regulations to protect the environment and manage coastal resources among states may be similar, subtle differences in code and permitting procedures could add conflict, confusion, and inconsistency to the general process of siting offshore projects (Firestone et al. 2004).

The following sections outline which state laws may apply based on the experiences of Massachusetts and New York, the only two states that are currently in the process of reviewing offshore wind proposals adjacent to their waters.

MASSACHUSETTS

Cape Wind Associates, LLC (Cape Wind), first proposed an offshore wind farm in Nantucket Sound, outside Massachusetts state waters, in 2001. This large scale wind energy generation project has been sited in a 24-square mile area in federal waters, and was chosen by Cape Wind based on intensity of sustained winds, water depths, and its accessibility to the transmission grid. The project would be comprised of 130 offshore wind turbine generators (WTGs), a centrally located Electrical Service Platform (ESP), and transmission cables that would connect the wind farm to the mainland grid on Cape Cod. Each turbine would extend approximately 420 feet above the water surface, to the top end of the turbine blade. WTGs would be placed in parallel rows, spaced between 0.34–0.54 nautical miles apart (USACE 2004), and would produce energy independently with interconnecting cables terminating on the ESP. From there, two 115 kV submarine transmission circuits would then bring the energy from the ESP to the mainland, at a distance of 12.2 miles (USACE 2004). The wind farm will be capable of producing an average annual output of approximately 170 megawatts, with a maximum capacity of 454 megawatts (USACE 2004). While the entire project has yet to receive full approval, Cape Wind has already gained permission from the USACE to construct a research/data tower. ISO New England, which operates the transmission grid and wholesale power market from Maine to Connecticut, has also granted approval for the Cape Wind project to connect to the regional grid.

Permission to construct the offshore wind farm depends on compliance with applicable state laws and the cooperation of many state and local agencies that have jurisdiction over the project. Table 1 outlines the different state, regional, and local agencies involved in permitting the Cape Wind project, where their jurisdiction comes from, and what their requirements are of an offshore wind project.

Many of these laws and jurisdictions are straightforward; state and local agencies already have laws to govern private development and to protect natural resources. What is notable about offshore wind is that, initially, it was uncertain how permitting and review processes would proceed since a direct regulatory framework for offshore wind was non-existent. Since the Cape Wind proposal was the first in the U.S., the state of Massachusetts was the first to address these jurisdictional and permitting issues for offshore wind. State and local officials worked closely with federal agencies from the start, and found ways to make the process more efficient. For instance, Massachusetts requires that projects undertake a state environmental review if a project requiring state permits is likely to cause environmental damage. That review process, MEPA, includes an analysis of project alternatives, environmental impact assessments, determinations that the project is consistent with state regulations and policies, and appropriate mitigation measures. In this case, since the federal EIS under NEPA and the state MEPA reviews are similar, state and federal authorities decided to reduce overlap and ensure consistency with one another by issuing one review document. The federal EIS for Cape Wind will therefore fulfill the regional, state and federal environmental assessment requirements.

Table 1: Agencies, Laws, and Requirements
for Offshore Wind in Massachusetts

	Agency (legal authority in parentheses)	Requirement
State Environmental Impact Review	Massachusetts Environmental Policy Act Office (MassachusettsGeneral Law Chapter 30, Section 61–62H; State Regulations: 301 CMR 11.00)	• Environmental Notification Form (ENF) • Draft and Final Environmental Impact Reports (DEIR/FEIR) • Issuance of Certificate
State Permit Reviews	Massachusetts Energy Facility Siting Board (164 MGL Section 69G-J; State Regulations: 980 CMR 1.00–12.00; MOU with Executive Office of Environmental Affairs relative to the state CZMP)	• Petition to Construct Jurisdictional Facilities • Certificate of Environmental Impact and Public Need
	Massachusetts Department of Environmental Protection (DEP) Waterways Program (MGL Chapter 91; State Regulations: 310 CMR 9.00)	• Chapter 91 Waterways License
	Massachusetts Department of Environmental Protection (DEP) Wetlands Program (Section 27 of Mass Clean Water Act; MGL c. 21 26–53, State Regulations 314 CMR 4.00 and 9.00)	• Water Quality Certification • Superceding Order of Conditions
	Massachusetts Coastal Zone Management Office (Federal Coastal Zone Management Act 16 USC 1451–1465; State CZMA 301 CMR 20.00–21.00)	• Federal Consistency Certification
	Massachusetts Highway Department (MGL Chapter 81, Section 21)	• Permit to Access State Highway and Access Agreement
	Massachusetts Historical Commission/Massachusetts	• Permit for Upland Reconnaissance

Table 1: Agencies, Laws, and Requirements for
Offshore Wind in Massachusetts *(continued)*

	Agency (legal authority in parentheses	Requirement
	State Archaeologist (MGL Chapter 9, Section 27C; State Regulations 950 CMR 70.00)	Archaeological Survey • Permit for Upland Intensive Archaeological Survey
	Massachusetts Board of Underwater Archaeology (MGL Chapter 6, Section 179–180; State Regulations 312 CMR 2.0–2.15)	• Reconnaissance Permit • Excavation Permit
State Regulatory Reviews	Massachusetts Division of Marine Fisheries (Federal Magnuson Stevens Act, 16 USC 1856; State fisheries statute, MGL Chapter 130; State Regulations: 322 CMR Sections 1.00–12.00)	• Regulatory Review
	Massachusetts Department of Conservation and Recreation (132A MGL Sections 13, 16, 18; State Regulations 302 CMR 5.00)	• Regulatory Review
	State Historic Preservation Office (MGL Chapter 9 Section 27C; State Regulations 950 CMR 70.0 and 71.00)	• Regulatory Review
Regional Jurisdiction and Regulatory Review	Cape Cod Commission (Cape Cod Commission Act; Regional Policy Plan)	• Development of Regional Impact Review
Local Jurisdiction and Regulatory Reviews	Yarmouth Conservation Commission (MGL Chapter 131, Section 40; State Regulations 310 CMR 10.00; Rivers Protection Act, Chapter 258 of 1996 Acts; Yarmouth Wetlands Bylaws and Regulations Chapter 143)	• Notice of Intent Issuance of Order of Conditions

---

**Table 1: Agencies, Laws, and Requirements for
Offshore Wind in Massachusetts *(continued)***

Agency (legal authority in parentheses	Requirement
Barnstable Conservation Commission (MGL Chapter 131, Section 40; State Regulations 310 CMR 10.00; Rivers Protection Act, Chapter 258 of 1996 Acts; Barnstable Wetlands Protection Ordinance Article 27)	• Notice of Intent Issuance of Order of Conditions
Yarmouth Department of Public Works (Local Regulations)	• Street Opening Permit
Barnstable Department of Public Works (Local Regulations)	• Street Opening Permit

Adapted from (USACE 2004)

Sections 6.0, 8.0 and 9.0 of the federal Draft EIS are specific to the state MEPA and CCC requirements. It should be noted that the MMS — originally a cooperating agency in the review process — has taken over as the lead regulatory agency for the EIS. The USACE, however, remains a key agency due to the required Section 10 permit under the RHA. MMS will also complete leasing arrangements for the Cape Wind project.

NEW YORK

A second offshore wind farm has been proposed in federal waters off of Long Island, NY. Long Island Power Authority (LIPA) and Long Island Offshore Wind Park, LLC, submitted an application in the spring of 2005 to the USACE for an offshore wind generating facility in the Atlantic Ocean, 3.6 miles south of Jones Beach Island (USACE Public Notice 2005–00365-L4). This proposed facility is smaller than Cape Wind; it would consist of 40 WTGs over an 8-square mile area (USACE Public Notice 2005–00365-L4). This project is still in its initial stages, and is far behind Cape Wind in the approval process. Since the activity is proposed in federal waters, it is likely that the USACE (or MMS, when they actively resume responsibility of the project) will use the Cape Wind EIS as a model. In fact, many have argued that a Programmatic EIS should be used when evaluating proposed offshore wind projects (e.g. Santora et al. 2004).

Like Massachusetts, New York has its own state laws that will apply to offshore wind. According to the application submitted to the USACE, the developers must obtain permits from the New York State Department of Environmental Conservation, Office of General Services, Department of State, and Department of Public Service Commission (USACE Permit Application 2005). The USACE has also indicated that the project will need review by the New York State Public Service Commission, New York State Office of Parks, Recreation, and Historic Preservation, Town of Babylon, and Town of Oyster Bay (USACE Public Notice 2005–00365-L4). Other state agencies may have regulatory review or will act as cooperating agencies in the EIS process; a full analysis of applicable state laws and agencies will be discussed in the EIS when it is completed. Table 2 outlines the preliminary scope of agencies identified by the USACE as being involved in offshore wind in the state of New York.

An interesting part of the way NY deals with offshore wind is through an explicit lease or easement for any part of the facility occurring within the three mile state jurisdiction. Not only does an application have to be submitted to the Office of General Services, but the NYSDEC must review any proposed lease, easement or permit to ensure protection of the environment or natural resources. The Secretary of State may also review such proposals with regard to coastal management (Bailey et al. 2003).

A legal analysis completed in 2003 for the applicant, LIPA, suggests that additional New York state laws and jurisdictions may apply. The analysis maintains that in addition to the DEC's responsibilities under the Tidal Wetlands Act, the agency also has jurisdiction under NYS ECL Article 15, "Use and Protection of Waters" and under NYS ECL Article 34, "Coastal Erosion Management." A previous report indicated that the New York State Public Authorities Control Board may also have authority to approve the use of funds if an offshore wind farm is to be built, owned and operated by LIPA (Freedman 2001).

Significantly absent in the above table, but mentioned in the 2003 legal analysis, is the State Environmental Quality Review Act (SEQR) (modeled after NEPA and similar to Massachusetts's MEPA). SEQR requires state and local agencies to conduct an environmental review when considering permits or approvals. In this case, if the project falls under certain state law (NYSPSL Article VII and X proceedings), it will be exempt from SEQR. This does not mean that the project will be exempt from NEPA, however. In cases where both NEPA and SEQR apply, there are statutory

**Table 2: Agencies, Laws, and Requirements
for Offshore Wind in New York**

	Agency (legal authority in parentheses)	Requirement
State Permit Reviews	Department of Environmental Conservation (Tidal Wetlands Act, NYS Environmental Conservation Law Article 25)	• Navigable Waters (Excavation and Fill) • Tidal Wetlands • 401 Water Quality Certification
	Office of General Services (NYS Public Lands, Article 6)	• Lease, License, Easement or other Real Property Interest (for state owned lands under water)
	Department of State (Waterfront Revitalization of Coastal Areas and Inland Waterways Act, Article 42 NYS Exec. Law Section 910 *et seq.*)	• Coastal Zone Consistency Certification
	Department of Public Service Commission (NYS Public Service Law, Article VII)	• Article VII Certificate, "Opinion and Order adopting Joint Proposal and Granting Certificate of Environmental Compatibility and Public Need" for underwater cables
	Office of Parks, Recreation and Historic Preservation	• Easement
Local Jurisdiction and Regulatory Reviews	Town of Babylon	• Easement
	Town of Oyster Bay	• Easement

Source: (USACE Permit Application 2005; USACE Public Notice 2005)

mandates on both the state and federal levels for cooperation in planning, environmental research and studies, public hearings, and environmental assessments—similar to the approach currently being taken in Massachusetts.

State Coastal Policies

Many of the subtle differences in the way states handle offshore wind will involve coastal policy. In fact, the basis of the federal Coastal Zone Management Act is to allow states to develop appropriate coastal programs and policies based on their particular coastal and human resources. Table 3 gives a brief illustration of the different state coastal policies that apply to offshore wind in Massachusetts and New York. In each case, the offshore wind proposal will be evaluated against each of these policies to ensure that the project is compliant. Local coastal policy will also apply; for instance, the Cape Wind project must comply with the Cape Cod Commission's Regional Policy Plan. In New York, local policies also exist; however, the LIPA project has not been cited in any municipalities with such Local Waterfront Revitalization Programs.

A full analysis of how offshore wind proposals may or may not be consistent with the above coastal policies is beyond the scope of this chapter. However, the Draft EIS (DEIS) for the Cape Wind project indicates that the project is consistent. The DEIS states that the project "has been designed to be consistent with the CZM program policies and principles" and gives a description of how the project complies with each of the relevant policies (USACE 2004). Similarly, the New York State Coastal Management Program has released a preliminary Federal Consistency Assessment Form that explains how the proposed LIPA project would comply with each applicable coastal policy in New York.

Discussion

Regardless of whether an offshore wind farm is proposed in federal or state waters, such development will undoubtedly have an effect on coastal states. A coastal state's position on ocean governance issues will usually reflect the interest and concerns of its coastal population—meaning that the state will tend to be more concerned about the well-being of fisheries, tourism, water quality, and beaches than the federal government (Cicin-Sain and Knecht 2000). Considering that offshore wind projects will

Table 3: Coastal Policies in Massachusetts and New York

Massachusetts Coastal Policies Applying to Offshore Wind	New York Coastal Policies Applying to Offshore Wind
Habitat Policy #1— Protect coastal resource areas including salt marshes, shellfish beds, dunes, beaches, barrier beaches, salt ponds, eelgrass beds and fresh water wet-lands for their important role as natural habitats.	Policy #2: Facilitate the siting of water dependent uses and facilities on or adjacent to coastal waters.
Energy Policy #1— For coastally dependent energy facilities, con-sider siting in alternative coastal locations. For non-coastally depen-dent energy facilities, consider sit-ing in areas outside of the coastal zone. Weigh the environmental and safety impacts of locating proposed energy facilities at alternative sites.	Policy #7: Significant coastal fish and wildlife habitats will be protected, preserved, and where practical restored so as to maintain their viability as habitats.
Energy Management Principle #1— Encourage energy conservation and the use of alternative sources such as solar and wind power in order to assist in meeting the energy needs of the Commonwealth.	Policy #8: Protect fish and wildlife resources in the coastal area from the introduction of hazardous wastes and other pollutants which bioac-cumulate in the food chain or which cause significant sublethal or lethal effect on those resources.
Public Access Policy #1— Ensure that developments proposed near existing public recreation sites minimize their adverse effects.	Policy #11, 12, 17: Buildings and other structures will be sited in the coastal area so as to minimize damage to property and the endangering of human lives caused by flooding and erosion; Activities or development in the coastal area will be undertaken so as to minimize damage to natural resources and property from flood-ing and erosion by protecting natural protective features including beaches, dunes, barrier islands and bluffs; Non-structural measures to minimize damage to natural resources and property from flooding and erosion shall be used whenever possible.

Massachusetts Coastal Policies Applying to Offshore Wind	New York Coastal Policies Applying to Offshore Wind
Protected Areas Policy #3 — Ensure that proposed developments in or near designated or registered districts or sites respect the preservation intent of the designation and that potential adverse effects are minimized.	Policy #15: Mining, excavation or dredging in coastal waters shall not significantly interfere with the natural coastal processes which supply beach materials to land adjacent to such waters and shall be undertaken in a manner which will not cause an increase in erosion of such land.
Coastal Hazard Policy #1— Preserve, protect, restore, and enhance the beneficial functions of storm damage prevention and flood control provided by natural coastal landforms, such as dunes, beaches, barrier beaches, coastal bank, land subject to coastal storm flowage, salt marshes, and land under the ocean.	Policy #19, 20: Protect, maintain, and increase the level and types of access to public water-related recreation resources and facilities; Access to the publicly-owned foreshore and to lands immediately adjacent to the foreshore or the water's edge that are publicly owned shall be provided and it shall be provided in a manner compatible with adjoining land uses.
Coastal Hazard Policy #2 — Ensure construction in water bodies and contiguous land areas will minimize interference with water circulation and sediment transport. Approve permits for flood or erosion control projects only when it has been determined that there will be no significant adverse effects on the project site or adjacent or downcoast areas.	Policy #23: Protect, enhance, and restore structures, districts, areas or sites that are of significance in the history, architecture, archaeology or culture of the state, its communities, or the nation.
Ports policy #3 — Preserve and enhance the capacity of Designated Port Areas to accommodate water-dependent industrial uses, and prevent the exclusion of such uses from tidelands and any other DPA lands over which a state agency exerts control by virtue of ownership, regulatory authority, or other legal jurisdiction.	Policy #24, 25: Prevent impairment of scenic resources of statewide significance; Protect, restore or enhance natural and man-made resources which are not identified as being of statewide significance, but which contribute to the overall scenic quality of the coastal area.

Table 3: Coastal Policies in Massachusetts and New York *(continued)*	
Massachusetts Coastal Policies Applying to Offshore Wind	**New York Coastal Policies Applying to Offshore Wind**
	Policy #27: Decisions on the siting and construction of major energy facilities in the coastal area will be based on public energy needs, compatibility of such facilities with the environment, and the facilities.
	Policy #29: Encourage the development of energy resources on the OCS, in Lake Erie and in other water bodies, and ensure the environmental safety of such activities.
	Policy #37: Best management practices will be utilized to minimize the non-point discharge of excess nutrients, organics and eroded soils into coastal waters.
	Policy #30: Municipal, industrial, and commercial discharge of pollutants, including, but not limited to, toxic and hazardous substances, into coastal waters will conform to state and national water quality standards.
	Policy #44: Preserve and protect tidal and freshwater wetlands and preserve the benefits derived from these areas.

have to traverse through state waters, connect to mainland grids, co-exist with adjacent land and ocean uses, and be viewed from state shorelines, it is reasonable to expect that state and local governments should have a substantial role in their regulation.

Martin and Smith (2004) point out that certain sections of prevailing offshore oil and gas legislation affirm the rights of state and local governments in decision-making. For instance, subsection 1332 (4) of OCSLA requires that states receive sufficient assistance in dealing with adverse consequences from a given use of the OCS, and subsection 1332 (5) requires that the rights and responsibilities of all states (and where appropriate, local governments) to preserve and protect their marine, human, and coastal environments should be considered and recognized (Martin and Smith 2004). Amendments were made in 1978 to OCSLA, partly to "bring state and local governments into much clearer and statutorily specified consultative roles at various points" in the decision-making process (USCOP 2004, 313). Because of those amendments, and the 1990 amendments to the CZMA, leasing for oil and gas on the OCS now requires consultation with coastal states and localities at a number of points in the decision making process. While the Energy Policy Act (Section 388 (a)(7)) asserts coordination and consultation with a Governor or executive of any state or local government affected by a lease, easement, or right-of-way for a renewable energy project on the OCS, specifics have yet to be determined. Regulations for oil and gas identify specific points in the process where state and local governments are involved, and offshore wind regulations should do the same.

While states cannot have direct control over developments on the federal OCS, they can be proactive about how they manage proposals in their waters. For instance, Rhode Island has identified in its Coastal Resources Management Program six zones that are directly linked to the characteristics of adjacent shorelines, based on the concept that activities on the adjacent mainland are the primary determinant of the uses and qualities of any specific water site (RICRMC 1996). Type 1 waters are those adjacent to natural, undisturbed areas and are considered zones of "conservation," where many uses are prohibited, including dock construction. Types 2 and 3 have increased uses, such as dock construction or boating. Type 4 waters are areas known as "multipurpose," and signify open waters of the bays and sounds where a wide variety of uses are permitted. Type 5 waters are those of commercial and recreational harbors, and Type 6 waters are commercial navigation channels or adjacent to industrial waterfronts, where precedence is given to industrial and commercial activities (RICRMC 1996). This example highlights how one state classified its waters to allow for appropriate development and human use while accounting for environmental protection and compatibility with adjacent lands.

Such planning can also take place on a regional level, as recommended by the U.S. Commission on Ocean Policy (2004). While the federal government is clearly attempting to better manage offshore wind, existing laws are still inadequate to manage large-scale offshore wind development on a regional or national basis. Unless federal and state authorities establish decision criteria to evaluate proposed offshore wind developments, no standards will exist on which to base permitting decisions. Similar scale projects require specific decision criteria, which are usually detailed by

Congress and tailored to the issues associated with the type of activity proposed (Martin and Smith 2004). No guidelines or standards are in place for operating, maintaining, or evaluating offshore wind facilities (Martin and Smith 2004) on either the federal or state levels, and regional coastal areas have not been inventoried to determine where development is most and least appropriate (Santora et al. 2004).

The latter problem is a significant one. With no system to address the planning of offshore wind on a broader scale, it is impossible to ensure that such facilities will not cause cumulative impacts regionally (Santora et al. 2004). The siting of wind farms is currently based on criteria developed by private developers, and there is no overall strategy or design plan for how, when, and where offshore wind development should take place in U.S. waters (Santora et al. 2004; USCOP 2004). Currently, offshore wind development is not being considered in an ecosystem or regional management context. Treating ocean regions as unified ecological areas will allow for appropriate scale planning to protect against cumulative impacts and to ensure maximum output and efficiency of energy production. Economies of scale mean that larger wind farms will be required (see Krohn 2002) to make offshore wind cost-effective. The result should not be a scattering the seascape with offshore wind farms sited independently from each other.

The USCOP recognized the need for comprehensive management for offshore renewable energy, and even the need for an offshore management regime that considers all uses within a larger planning context. Such a strategy will be able to appropriately weigh the benefit of the nation's energy needs against the potential adverse effects on other ocean uses, marine life, and the ocean's natural processes (USCOP 2004).

Conclusion

Several states are taking renewable energy seriously, and are now considering the possibilities of sustainable energy from the oceans. Massachusetts and New York have passed Renewables Portfolio Standards (RPS) to provide four and 25 percent of energy from clean sources by 2009 and 2013, respectively, and are now looking toward offshore wind to help fulfill those renewable energy requirements.

Each state will approach offshore wind differently — according to its leadership, values, and stakeholders. Massachusetts is a telling example. While the state clearly took a step toward investing in renewable energy by passing a RPS, wholehearted support remains lacking for the Cape Wind project, which could significantly contribute to meeting renewable energy goals. While valid arguments supporting and opposing offshore wind exist, the Cape Wind debate may be focused more on visual impacts and not-in-my-backyard issues than the true sustainability of offshore wind as an energy source.

Offshore wind has clearly gained momentum in the U.S., however it is still an industry with which state and federal governments, as well as private companies, have little experience. As a result, states should critically analyze how offshore wind development could impact their natural resources, stakeholders, and economies to ensure that when proposals arise, they are equipped with the knowledge of potential benefits, alternatives, or mitigation measures. Rather than taking a reactive approach, states should discuss the sustainability of offshore wind in advance, and proactively evaluate whether or not offshore wind is feasible and appropriate in their waters.

Notes

1. Additional observations show that wind speeds offshore are still higher than those located a bit further out than 10 meters; mean wind speeds 2 and 11 km offshore are 6% and 25% higher than 30m off the coast and 5% and 24% higher than 50m off the coast.

References

Bailey, Bruce, Skip Brennan, Brent Kinal, Mike Markus and Jason Kreiselman. 2003. Long Island's Offshore Wind Energy Development Potential: Phase 2 Siting Assessment. Prepared by AWS Scientific, Inc. for Long Island Power Authority.

Beatley, Timothy, David J. Brower, and Anna K. Schwab. 2002. *An Introduction to Coastal Zone Management.* 2nd Ed. Washington, D.C.: Island Press.

Christie, Donna R., and Richard G. Hildreth. 1999. *Coastal and Ocean Management Law in a Nutshell.* 2nd Ed. St. Paul, MN: West Group.

Cicin-Sain, Biliana and Robert W. Knecht. 2000. *The Future of U.S. Ocean Policy: Choices for the New Century.* Washington, D.C.: Island Press.

Department of Trade and Industry (DTI) 2002. Future Offshore: A Strategic Framework for the Offshore Wind Industry. U.K. Department of Trade and Industry. Available at *http://www.dti.gov.uk/energy/leg_and_reg/consents/future_offshore/FutureOffshore.pdf.* Accessed November 4, 2005.

Firestone, Jeremy, W. Kempton, A. Krueger, and C.E. Loper. 2004. Regulating Offshore Wind Power and Aquaculture: Messages from Land and Sea. *Cornell Journal of Law and Public Policy* 14(1): 71–111.

Flynn, Aaron M. 2005. Wind Energy: Offshore Permitting. CRS Report for Congress, Updated March 30th, 2005.

Freedman, Jeffrey M. 2001. Offshore Development of Wind Energy Facilities: Jurisdictional and Regulatory Analysis. Prepared For AWS Scientific, Inc.

Gaudiosi G. 1999. Offshore wind energy prospects. *Renewable Energy* 16: 828–34.

Hartland, Nathaniel D. 2003. The Wind and the Waves: Regulatory Uncertainty and Offshore Wind Power in the United States and United Kingdom. *U. Pa. J. Int'l Econ. L.* 24: 691.

Hartnell, G. and D. Milborrow. 2000. Prospects for offshore wind energy. A report written for the EU (Altener contract XVII/4.1030/Z/98–395) by The British Wind Energy Association (BWEA).

Krohn, Soren. 2002. Offshore Wind Energy: Full Speed Ahead. Danish Wind Industry Association.

Martin, Guy R., and Odin A. Smith. 2004. World's Largest Wind Energy Facility in Nantucket Sound? Deficiencies in the Current Regulatory Process for Offshore Wind Energy Development. *Boston College Environmental Affairs Law Review* 31: 285–323.

Musial, W. and S. Butterfield. 2004. Future for Offshore Wind Energy in the United States. Proceedings of EnergyOcean 2004 Conference, NREL/CP-500–36313.

New York State/U.S. Army Corps of Engineers. 2005. Joint Application for Permit. Applicant: Long Island Offshore Wind Park, LLC/Long Island Power Authority. DEC Application #2005–00365. April 26, 2005.

Offshore Wind Energy Collaborative. 2005. A Framework for Offshore Wind Energy Development in the United States. Report from a workshop organized and supported by the U.S. Department of Energy, GE, and the Massachusetts Technology Collaborative. Available at *http://www.masstech.org/offshore/final_09_20.pdf.* Accessed November 4, 2005.

Pelc, R., and R.M. Fujita. 2002. Renewable energy from the ocean. *Marine Policy* 26:471–479.

Pryor, S.C. and R.J. Barthelmie. 2002. Statistical analysis of flow characteristics in the coastal zone. *Journal of Wind Engineering and Industrial Aerodynamics* 90: 201–221.

Rhode Island Coastal Resources Management Council. 1996. The State of Rhode Island Coastal Resources Management Program As Amended. Available at *http://www.crmc.state.ri.us/pubs/programs/redbook.pdf.* Accessed November 4, 2005.

Russell, Rusty. 2004. Neither Out Far nor in Deep: The Prospects for Utility-Scale Wind Power in the Coastal Zone. *Boston College Environmental Affairs Law Review* 31: 221–261.

Santora, Christine, Nicole Hade, and Jackie Odell. 2004. Managing offshore wind developments in the United States: Legal, environmental and social considerations using a case study in Nantucket Sound, Massachusetts. *Ocean and Coastal Management* 47: 141–164.

U.S Army Corps of Engineers, New England District. 2004. Draft Environmental Impact Statement, Section 10 Rivers and Harbors Act Permit Application, Action ID NAE-2004–338–1 (formerly #200102913) Environmental Impact Report (EOEA File #12643) Development of Regional Impact Review (JR #20084) for the Cape Wind Energy Project, Nantucket Sound, Massachusetts.

_____, New York District. 2005. LIPA Offshore Wind Park Application, Public Notice Number: 2005–00365-L4. Issue Date: June 9, 2005.

About the Contributors

Clinton J. Andrews is an associate professor in the Edward J. Bloustein School of Planning and Public Policy at Rutgers University, New Brunswick, New Jersey, where he directs the graduate program in Urban Planning. He is affiliated with Rutgers' New Jersey Sustainable State Institute, Center for Energy, Economics and Environmental Policy, and Environmental and Occupational Health Sciences Institute. Dr. Andrews' books include *Regulating Regional Power Systems, Industrial Ecology and Global Change,* and *Humble Analysis.* He currently holds leadership positions in the Institute for Electrical and Electronics Engineers (IEEE) and the International Society for Industrial Ecology. Dr. Andrews was educated at Brown and MIT in engineering and planning.

Justin R. Barnes is a graduate student in the environmental policy program at Michigan Technological University and is affiliated with the Sustainable Futures Institute. His research interests include barriers to the development of renewable energy.

Jessica Boscarino is a Ph.D. candidate in political science at the Maxwell School of Syracuse University. She holds a master's degree in international relations. Her research interests include environmental politics and the role of advocacy groups in the policy process. Her current research examines the strategic actions of environmental organizations in promoting sustainable forestry practices.

Nicholas A. Hiza has worked in renewable energy development and research since 2002. He is currently project development manager at Greenlight Energy, Inc., where he oversees development efforts in the northeast. With experience ranging from GIS-based assessments of regional resources to the siting, permitting, and development of large-scale wind power facilities, Mr. Hiza has worked with groups in a number of sectors including private developers, non-profits and educational institutions. He is interested in how better assessments of resource availability can inform smarter policies.

Catherine Horiuchi is an assistant professor of public administration in the University of San Francisco's College of Professional Studies, where she teaches courses in statistics, policy analysis, organizational theory, and emerging technologies and e-government. Dr. Horiuchi's research agenda is focused on energy and technology policy.

Paul Komor is a lecturer in the Environmental Studies Program and the School of Engineering at the University of Colorado at Boulder and is a senior advisor at E Source. He has also been a project director at the U.S. Congress' Office of Technology Assessment and has taught at the Woodrow Wilson School at Princeton University. Dr. Komor holds an M.S. and Ph.D. from Stanford University.

W. Henry Lambright is a professor of public administration and political science and director of the Science and Technology Policy Program of the Center for Environmental Policy and Administration, the Maxwell School, Syracuse University. He has written or edited seven books and numerous articles relevant to science and technology policy or the environment. Dr. Lambright's books include *Powering Apollo: James E. Webb of NASA and Space Policy in the 21st Century.*

Sarah Pralle is an assistant professor of political science at the Maxwell School of Syracuse University, where she specializes in the study of public policy and environmental politics. Dr. Pralle's current research compares the strategies of environmental advocacy groups in the United States and Canada. Her work has appeared in the *Journal of Public Policy* and *Political Science Quarterly.*

Dianne Rahm is a professor of public administration at the University of Texas, San Antonio. Dr. Rahm has written or edited five books and numerous articles relevant to science and technology policy or energy and the environment. Her recent books include *United States Public Policy: A Budgetary Approach* and *Toxic Waste and Environmental Policy in the 21st Century United States.*

Christine Santora is a research associate at the Pew Institute for Ocean Science in New York City. She obtained a master's degree in marine affairs from the University of Rhode Island in 2002, and is now working on various fishery management issues for PIOS. Her master's thesis focused on the management of sea turtle bycatch in an inshore gillnet fishery in North

Carolina and she has worked on other marine policy issues such as offshore wind and dredged material disposal.

Barry Solomon is a professor in the environmental policy program at Michigan Technological University and is affiliated with the Sustainable Futures Institute. Dr. Solomon's research interests include barriers to the development of renewable energy and emissions trading systems. Some of his work has been supported by a grant from the Biocomplexity Program of the National Science Foundation to investigate the development of ethanol from lignocellulosic biomass in the Upper Midwest States.

Index